It is difficult for dedicated organic gardeners not to sound inspirational, but the fact is, the world we live in is toxic. To be more specific, there are now manmade poisons in everything that grows—plant, animal and fish; there is poison in our air and in our water. The human animal itself now carries a sufficient concentration of DDT so that, in certain areas, its milk is actively dangerous to its young.

In the circumstances, if one has even a small plot, it makes the utmost sense to be doing organic gardening. You might be lucky enough to own several acres, but if not, even a pot of herbs on a windowsill is better than nothing.

The information is all here for you to use—for a tiny plot, a suburban garden, a small farm—with specific details about the value and the growing of specific vegetables and fruits.

And for those unfortunate enough not to be able to grow anything of their own, there is a complete list, by area, of sources for organic foods by mail.

Grow it! Do it!

THE BASIC BOOK OF ORGANIC GARDENING

Edited by
ROBERT RODALE
and
BRIAN FURNER

PAN/BALLANTINE
33, Tothill Street,
London S.W.1

Most of the text was written especially for this
edition and is based on material which has appeared in
Organic Gardening Magazine, Rodale Press, Inc.

Copyright © 1971 by Rodale Press Inc.
First published in the United States of America
by Ballantine Books Inc., 1971.
This revised edition published by Pan/Ballantine,
London, 1972.
SBN 345 09709 2
Cover design by David Larkin

Printed in Great Britain by
Richard Clay (The Chaucer Press) Ltd,
Bungay, Suffolk.

CONTENTS

Part I

WHAT IS AN ORGANIC GARDENER?

An organic gardener knows that soil is not inert or dead but is full of living organisms and needs careful treatment. To have healthy, health-giving crops an organic gardener feeds his plot of soil with animal and vegetable wastes, and in cultivating his soil an organic gardener tries to work with nature and not against her.

For building up soil fertility and maintaining it an organic gardener relies mainly on home-made garden compost. Chemical fertilizers and poisonous insecticides are avoided by an organic gardener because he knows that these artificial stimulants and disinfectants are harmful to the soil itself, to the wildlife which shares his garden, and to his family and himself.

Not only does his truly fertile soil provide him with foods rich in vitamins and minerals necessary for good health but the produce has real flavour—the flavour that is often said to be lacking these days. True, real natural flavour is lacking from chemicalized, poison-sprayed, processed foods.

Finally—and most important—the organic gardener knows that he is a living, contributing part of the cycle of life. He does not merely take. He is a giver, a sharer, a restorer.

HOW TO BE AN ORGANIC GARDENER

It's easy to be an organic gardener! In fact, it's so easy that we sometimes wonder why *all* gardeners aren't organic gardeners. Our prediction is that once everyone has a chance to see organic methods demonstrated, there will be few *artificial* gardeners left.

The main reason why organic gardening is easy and produces good results is because it forces people to pay attention to their soil and build its fertility. Organic gardening is basically organic soil building. We all know that probably 90 per cent of all garden failures are caused by poor soil. By improving the fertility of the soil, the organic gardener prevents the major cause of poor gardening results.

The first step in becoming an organic gardener is to think about the step you are taking. Consider that you are embarking on a new adventure—a voyage of discovery into the world of nature's wonders. You are going to create in your own garden an environment for plant life that is supremely fertile and natural in conception. You are going to grow plants that are superior in size and in nutritional quality to the average produce available in the market—and immeasurably superior in taste.

Most important, think about the fact that your organic garden will be a demonstration of the *cleanliness* and spirituality of nature's design for life on this planet. Your organic garden will prove to you that our lives and the way we grow our food still are conducted best along the patterns set down by nature.

1. WHAT ARTIFICIAL FERTILIZERS DO TO THE SOIL

Artificial chemical fertilizers have no part in the organic method. They symbolize the basic objections to unnatural gardening and farming. True, artificial fertilizers supply food elements that plants use, but their method of doing so is unnatural. Feeding a plant artificial fertilizers is basically the same as feeding a person intravenously. You can get needed food elements into the organism, but you are not doing it the natural way.

The food elements in artificial fertilizers are almost all soluble, while in nature plants are accustomed to getting nutrients from many insoluble sources. This solubility of artificial fertilizers leads to trouble in the soil. It unbalances the soil's supply of nutrients.

Another objection to artificial fertilizers is that they introduce into the soil various unnecessary and even poisonous elements that are added to them in order to make their nutrients soluble. Soluble food elements occur rarely in nature; so man in his factories adds various acids and other processing chemicals to insoluble minerals to make them into soluble fertilizers. After years of continued use, these processing chemicals, which weren't really needed in the first place, build up in the soil and can even change its structure and tilth.

The first practical step you can take in becoming an organic gardener is never to buy artificial fertilizers. If you are already a gardener, stop using artificial fertilizers! Throw them out, give them away, sell them—the important thing is to stop using them.

CHEMICAL CALL-UP

Following the tragedy in Hertfordshire when a baby was severely burned after a lawn treated with sodium chlorate exploded into flames, gardeners at Ashford, Kent, have been advised to contact the council to arrange for the special collection of unwanted chemicals.

The council feels that reports of the accident may prompt people to dump their own stores of chemicals and weedkillers in dustbins and down drains.

Disposed of in this way the chemicals could cause a great fire risk at the municipal refuse dump or damage at the sewage works.

Front page of *Garden News*—10.9.71

2. Replacements for Artificial Fertilizers

The organic method of gardening is just what its name implies—*organic*. As an organic gardener you will gain a new familiarity with compost, manure, garbage, spoiled hay, straw, sawdust, peat moss, weeds, and all the other sources of humus for the soil. Just as artificial fertilizers symbolize man's vanity in setting up a chemical method of gardening, humus symbolizes the spirit of co-operation with nature that is the core of the organic method. As well as using waste products to rejuvenate and maintain soils at a high rate of fertility, organic gardeners in the United States sometimes make use of natural rock fertilizers, too.

3. What About Insecticides?

Poison sprays are obviously the most unnatural element introduced by man into his farms and gardens. Because they disrupt the balance of nature and can be serious health hazards, practically all organic gardeners shun such poisons. Poison sprays are particularly dangerous when used in gardens because your garden is where you live and that's where the persistent poisons of an impure environment can hurt you most.

Organic growing and non-use of pesticides go hand in hand. It has been shown time and again that plants and trees grown in fine organic soil do not suffer as much from insect and disease attack as plants growing on chemicalized soil. Scientific research has pointed out that many insects are the censors of nature—the destructive force whose purpose it is to kill off the weak so the strong can flourish.

Certainly, it is not logical to build a fine natural soil, rich in humus and free of the influence of chemical fertilizers, and then defile it with poison sprays.

One more thing to remember: When you decide to become an organic gardener, in your small way you have become part of a national energy—a real, honest-to-goodness, vigorous movement. Your decision to live compatibly with nature places you in the forefront of this serious effort to save the world. You have taken the first meaningful step away from the centric, superindustrial state towards a simpler, one-to-one relationship with the earth itself.

ORGANIC LIVING—WHY IS IT SO VITAL?

The idea of conservation and natural living is on the verge of being a vital necessity—a life preserver within reach of people almost drowning in the effluence of their own mistakes. The virgin land is no more. The quiet places in the country are being built up. The air and water are dirty almost everywhere.

Under the conditions of today, it isn't hard to think like an organic gardener. On the contrary, you wonder why everyone isn't composting his garbage and tending a poison-free plot of land. What can be more valuable now than a small garden, free of synthetic fertilizers and pesticide poisons, yielding food that tastes as good as the vegetables and fruits we were able to buy at the shop years ago? Valuable not only to the body but also to the spirit.

Even before the technological world became so oppressive and obvious, the organic gardening idea was a full-grown philosophy. In fact, the unpleasant conditions of pollution and degradation which so many people are experiencing today were predicted almost 40 years ago by the founders of the organic method. They could see evidence then of trouble on a small scale, and knew that the isolated, eroded fields and polluted crops of that time would mushroom eventually into a pall of illness across all of society. The organic gardening idea goes back a long way. Even more significantly, organic gardening as an idea goes far into the future, projecting the possibility of a pleasant and rewarding way of life in an increasingly synthetic world.

Sir Albert Howard, an English agricultural adviser to the Indian state of Indore, first thought out the concept of growing plants and husbanding animals without using synthetic chemicals. Partly, his development of natural gardening and farming was a reaction to necessity. The area of India where he worked was so poor that local farmers couldn't afford to buy imported fertilizers. Sir Albert had to devise ways to recycle the natural nutrients available locally—the manure of animals and the waste plant materials that would otherwise be burned or overlooked. He saw that many potential sources of plant nutrients weren't being used because the native farmers didn't understand their value.

Sir Albert's practical solution to the Indian farm problem was the Indore method of composting. He taught farmers to combine rough weeds and crop wastes in layers with high-nitrogen manure and a little soil, making a pile that soon heated up to over 150° as a result of the multiplication of bacteria and fungi. Lacking machinery and power, the native farmers had no mechanical means to deal with those wastes. By composting, however, they were able to break down stalks and leaves and to create a valuable soil conditioner and fertilizer that would replace the nutrients and humus removed from the soil by crops.

There was more to Sir Albert's thinking than just a solution to an immediate practical problem, however. He was disturbed by the trend of the scientific community towards advocating synthetic substitutes for many natural commodities, using the discoveries of the nineteenth-century German chemist, Justus von Leibig. Hailed as a pioneer of a new age of science, von Leibig had demonstrated the chemical simplicity of plant matter simply by burning it and then analysing the ash for nitrogen, phosphorus, and potash, ignoring the organic portion of the plant. The chemical fertilizer industry was created out of the ash of von Leibig's experiment. Farmers and gardeners were told that the chemical elements nitrogen, phosphorus, and potash (potassium) were all that mattered in the soil and that by replacing these chemicals in the form of powders they could ensure soil fertility indefinitely. This idea is known as the NPK theory where N stands for nitrogen, P for phosphorus, and K for potassium (kalium). As we know, the chemical fertilizer message spread around the world quite effectively, and became the foundation upon which the current industrial type of agriculture is built.

Sir Albert perceived in von Leibig's doctrine something extremely dangerous—the rupture of the cycle of life. Under the 'scientific' system of farming, soil became primarily something to hold up the plants so that they could be fed with artificial solutions. The age-old rhythms of nature that had built the soil were violated. Sir Albert began preaching that it was possible for thinking farmers to preserve the cycle of life by returning plant and animal wastes to the soil, countering insects by non-poisonous means, and by avoiding the synthetic, soluble fertilizers with their burden of toxic residues. If the cycle of life wasn't preserved, said Sir Albert, future generations would be faced with declining fertility, hunger, and increases in disease and pollution.

My father, J. I. Rodale, first read about Sir Albert Howard's ideas in the late 1930s. Even then, the United States was so industrialized and technologically 'advanced' that it was possible to see that what Sir Albert was predicting could easily come to pass. The American Dust Bowl experience of the Depression years was graphic evidence of the disruption of the cycle of life. But there were signs of trouble everywhere. Food quality was low. Pollution was intruding on our lives. Disease caused by physical degeneration—not just by microbes—was increasing. J. I. Rodale noted with dismay that the grim harvest predicted by Sir Albert and other philosophers of the conservation school was about to be reaped.

My father first used the word *organic* to describe the natural method of gardening and farming, mainly because compost, humus, and the organic fraction of the soil were emphasized so strongly. J. I. Rodale saw that this method was more than just a good way of cultivating soil and growing healthy crops. In 1942 he started publishing America's flourishing monthly magazine *Organic Gardening*, in which he proclaimed that to be *organic* was to know and to understand the lessons of nature in all ways, and to use that knowledge to evaluate all of the 'blessings' of science and technology. What good was it, he thought, to grow food without using chemical fertilizers or pesticides, and then to process that food so that its content of vitamins and minerals would be depleted seriously? In fact, not caring whether he was called an extremist or a crackpot, J. I. Rodale created what might now be called a *strict constructionist* interpretation of natural life under the banner of organiculture.

If it is synthetic, avoid it, he said. If it goes through a factory, examine it with special care. Follow the dictates of the cycle of life when growing things, he advised, and you will be blessed with foods of surpassing taste and quality that are less troubled by insects or disease.

Of course, there was originally much objection to the organic idea from the scientific community. Its members felt that anyone who said that all artificial fertilizers, pesticides, and foods were bad simply was not living in the twentieth century. Strangely, many 'chemical' people who expressed violent disagreement with organic gardening and farming as a practical technique, admitted that it made sense theoretically. 'Humus in the soil is important,' they said, 'but there isn't enough compost to go round.' Almost everyone agreed that old-fashioned, natural ways of growing things produced tastier foods, but few would admit that it was possible to grow them now on a large scale.

Events of the past few years have changed a lot of minds. Many people can now see the direct result of the misuse of our environment, and of the failure of industry and agriculture to understand the importance of the cycle of life. You no longer have to be a prophet or a visionary to perceive that the way our world is being abused is leading to trouble. Of course, there is still much opposition to the organic method. Those whose reputations or livelihoods depend on continuing chemicalization of land, water, and air tend to refuse to believe that only a deep and sympathetic appreciation of natural ways can lead to a better and more pure world. There are still people who say that DDT is needed, and won't hurt anyone. A number of local authorities in many parts of the world have, however, got the message and are showing a fine example to others. I am thinking particularly of garbage disposal. Instead of burning this useful, plant-rich organic material, go-ahead, with-it towns and cities are salvaging valuable metals for re-use and composting the rest for return to the land. How does your own local authority deal with household refuse? If the stuff is burnt, why not suggest to your local council that they get up to date, stop polluting, and start large-scale composting as in Jersey or Edinburgh?

I know, and I think you do too, that the organic way of living points down the right road, even though that road might have a few bumps and some hills to climb. Let's hope that everyone will soon start thinking as the organic gardeners and farmers have been thinking for 30 years.

ROBERT RODALE

PART II

SOILS AND SOIL BUILDERS

SOIL

1. WHAT IS SOIL?

Soil—what it is, how it is formed

The loose top layer of the earth's surface that supports the growth of plants, soil consists mainly of four parts—minerals, organic matter, water, and air.

An average topsoil of an active garden or farm might consist of about 25 per cent air, 25 per cent water, 49 per cent minerals, and only 1 per cent organic matter. In a virgin prairie soil, the organic matter could go to more than 10 per cent. There are some soils that might contain up to 20 per cent of organic matter. The amount of organic matter in the subsoil gradually goes down until, at a depth of about 30 feet, it may amount to only one-eighth of 1 per cent.

Profile

In discussing soil, the word *profile* means a side view of a vertical section of the earth. If we could slice away a section of it, we could then regard the profile and see the various layers down to bedrock. A soil profile is often visible at a place where a road has been cut through a hill. An average profile might consist of five or six layers, beginning with the rock below and going through the various stages of subsoil to the uppermost layer, or topsoil. These layers, called horizons, are extremely significant in their effect on the processes of plant growth.

How soil is formed

Originally the entire earth was one mass of rock, and the only living things were microbes—single-celled organisms. Through their activities, these bacteria and fungi liberated carbon dioxide and certain organic and inorganic acids, which have a solvent action upon rocks, beginning the process of their breakdown into soil. The dead bodies of these organisms were the beginnings of the organic matter that was mixed with the tiny fragments of rocks to form soil. The action of heat, cold, wind, rain, glacier movement, and other influences and biological factors took a hand in the further gradual breakdown. The difference in temperature between day and night, and between summer and winter, caused expansion and contraction which produced open seams in the rocks and detachment of fragments, permitting water to enter deeper into the rock.

Part of the process of soil formation consisted of the decaying remains of the low forms of plants such as lichens and mosses which soon began to cover the exposed rocks, digging their tiny tentacles into the rock. This slowly formed a film of soil over them. This bit of soil provided the foothold for the plants which are the next step up the evolutionary scale—the ferns—and gradually, as the soil thickened, other higher plants and trees began to grow, until there came into being overgrown jungles.

We must remember that without the soil organisms—the bacteria, fungi, actinomycetes, yeasts, etc.—no soil formation could take place. The making of soil is a biological process, meaning that living forces take a prominent part in it. We might say, therefore, that the process of soil formation consists of physical, chemical, and biological elements. The physical part is accomplished by the wind and the rain, the chemical by the excretions and respirations of the microbes, and the biological by the other activities of these organisms.

Soil has formed not only from the original bedrock but also by rock that has been moved by glacial and other forces. And soil formation is still going on. Soil is constantly being created by the same forces which formed it originally—climate, decaying plant matter, etc. Deep down at bedrock, some of the rock is still gradually turning to subsoil. It takes these processes perhaps 500 years to make 1 inch of soil, but man with his destructive farming practices can destroy an inch in only a few years of soil mining, that is, farming that only takes out, putting nothing back that has staying power. It has been estimated that in about 200 years of farming in the United States, over 60 per cent of the topsoil has been destroyed.

Soils are classified into groups, series, and types. The groups are based largely on climatic factors and associated vegetation, the series on parent material, and the soil types on the texture of the soil. The following information is based on government agricultural reports.

Texture

By texture is meant the relative amounts of the various sizes of particles making up the soil. These particles range in size from stones and gravel, through sand and silt to clay, the particles of which may be too small to be seen under the strongest microscope.

Structure

This refers to the grouping of individual particles into larger pieces, or granules. Good granulation or crumb structure of the heavier soils is essential to good results. Sandy soils show little if any granulation, due to the coarseness of their component particles. With soils containing a substantial percentage of clay, working them when wet results in destruction of the granular structure. Excessive tramping by livestock under the same conditions is likely to have a similar effect.

Alternate freezing and thawing, or wetting and drying, and penetration of the soil mass by plant roots are natural forces which favour the formation of soil granules, or aggregates. Such aggregation is developed most highly in soils near neutrality in their reaction; both strongly acid and strongly alkaline soils tend to *run together* and lose their structural character. Tillage also tends to break down the structure of many soils.

Porosity

Associated with both texture and structure is pore space, or porosity. These spaces may be large, as in the case of coarse, sandy soils or those with well-developed granulation. In heavy soils, containing mostly finer clay particles, the pore spaces may be too small for plant roots or soil water to penetrate readily. Good soils have 40 to 60 per cent of their bulk occupied with pore space, which may be filled with either water or air, neither of which can truly be said to be more important than the other.

Here, as in all other soil relationships, a satisfactory balance is important for productivity. Too much water slows the release of soil nitrogen, depletes mineral nutrients, and otherwise hinders proper plant growth. Too much air speeds nitrogen release beyond the capacity of plants to utilize it, and much of it is lost. In an overly aerated soil, the stored water evaporated the departure or difference from the overall soil description.

Soil groups

All soils are composed of particles varying greatly in size and shape. In order to classify them by texture as well as physical properties, four fundamental soil groups are recognized: gravels, sands, loams, and clays. (The last three make up most of the world's arable lands.)

The sand group includes all soils of which the silt and clay make up less than 20 per cent by weight. Its mineral particles are visible to the naked eye and are irregular in shape. Because of this, their water-holding capacity is low, but they possess good drainage and aeration and are usually in a loose, friable condition.

In contrast, particles in a clay soil are very fine (invisible under ordinary microscope) and become sticky and cement-like.

Texture of the loam class cannot be as clearly defined, since its mechanical composition is about midway between sand and clay. Professors T. Lyon and Harry Buckman in their book, *The Nature and Properties of Soils*, (New York, Macmillan) describe loams

> as such a mixture of sand, silt and clay particles as to exhibit light and heavy properties in about equal proportions ... Because of this intermixture of coarse, medium and fine particles, usually they possess the desirable qualities both of sand and clay without exhibiting those undesirable properties, as extreme looseness and low water capacity on the one hand and stickiness, compactness, and very slow air and water movement on the other.

Most farm and garden soils are in the loam classification. The majority of soils are mixtures; the most common class names appear on page 22: (Combinations are given when one size of particles is evident enough to affect the texture of the loam. For example, a loam in which sand is dominant will be classified as a sandy loam of some kind.)

Sandy soils	*Loamy soils*	
Gravelly sands	Coarse sandy loams	
Coarse sands	Medium sandy loams	
Medium sands	Fine sandy loams	
Fine sands	Silty loams and stony silt loams	
Loamy sands	Clay loams	

Clayey soils		
Stony clays	Sandy clays	Clays
Gravelly clays	Silty clays	

You can get a good idea of your soil's texture and class by rubbing it between the thumb and the fingers or in the palm of the hand. Sand particles are gritty; silt has a floury or talcum-powder feel when dry and is only moderately plastic when moist, while the clayey material is harsh when dry and very plastic and sticky when wet.

Observe Professors Lyon and Buckman: 'This method is used in all field operations, especially in soil survey, land classification and the like. Accuracy ... can be acquired by the careful study of known samples.'

The ideal structure is granular, where the rounded aggregates (or clusters) of soil lie loosely and readily shake apart. When the granules are especially porous, the term *crumb* is applied.

Water

Soil water occurs in three forms, designated as hygroscopic, capillary, and gravitational. The hygroscopic soil water is chemically bound in the soil constituents and is unavailable to plants. Gravitational water is that which normally drains out of the pore spaces of the soil after a rain. If drainage is poor, it is this water which causes the soil to be soggy and unproductive. Excessive drainage hastens the time when capillary water runs short and plants suffer from drought.

It is the capillary water upon which plants depend very largely for their supply of moisture. Hence, the capacity of a soil to hold water against the pull of gravity is of great importance in ordinary agriculture. Organic matter and good structure add to this supply of water in soils.

But plants cannot extract the last drop of capillary water from a soil, since the attraction of soil materials for it is greater than the pull exerted by the plant roots. The point at which these two forces are just equal is called the *wilting coefficient* of a soil. This term is used to express the percentage of water in a soil at the time the loss from transpiration exceeds the renewal of the water by capillary means. Medium-textured loams and silt loams, because of their faster rate of movement of moisture from depth to the root zone, and the fact that they can bring up moisture from greater depths than either sands or clays, provide the best conditions of available but not excessive soil moisture for best plant growth.

Erosion

Generally erosion works this way: first, the main loss is by sheet erosion; each time it rains, the run-off water removes a thin layer of surface soil. Then, as the top-soil becomes thinner, miniature gullies appear. After most of the surface soil is gone, gullies become the main problem.

Usually there's a clear difference between the topsoil and subsoil. The subsoil is finer textured, more plastic, and lighter in colour than the topsoil. Here's how erosion is classified:

No apparent erosion. All or nearly all the surface soil is present. Depth to subsoil is 14 inches or more. The surface may have received some recent deposits as the result of erosion from higher ground.

Slight. Depth to subsoil varies from 7 to 14 inches. Ploughing at usual depths will not expose the subsoil.

Moderate. Depth to subsoil varies from 3 to 7 inches. Some subsoil is mixed with the surface soil in ploughing.

Severe. Depth to subsoil is less than 3 inches. Surface soil is mixed with subsoil when the land is ploughed. Gullies are beginning to be a problem.

Very severe. Subsoil is exposed. Gullies are frequent.

Very severe gullies. Deep gullies or blow-outs have ruined the land for agricultural purposes.

There is a direct relationship between erosion and a soil's ability for intake of air and water. For example, when the soil surface becomes compacted, the danger of erosion increases, while the intake of water and air decreases.

Soil series

This refers to a subdivision of soil groups. A series is often given the name of a town, river, or other geographical feature near which the soil was first identified. Thus, members of the same soil series, or subdivisions, signify soils which have developed from the same kind of parent material and by the same process.

2. THE SOIL IN YOUR GARDEN—HOW TO MAKE IT RIGHT FOR PARTICULAR PLANTS

Why do azaleas flourish where iris will produce nary a flower? Why can you grow armfuls of huge carrots in the same patch where cabbages never form tight hearts? The answer to this rather puzzling problem is surprisingly simple. Plants, like all of nature's creatures, have their own special needs. Fundamentally, there are three soil conditions; acid, neutral, and alkaline. A plant that thrives in a light acid soil may go fruitless in a rich loam that is not acidic. Once you have determined the needs of your favourite plants, you are well on your way to peak garden yields.

Although some plants, especially herbs, will thrive in almost any type of soil, most of the more popular plant families are mighty choosy about their environment.

If your flower gardens are lush with azaleas and rhododendron, but your efforts to get a vegetable patch going have met with failure, your soil may be overly acidic. This condition must be changed if you want to raise beets, broccoli, lettuce, and many other neutral to alkaline-loving plants. Crushed limestone or crushed chalk known as 'lime' by gardeners is used to lower soil acidity so that the soil has the correct pH (acidity–alkalinity scale) for plants which just can't bear over-acid conditions.

How is the need for lime determined? Most crops do best on soil within a 6·5 to 6·8 pH range—that is, just slightly acid. If it is lower than that—even only a little— the difference in yield can be tremendous. Maize, for example, that will yield 100 bushels to the acre at a pH of 6·8, will return but 83 bushels when this drops to 5·7. Food value in what is produced is affected, too. Crops supplied the right amount of calcium are richer in minerals and in protein.

The way to find out whether or not your soil needs lime, and how much, is by an accurate soil test. Adding it by guesswork is definitely a mistake. (Too

much can be as detrimental as a deficiency.) Thorough
soil tests are seldom needed for our garden soils. They
are of greater use to farmers wishing to embark on the
cultivation of specific crops. Private soil-testing com-
panies are around but their work is pricey. Some government experimental stations will oblige with a soil test if
you need one. There are also cheap Soil Testers in garden shops if you just wish to check up on the acidity–
alkalinity rating of your own garden soil. Bear in mind
that different parts of the garden may have different pH
values. In general, wherever you find mosses, ferns, pine,
laurel, and azaleas do well soil conditions are acidic. If
you wish to increase the acidity of patches of garden for
growing subjects which prefer acidic soils, use horticultural peat lavishly. It would be wrong to place too much
emphasis on the whole subject of acidity–alkalinity in
the garden. In Britain it is very rare for a garden soil to
be excessively acidic or excessively alkaline and most
food crops in which the organic gardener is interested
need soils which are neutral to slightly acid. With the
aid of a garden compost dressing and the judicious use
of lime it is not difficult maintaining our garden soils at
the correct rating.

pH Preference of Common Plants

Quite acid (pH of from 4·0 to 6·0)

Azalea	Heath	Pine
Blackberry	Heather	Potato
Blueberry	Lily	Radish
Chrysanthemum	Lily of the valley	Raspberry
Cranberry	Marigold	Rhododendron
Evergreens	Mountain laurel	Spruce
Ferns	Mosses	Yew
Flax	Oak	

Slightly acid (pH 6·0 to 6·5)

Apple
Apricot
Barley
Bent grass
Bluegrass
Cherry
French bean
Gardenia
Gloxinia
Gooseberry
Grape

Kale
Millet
Mustard
Oats
Pansy
Parsley
Parsnip
Pea
Peach
Pear
Pumpkin

Rape
Rhubarb
Rye
Salsify
Strawberry
Sweet corn
Tomato
Turnip
Vetch
Wheat

Neutral to alkaline (pH 7·0 to 7·5)

Alyssum
Asparagus
Beet
Broccoli
Brussels sprouts
Cabbage
Carnation

Carrot
Cauliflower
Celery
Clover
Cucumber
Iris
Leeks

Lettuce
Melon
Onion
Quince
Spinach
Swiss chard
Vegetable marrow

3. SOME USEFUL SOIL BUILDERS

Organic gardening cheapens the cost of home food production because the system is based on the use of garden compost made from garden and household wastes. The making and the use of garden compost is so important. That is why it has a chapter of its own. Apart from garden compost there are other waste products which are worth knowing about. These soil builders come in handy if you have a large garden and have insufficient garden compost to build up and maintain it in peak-fertility condition. They are also of use if you have just taken over a garden and although you have no garden compost ready for use yet you want to make a start at growing things organically.

Unless otherwise noted, these fertilizers can either be worked into the soil in spring or autumn, top-dressed around growing plants, added to the compost heap, or used as a mulch.

Blood meal and dried blood

This is blood collected in slaughterhouses, later dried and ground. Blood meal analyses 15 per cent nitrogen, 1·3 per cent phosphorus, 0·7 per cent potash; dried blood contains 12 per cent nitrogen, 3 per cent phosphorus.

These materials can be used directly in the ground or composted. Because of its high nitrogen content, use very sparingly. A sprinkling is enough to stimulate bacterial growth; available in nurseries or wherever garden products are sold.

Bone meal

Years ago, so I am told, British fertilizer manufacturers imported human and horse bones from handy European battlefields; nowadays the main source is the slaughterhouse. Consisting mostly of calcium phosphate, the phosphorus and nitrogen content depends mostly on the kind and age of the bone. Raw bone meal has between 2 and 4 per cent nitrogen, 22 to 25 per cent phosphoric acid. The fatty materials in raw bone meal somewhat delay its breakdown in the soil.

Steamed bone meal contains 1 to 2 per cent nitrogen, up to 30 per cent phosphorus, available in hardware stores, local nurseries, or usually wherever garden products are sold.

Composts—manufactured composts

Manufactured composts are quite unlike home-made garden compost and should be used according to the suppliers' instructions. This is advisable because they may be richer in nitrogen or another plant food than the compost you make yourself. Apart from municipal composts made and sold by some local authorities there is also 'Pompost'. This is prepared from apple and other fruit wastes.

Cottonseed meal

This is made from the cottonseed which has been freed from lints and hulls and then deprived of its oils. (Cottonseed cake is one of the richest protein foods for animal feeding.) Its low pH makes it especially valuable for acid-loving crops. Cottonseed meal analyses 7 per cent nitrogen, 2 to 3 per cent phosphorus, and 1·5 per cent potash. An excellent organic fertilizer but only available if you live near a processing factory dealing with cottonseed.

Grass clippings

Fairly rich in nitrogen, grass clippings are useful as a green manure to be worked into the soil, for adding to compost heaps, or for mulching. Clippings from most lawns contain over 1 pound of nitrogen and 2 pounds of potash for every 100 pounds of clippings in the dry state. We live in a hungry world where every square foot of fertile soil is needed for food production. Because, apart from some increase in prices, Britain is not yet affected by the world food shortage a large proportion of gardeners do what the politicians do—put this very worrying subject out of mind. Instead of using most of the garden for growing healthy, home-grown fruit and vegetables many gardeners grow grass. The British lawn is often an attractive sight but with world hunger already a menace, for how long can this green luxury be permitted? From these handsome, cared-for lawns thousands of tons of unwanted clippings are mown each summer. Those of your neighbours who practise grass culture and precious little else in their gardens will be delighted to let you have regular supplies of lawn mowings. If you live near a park or a golf course groundsmen may be eager to get rid of stacks of smelly mowings, too. Ascertain if such large tracts of grassland have been treated with selective weed killers. Refuse offers of mowings from grassland where these weed killers have been used. The residues of these chemical compounds may harm your garden soil and kill or maim the crops of which you are so proud.

Hops—spent hops and malt dust

If you work in or live near a brewery you may be able to get brewery wastes. Most are now sold for adding to animal-feeding stuffs and to manufacturers of hop-based garden fertilizers. These are fortified with chemical or organic plant foods. If you can get spent hops from a brewery stack them and leave for several months before applying at the rate of one pailful to the square yard. Best applied after rain in the autumn. On a truly organic soil may also be used as a summer mulch. Ideal for mixing and stacking with poultry or pigeon droppings. Malt dust ('Culms') consists of barley rootlets and shoots. The moisture content is low and the NPK values are around 3 per cent nitrogen, 1·5 per cent phosphorus, and 2 per cent potash. May be used in small quantities around growing plants but always after rain has wetted the soil well.

Hulls and shells

Hulls and shells of cocoa beans, buckwheat, oats, rice, and cottonseed are commonly used as a fertilizer and mulch. They decay readily and may be spaded into the ground. The coarse shells are excellent as mulches, while the finer ones (sometimes almost in dust form) can be applied to lawns and elsewhere with a spreader. Hulls and shells make an exceptionally attractive mulch, and are most effective when about 1 inch thick. Ask at any local processing plant for wastes of this sort.

Leaf mould

Park keepers often burn valuable autumn leaves. Prevent this from happening—if you can—by collecting leaves (with permission) from a local park. The road where you live may also be a source of lots of autumn leaves each season. Highways departments of local authorities are sometimes keen to support organic gardeners by delivering loads of autumn leaves free of charge. Stack the leaves in a large pile. Sprinkle a little lime on and off when stacking unless you plan to use the leaf mould around acid-tolerant plants only. Cover with a large sheet of tarpaulin or strong black plastic and weigh down to retain the sheeting in position. Partial rotting occurs within 6 months. It takes a year or two for the pile to rot down to produce first-class leaf mould for spreading over the garden soil. Leaf mould from deciduous trees has been found to be somewhat richer in potash and phosphorus than that made from conifers. Nitrogen content varies and is sometimes as high as 5 per cent.

Leaves

Leaves are an abundant source of humus and mineral material, including calcium, magnesium, as well as nitrogen, phosphorus, and potassium. They are especially valuable for use around acid-loving plants such as azaleas, rhododendrons, and hollies. They may be applied directly to the soil, as a mulch, for leaf mould, and for composting.

Manure, fresh

This has been a basic fertilizer used for centuries. Some manures, such as horse, hen, sheep, and rabbit, are considered *hot* manures because of their relatively high nitrogen content. Rabbit manure, for example, analyses 2·4 N, 1·4 P, and 0·6 K. It's best to allow these manures to compost before applying directly to plants. Cow and pig manure, relatively wet and correspondingly low in nitrogen, are called *cold* manures, and ferment slowly. All manures are excellent and should be included in an organic fertilizing programme, when available.

Manure—composted

Commercially produced composted manures are concentrated. They should not be used as lavishly as manures you may obtain from a local farmer. In fact, they are best considered as fertilizers for use to the manufacturers' instructions. Composted horse manure is widely advertised. Manures of this sort may be made from dung from stables or they may be wastes of the mushroom industry. If prepared from spent mushroom beds the manures will probably contain some residues of chemical preparations used in mushroom culture. Some years ago composted poultry manure from hen batteries was around. Concentrated manures of this sort are useful activators for the compost heap.

Peat

This is partially decomposed remains of plants accumulated over centuries under relatively airless conditions. There are several types. Granulated sedge peat is very popular among gardeners. Although this is the most widely advertised organic gardening product it contains very little in the way of plant foods. Horticultural peat is expensive. If used in fairly large quantities peat can increase the water-holding property of a light, sandy soil and also open up a sticky clay one. Garden compost does both jobs equally effectively but does not arrive at the door in a large plastic sack! Sedge peat is also used as a soil cover (a mulch). A rose bed looks fine and weed-free in a peat mulch.

Sawdust

A very useful mulch material which should be used more widely but only if the garden soil has been brought up to organic peak fertility. Many gardeners fear that the use of sawdust may lead to a soil nitrogen deficiency so before using sawdust they side-dress with a nitrogenous fertilizer like dried blood. However, a recent *Organic Gardening* survey showed that many sawdust users among organic gardeners never apply extra nitrogen and are satisfied with results. Some gardeners stack raw sawdust and use it only when it has aged and darkened; others use the stuff raw. I have seen exhibition-quality cabbages and leeks grown in well-composted soil and mulched with sawdust straight from the saw mill.

Seaweed and kelp

Both are high in potash (about 5 per cent) and trace elements. Many seaweed users apply it fresh from the sea; others prefer washing first to remove salt. It can be used as a mulch, worked directly into the soil, or placed in the compost heap. There are several commercial seaweed horticultural preparations in the shops.

Sludge

Activated sludge, produced when sewage is agitated by air rapidly bubbling through it, contains about 5 per cent nitrogen, 3 to 6 per cent phosphorus, that is similar to cottonseed meal. Digested sludge, formed when sewage is allowed to settle over filter beds, has about the same fertilizer value as barnyard manure—2 per cent for both nitrogen and phosphorus. Sludge is usually on the acid side. It can be worked into the soil in autumn or in early spring at time of initial cultivation.

Straw and hay

When straw was cheaper it was much recommended to the organically-minded gardener for stacking around compost heaps, for mulching, and, when partially decayed, for adding to compost heaps. Spoilt straw is usually burnt by farmers who are either ignorant of its value or just can't afford the labour costs involved in composting it. If you can get spoilt straw enquire as to what chemical sprays were used when the corn was being grown. If the names of the sprays sound pretty grim, refuse the offer. You don't want your compost heaps and your soil contaminated by poisonous chemical residues. Spoilt hay is unlikely to contain much in the way of spray residues but will undoubtedly contain a lot of weed seeds. Do not let this put you off. The seeds will be of common annual weeds. If you add some of the hay now and then to your compost heaps a proportion of the seeds will be killed during the fermentation process. The rest will pop up as seedlings after the garden compost has been applied to your soil. All will be killed when you start hoeing.

Water weeds

If unpolluted streams, ponds, and ditches are being cleaned near your garden ask the chap doing the job to let you collect some of the raked-out water weeds. Drain and leave the weed to wilt for 48 hours—preferably before you start carting it home. The wilted weed will be lighter to handle and carry. Add now and then to the compost heap when building. This is ideal for mixing with straw or other dryish ingredients you have collected for compost making. Never dig into the garden soil smelly, uncomposted water weed.

Wood ashes

Containing 1·5 per cent phosphorus, 7 per cent or more potash, wood ashes should never be allowed to stand in the rain, as the potash would leach away. They can be mixed with other fertilizing materials, side-dressed around growing plants, or used as a mulch. Apply about 5 to 10 pounds per 100 square feet. Avoid contact between freshly spread ashes and germinating seeds or new plant roots by spreading ashes a few inches from plants. Wood ashes are alkaline. If your garden soil is sticky clay do not be heavy-handed with wood ash. The ash can make the clay even stickier. Some organic gardeners consider wood ash should never be used straight but added in small quantities to the compost heap.

Wood shavings

Like sawdust, wood shavings are useful in the garden. They have a higher nutrient content than sawdust. A good use for wood shavings in gardens and on allotments is as a cover over temporary paths which then remain weed-free for from 1 to 2 years. The shavings gradually rot and increase the moisture-holding capacity of the soil. Often obtainable from saw mills free of charge.

4. ABOUT ANIMAL MANURES

Old-time gardeners were all-organic. They based the re-fertilization of their soils on animal manures. Some had plentiful supplies and their soils were rich and their crops fine; others used less and their results were nothing like as good. Animal manures are acidic. To keep the soil more or less neutral old-timers limed regularly.

Twentieth-century organic gardeners do not keep their garden soils up to scratch by using animal manures.' They are so expensive—unless you know a local farmer, poultryman, or pigeon fancier who is glad to see you cart the stuff away. In nature's own build-up of soils the animal wastes content is low when compared with the high amount of vegetable wastes. Animal manures are therefore not needed in vast quantities in the garden. In fact the excessive use of animal manures can lead to unbalanced soil conditions and to sick plants. The modern organic gardener makes use of relatively small quantities of animal manure during compost making and seldom applies vast quantities of dung to the soil.

5. Some Major Sources of Organic Fertilizers, Mulches, and Conditioners

There are six major sources of organic fertilizers, mulches, and conditioners available in such profusion that the categories overlap—what you can't get in one, you can obtain in another. If animal manures are in short supply in your area do not worry. They are not a necessary factor in twentieth-century organic gardening. But most organic gardeners feel that apart from wildlife droppings a little extra animal matter is of help. Some add dried blood to the compost heap. Budgie, hamster, guinea pig, or pet rabbit droppings are even better. The organic gardener is resourceful and he is always on the lookout for likely sources of organic animal and vegetable wastes. Here are some of the many useful waste products to be had:

1. *Animal manures:* horse, cattle, pig, poultry, pigeon, rabbit.
2. *Processors' vegetable wastes:* spent hops, various vegetable wastes from food processors and from factories making animal feeds or dealing in wool, cotton, and jute.
3. *Compost:* municipal composts and other commercial composts.
4. *Local vegetable wastes:* autumn leaves, spoilt hay and spoilt straw, greengrocers' wastes, and, of course, all plant (including weeds) remains from your garden and from other gardens where these wastes are not wanted.
5. *Wood wastes:* sawdust and wood shavings.
6. *Water weeds:* seaweeds and weeds from unpolluted streams, rivers, ponds, and ditches.

Animal manures, chief source of nitrogen

Because animal manures are in short supply nowadays their use is usually restricted to activating garden compost heaps. Animal manures are noted for their high nitrogen content. Should you be so fortunate as to be able to obtain large quantities of any sort of dung from local farmers or poultry keepers use it with reserve. Small quantities of fresh manure can be applied to compost heaps during building. Large quantities are best stacked in layers a foot thick and each layer covered with an inch of topsoil. When the pile is 5 to 6 feet high cover with a sheet of 500-gauge polythene to prevent leaching by rain of valuable minerals and to prevent the neighbours from complaining to the local authority about the muck-heap stench from your dung heap. After the pile has heated up, fermented, and sunk to almost half its original volume the composted manure may be spread on to or forked into the ground before you get down to sowings and plantings. If the dung was from a poultryman or pigeon fancier, use it very sparingly—preferably as a fertilizer top-dressing. If used with little discretion bird droppings can lead to a sticky soil condition and to pest-ridden crops. Where animal manures are used in quantity liming will very probably be necessary each winter or every second winter to counteract soil acidity. When used in ordinary compost heaps the amount of dung is so little and is so well mixed with large quantities of other fermented wastes before it reaches the garden soil that there is little danger of any soil acidification occurring. So in many organic gardens the practice of liming is found to be unnecessary.

6. Getting Humus into the Soil

There are two ways to get humus into the soil; you can put it there, or you can grow it in. Which is best for you?

The method depends on the kind of place you have, where it is, how big, and the kind of soil you have to work with. To maintain soil fertility, texture, and structure, you can spread compost, animal, and vegetable manures, and then work them under. But if your soil is extremely poor, too much sand or clay, you should consider green manuring or cover cropping seriously.

What some Organic Gardening *readers report*

Sheet composting is an efficient, quick way to add organic material to the garden patch. Instead of being composted in heaps, materials are spread directly over the planting area and turned under with a rotary tiller. It provides a highly concentrated organic mixture of animal manures, crop residues, rock minerals, and soil which creates a balanced condition for healthy, vigorous plant growth.

Down in Florida, 'where spring is fall and the end of the growing season is June', Jeanne Wellenkamp follows a programe of 'sheet composting combined with organic minerals and green manuring'.

First, year-old chicken manure is combined with granite dust, phosphate rock, and bone meal 'in amounts determined by the crop that will follow'. These are worked into the soil at the same time, weather permitting. Otherwise they are worked in singly.

About July 1, a nitrogen-fixing legume, sesbania, is planted as a cover crop, 30 pounds of seed to the acre. Six weeks later, about August 15, 'when this green manure has shot up to 8 to 10 feet and is beginning to bloom, it is cut down, chopped and ploughed in.' In 3 weeks the fields are ready for cultivation and planting.

In the meantime, Mrs Wellenkamp notes, 'the earthworms have been having a field day for themselves and millions of them are propagating in the sweet sesbania compost'.

Up in Needham, Massachusetts, Jerome Sisson likes sheet composting for another reason, 'It's a one-time operation that doesn't call for the periodic all-summer attention required in maintaining a compost-heap,' he writes. 'Besides saving time and effort, the spread-and-turn-under system allows the gardener to make direct, soil-enriching use of many materials—probably more than he would process into compost,' he stresses.

Two different systems of sheet composting are used by Mr Sisson. First, he spreads weeds, manure, and other organic materials over the garden and field where they are worked into the soil to decompose. Second, he spreads 'about 8 cubic yards of ground leaves over my 30-by-30 garden where they lie 1 to 2 inches deep'. After spreading a generous application of ground limestone, he works them in 'thoroughly with a rotary tiller, and then I leave the rest to Mother Nature'.

What about garbage—and the compost pile?

But the now classic compost pile cannot be either ignored or neglected. Maybe it does take longer to make finished compost this way, 14 days with considerable turning, and then maybe you do have to haul it away and spread it. But in the summer's greatest heat, we have made good, usable compost in 6 days with our open-hearth composting technique. The trick is to raise the pile off the ground, with about 12 inches of space under it. Convection does the rest. As the heap heats in the blazing sun, cool air is sucked in at the bottom and pulled up through the pile, aerating it completely.

This rapid conversion of compostable material permits us not only to make good and full use of our kitchen garbage, it also allows us to maintain a schedule of successive midsummer and late summer plantings. Into the new planting rows or into the second plantings, go spadefuls of compost with the seeds or seedlings to give them a good start. We like this system which gives us late tomatoes and corn, and also side-dressings and booster feedings right through the summer.

As for the garbage, since it is necessary to any organic gardening programme, don't treat it as though it were a nuisance. Mix it with straw, hay, wood chips, sawdust; get it into your compost pile, and put it to work out in the garden rows!

It's an old trick, using garbage on 'hard spots'

Kitchen wastes are a good supply for our compost, but out in Michigan, Marilyn Pearce also buries garbage directly in the paths of her garden. 'Lifting up the spoiled hay mulch which covers all the pathways, I dig a hole and bury some of the kitchen wastes,' she writes. The mulch is then replaced and she leaves her 'small shovel right in place to know where to dig next time'.

Come spring, compost is placed 'all over the garden which we work into the soil with a rotary tiller. By now the former sand we began with has turned into rich-looking soil,' she notes, 'a pleasure to dig into with your hands.'

'Organic cores' beat harsh Texas conditions

Another organic gardener, Fred L. Christen, writes from Texas that 'hardpan is what the building contractor leaves after he is finished with his heavy equipment'. Confronted with such a situation, Mr Christen bought a 6-inch posthole auger and started to plan in 2-foot-deep holes filled with 'organic cores'.

Each hole was filled with 'a mixture of compost and uncomposted organic materials', watered down to drive out the air, and then a plant was set down right on top. Only organic material was used to fill the hole, and the removed soil was 'thrown on the compost pile for the worms to aerate'.

The results, he reports, were 'spectacular'. Although it was one of the hottest Texas summers on record, '38 days reached 100 degrees or higher', the peppers and tomatoes thrived, and insects were 'only a slight problem'. When he checked out the root systems at the end of the season, he found them 'healthy and husky, ample testimony to how well the method works!'

The 'hole method' was also used to save peach trees,

writes an Oklahoma hardpan gardener, Mrs. Marjorie Bingham. Although they were badly stunted, the trees responded to holes dug around them and filled with fresh cow manure. 'The results have been wonderful', she notes, adding that the 'hardpan presents such a barrier to roots that very little growth occurs unless it is broken.'

Cover cropping saves manure

The Binghams also report that the 'first cover crop planted was so scant that it was scarcely worth turning under, although one of our first purchases was a rotary tiller which has since proved invaluable'. However, by continuing to plant cover crops, and practise green manuring and sheet composting, 'the soil gradually improved'. The Binghams estimate they have spread about 40 tons of manure and litter on the orchard and garden. Manure, which at first 'seemed almost a must in order to start production', is no longer relied on to maintain soil fertility. 'We always have a winter cover crop such as rye and vetch,' Mrs Bingham reports.

The advantages of green manuring your garden plots are many and they add up to better crops because it encourages a normally functioning soil microbial life. Here they are:

1. *Adding nitrogen* to the soil for use by productive crops.

2. *Increasing fertility* by mobilizing minerals and building up organic matter.

3. *Reducing losses* caused by erosion.

4. *Improving physical condition* of the soil, thus permitting a more efficient use of plant nutrients.

5. *Conserving nutrients* by cutting down losses caused by leaching.

Hairy vetch is the 'most dependable' green manure crop, write T. Hayden Rogers and Joel E. Giddens in their joint USDA article, 'Green Manure and Cover Crops'. In a 6-year planting experiment conducted in Alabama, vetch was superior to commercial nitrogen fertilizer. Other studies revealed that the 'residual effect of vetch preceding corn in a cotton-corn rotation was equivalent to 214 pounds of seed cotton'.

Green manure crops may be used with considerable success in rotating vegetables, the authors report. Green manure 'increased the yield of potatoes an average of 53 bushels an acre' in experiments conducted over a period of 16 years in Maine. When the green manure crop was removed, 'the yield of potatoes was reduced 38 bushels'. Green manuring is quite profitable from the commercial aspect. 'The average value of the organic treatment on all vegetables studies was $135 an acre above costs.'

Your choice

By now it should be fairly obvious that what you do to maintain soil fertility and structure in your garden is up to you and depends on what you've got to work in terms of soil and the weather conditions that prevail in your area. In any case, use what is abundant and cheap locally. Grow a cover or green manure crop, sheet compost, bury garbage or compost to break up hardpan. Do them all, but *do what conditions demand* and then check results *honestly and carefully*!

And, if you really want to add humus, don't forget to mulch. It also puts humus in the soil, which is dragged down by the worms and broken up into layers, just like on the forest floor, below the mulch. Also, plant some deep-rooted annuals for show and soil improvement.

Their roots aerate the soil and, after they die, turn into humus down in the deeper topsoil and subsoil.

7. WHAT'S AN EARTHWORM WORTH?

Call him a wriggler, an angleworm, fish bait, or anything else you may choose, the earthworm is a valuable adjunct in the soil's expression of fertility. He digests the soil, eats it, and conditions it. Our topsoils have practically been made by earthworms. That is why Aristotle called them the intestines of the soil. Their castings are far richer minerally than the soil which they ingest. It is said that an average earthworm will produce its weight in castings every 24 hours. They burrow into the ground, as far as 6 feet down, aerating the soil, making holes for rain to penetrate. They break up hardpans, which have been created by chemical fertilizers and artificial horticultural practices. Each year their dead bodies furnish a considerable amount of valuable nitrogenous fertilizer, which may amount to more than 1,000 pounds per acre in a highly 'organic soil'.

An earthworm-worked soil will absorb a 2-inch rainfall in 15 seconds due to its porous consistency and sponge-like structure, whereas its neighbouring clay soil takes sometimes as long as 2 hours for the same amount to sink in. Every earthworm burrow hole is a watering tube.

These subterranean workers aerate the soil, allowing the much-needed air to penetrate to the roots. In turn, this oxidizes and nitrifies the earth. It dissolves the soil and makes it soluble in the water that carries the food to the plant roots. I have seen an earthworm take a fairly good-sized globule or tiny clod of earth and watched its passage through its body. It draws leaves and other green matter below the surface, much of which decays and enriches the soil. Many roots use the long tunnels as a means to get to lower levels. As these tunnels are lined by the worms with a fertile liquid casting, the roots benefit accordingly.

As the life of the earthworm is a bare year or two, their dying and decaying bodies furnish a substantial amount of fertilizer each year. The worms have a very high nitrogen content as well as a potent oil which immeasurably enriches the soil. Some earthworm breeders, incidentally, claim that persons with eczema of the hands have cured it by running their hands through the soil of the earthworm boxes which seem to be impregnated with this oil.

Worm castings are richest humus

Earthworm castings are the finest form of humus known. At the Connecticut Experimental Station, it was found that the nitrogen in these castings is almost five times greater than in the ordinary topsoil, the phosphate seven times greater, potash eleven times, and magnesium three times. California flower-growers pay a high price for earthworm castings. They report this material as the best they have ever been able to secure for raising flowers. Experts from Great Britain have estimated that in the intensive 6-month cotton-growing season, following the overflowing of the Nile, earthworm castings amounted to almost 120 tons per acre. This is more than eight times the figure given by Darwin, and would seem to indicate an earthworm population of about 1,500,000 an acre. Such a gargantuan quantity of worms is made possible by the organic material (their food), which the overflowing Nile deposits on the land.

Darwin's figures of the number of earthworms per acre were very conservative. In Ohio, government investigators found 1,000,000 worms per acre on bluegrass pasture. Here the topsoil was over 18 inches thick, whereas in England Darwin found the upper layer of rich soil where he conducted his researches only 5 or 6 inches deep. Government investigators in Oregon found earthworm populations from 500,000 to 1,500,000 per acre.

More than a thousand types of earthworms

There are over 1,100 species of earthworms, but for our purposes we need consider only two. This group doesn't include cutworms, which are really caterpillars, nor wireworms. Neither do they include the parasitic nematodes—threadworms or roundworms so small that they are barely seen by the naked eye. Eelworms are in the same class.

We are concerned mainly with two types of earthworms: the rain worm, which works in the soil, and the smaller, thinner reddish type, which lives on fresh manure and in compost heaps. The soil-inhabiting rain worm will not thrive in a compost heap, and vice versa. When a heap is first made, no earthworms will be seen. They soon begin to propagate (the red type), and when the heap turns to humus they die and decay. Where semi-decayed compost is spread on the land most of the red earthworms in it die at once; some continue to live for as long as fairly large amounts of decaying matter are present. It is then time for the rain worm to take over and to convert the decayed organic matter in the soil into humus. Sometimes when a compost heap is in the final stages, soil-inhabiting rain worms may migrate into it.

Chemicals and earthworms don't mix

Organic matter and mineral rock fragments are the earthworm's natural food. Where strong chemical fertilizers are used, conditions distasteful to earthworms arise and their numbers decrease to the vanishing point. Ammonium sulphate, a fertilizer extensively used by farmers, is particularly harmful to these soil workers. In fact ammonium sulphate is a known worm killer and is used for that purpose to kill worms on golf-course putting greens!

Many other chemical fertilizers are slowly but definitely killing off the earthworm population. This was proven at the research laboratory at Dornach in Switzerland, where experiments showed that earthworms did not like soil saturated with artificial fertilizer, and if given an opportunity chose earth fertilized with biodynamic compost, in preference even to soil that was not fertilized at all.

Strong insect sprays containing lead, arsenic, copper, lime sulphurs, and tar oil, etc., are even more destructive to earthworms. In tracts of potato-growing land where many of these sprays are doused periodically on the land, nary an earthworm can be found. What is equally as bad is the fact that much of the bacteria population is adversely affected. The result is that the soil becomes almost sterile, and the farmer is working in a dead medium. Therefore, each succeeding year requires the use of progressively more spray and more chemical fertilizer to get the necessary yield.

Likewise in vineyards or orchards which have been intensively treated with sprays for many years, no earthworms are to be found. In such places, the earth becomes hard-packed and extremely difficult for cultivation. Bird life will move away because of the lack of its usual food, the earthworm, and the land will suffer further because birds destroy fabulous amounts of noxious insects and their larvae.

'Bacteria test' shows worm's value

The boring into the soil of earthworms increases the porosity and aeration of the soil. This is of great aid to other kinds of soil life, such as bacteria, for example. In well-worked soil there is to be found about 600 pounds of bacteria to the acre. Where earthworms are absent, the bacteria population greatly decreases, to the serious detriment of the soil's fertility.

Bacteria is a potent factor in the formation of humus. It gives the soil the power to quickly digest organic matter. Place a piece of sacking on top of the soil that is saturated with bacteria. It will be eaten up by the soil and completely disappear from the surface in a few months. Do the same thing on land strongly chemicalized and sprayed. It will remain for years. That type of soil has lost its natural powers of digestion. It is sterile. It is dead.

Where any one item in nature's cycle is disturbed, it will be found that others are automatically affected. Nature consists of a chain of conditions, interrelated and interlocked. Remove any one factor and you will find that she cannot do her work efficiently and becomes less friendly to man. It never fails.

COMPOST

1. GARBAGE IS GOLD; COMPOST IS BEAUTIFUL

At the very base of the organic method lies compost. In its many forms and variations, compost is the beautiful substance which gives fertility to soil, productivity to plants, and health to man. It is the combination soil conditioner–fertilizer of the organic gardener, and the hub of all his gardening activities. If you are a successful compost maker, chances are 100 to 1 that you are a successful organic gardener.

In the past two decades, there has been a great amount of research in composting methods, resulting in the 14-day method, sheet composting, anaerobic methods, and many more variations of these. Behind them all, however, lies the original Indore method, invented by the father of organic gardening, Sir Albert Howard. The Indore method is still the most widely used, and is still practical and productive.

Sir Albert Howard found that by layering different organic materials, decomposition took place more quickly and more completely. He first placed down a 5- or 6-inch layer of green matter, then a 2-inch layer of manure (blood meal, bone meal, sewage sludge, or other high-protein material may be substituted), and a layer of rich earth, with a sprinkling of lime. This simple formula produced a crumbly compost, rich in nutrient value and valuable as a soil structure builder. In further research, Howard found that a heap 5 to 10 feet wide, and 5 feet high was ideal (the length is optional). He also found that decomposition was facilitated by aeration, and so he placed pipes or thick stakes through the pile as it was being built, then pulled them out when the heap was 5 feet high. He then lightly pressed the entire outside surface to prevent blowing, formed a shallow basin on top to catch rainwater, covered the entire surface with a thin layer of earth, and left it to decay.

Organic gardeners are not hide-bound to that original, successful research carried out years ago by Sir Albert Howard. They build on his work and get down to compost making in ways which suit them. Take the example of *Organic Gardening* reader O. A. Severance of Watertown, New York, who transformed a completely unproductive piece of land into a lush garden by using only his home-made garden compost by his own method. Mr Severance makes compost in a pit, surrounded by a wall of loose field stone 7 feet square on the inside and 2 feet high. The wall is laid on top of the ground, and the soil inside is dug out a foot deep.

Into this pit go hen and stable manure, leaves, weeds, garbage, lawn clippings, sunflower stalks, some sod, and ground limestone. This pit, layered according to Howard's Indore process, is level with the top of the stones when it is completed. Severance turns the pile in 3 weeks when he estimates the temperature has reached 150°. Four weeks later he turns the pile again, in order to be sure all material has a chance to get into the centre of the heap where decomposition is proceeding most rapidly. In a total of 3 months, he takes out well over 2 tons of finished compost. In this way he can make two piles each season.

From experimenting, gardeners often find ways to improve the Indore method, at least in their own gardens. Lois Hebble of Decatur, Indiana, uses a strip composting method. In the middle of the growing season, she lays heaps of organic materials on top of vegetable rows from which she has just harvested early crops. The material is partially composted by the next spring, but is not broken down enough for small seeds. Into these rows she plants melons, squash, or cucumbers.

'For each hill,' says Mrs Hebble, 'I scoop out a small hole and fill this with a shovelful or two of garden soil, then plant the seeds in this. Later in the summer, just before the vines start spreading out too much, I cover the strip with a good weed-smothering layer of old hay. By the following spring, the soil under this strip has become mellow and homogenized enough to plant the smaller seeds. This method also keeps the garden crops in constant rotation.'

Other gardeners use variations of the earthworm bed, sheet composting, mulching, pits, bins, plastic, shredding, and numerous devices in trying to find the best method for them. You, too, can experiment with different methods to find *your* way of composting. But remember that the key to success is the Indore method. Learn it well and anything is possible.

2. HELPFUL HINTS ON COMPOST MAKING

When to make compost

In temperate-climate zones, autumn is generally the most suitable time to make compost. Among the reasons for this are:

1. Garden production is completed for the season; time and attention can more readily be given to preparing humus.

2. Plant wastes, leaves, and various other organic materials are plentiful and easily available.

3. Either finished or partially decomposed compost can be readied and applied to all sections of the garden with minimum effort or interference and with ample time to replenish the soil well before spring planting.

October and November are excellent for making compost heaps or pits because at no other time of the year are plant materials more abundant for this purpose. Garden wastes, autumnal leaves, roadside weeds, wastes from food-processing plants, and other materials are easy to obtain at this time of year. Also by making the compost heap then, the compost will be ready for use at spring garden-making time.

Compost, however, can and should be made during any part of the year. In subtropical climes, any time is best for compost making. In the North, however, you often have extremely dry summers, when the decaying process is held up. We recently made a pit of compost of very resistant ingredients—shredded corncobs and leaves—in the middle of the winter, and by July it had been turned into wonderful compost, with earthworms doing the mixing. During the winter warm spells, compost can be made in a pit. The pit sides keep it warm and accelerate the decay processes in the winter. It wouldn't pay to assemble a compost heap in the open.

For winter composting, pile up the manure with a covering of soil and sacking or polythene sheeting. Also have available, in a protected place, topsoil and green matter that are not frozen. Leaves that have been gathered in the autumn are excellent.

If you do have to make a compost in the open during winter, choose a protected place, as on the south side of a building or wall. An extra heavy layer of soil on top would help, or a very heavy hay or straw mulch a few feet thick to keep the heap warm.

Chopping and smashing

American compost makers go in for grinders and shredders, often power-driven. These reduce crude wastes to shreds and the making of garden compost with smaller particles can lead to a quick ferment and finished compost made in so short a time as from 3 to 5 days. Rapidly-made garden compost is believed to be of better quality than compost made over a period of months because there is less time for the dissipation of valuable gases and the leaching out of essential elements. We in

Britain have, as yet, no compost-making gadgets. Instead, it is the practice to smash thick stems of Brussels sprouts and broccoli with a hammer or the back of a spade and then to sever them into small sections using the blade of a spade. Paper, cardboard, and discarded clothing are torn into fairly small pieces before being added to a compost heap. By reducing the size of the ingredients and by making a heap quickly the fermentation process is much more rapid than when the wastes incorporated in the heap are large in size and the heap itself built up slowly.

Ventilating the heap

It is absolutely essential that the compost heap be well ventilated so that there is a sufficient flow of gases between the atmosphere and the interior of the compost heap. The soil organisms which break down the plant and animal residues and convert them into compost are aerobes, i.e. they must have the oxygen from the atmosphere to carry on their life activities. Placing a stake or a pole in the centre and building the heap around it is one way of ensuring that the heap is well ventilated. Alternatively a pole may be driven from top to bottom and in the centre of the heap after completion. Stakes and poles are then removed, leaving ventilation holes. For ventilating large heaps in market gardens or on farms the following method is suggested. As soon as the pits have been dug or the soil has otherwise been prepared for the compost heaps, a number of ordinary fence posts are set up and held in position by driving three small stakes around the base of each post. The posts are placed where the ventilators are desired. By using chalk or heavy pencil, marks can be made on the posts 8 inches apart to serve as a guide in building the various layers of the heap; 6 inches for plant material,

2 inches for the fresh manure, a sprinkling of raw ground limestone, and a $\frac{3}{4}$ inch or less of good earth. When the heap has been built to its usual height of 5 feet, the posts are pulled out to form the ventilating chimneys. To facilitate the removal of the posts, a board can be laid on the heap to serve as a walk, and a cross-piece nailed near the top of the post to serve as a handle to pull out the post. The size of the ventilator is determined by the size of the post used.

Where to make compost

There are no set rules on the best place to make compost. We know of gardeners with imagination who have set up a composting area on their front lawns in such a way that it added to the overall attractiveness. For the most part, though, gardeners prefer to do their compost making in the back garden, where the heap can be easily 'disguised' in some way.

The spot you choose for your composting site should be one which:

1. Is close to the kitchen garden where you will use most of the compost you make.
2. Can be reached easily by the family car or a wheelbarrow. You may bring quite a quantity of wastes home in the car boot and your neighbours will be the more inclined to let you have their garden wastes if they can barrow them into your garden and to the heap with ease.
3. Is kept tidy, fits in well with the garden plan and is never an eyesore.

There are a great many ways to improve the appearance of composting areas on your own home grounds. There are wooden bins specially designed for this purpose, where the slats are removable for easy withdrawal of the finished compost. Many gardeners we know use cement blocks, often without mortaring them together, around two or three sides of the heap. (Hay bales make an excellent 'door' on the fourth side.) Still others make use of hedges to 'fence off' their home fertilizer factories.

What you decide to do depends a great deal on the size of your grounds. If you have several acres; there's probably little need to think about disguising the heap; your main objective is to choose an idea that's accessible and large enough to make all the compost you need.

On the other hand, if you live in a highly developed suburban area with fussy neighbours, you'll want to be extra careful. Besides the camouflage techniques mentioned previously, you might want to think about making compost in pits.

Here's an idea which John Adamson of East Lansing, Michigan, sent in to us at *Organic Gardening*. What he suggests may help you with your own composting problems.

I've been trying to come up with a systematic arrangement for making regular use of kitchen and garden refuse. What I have in mind are sunken dual compost heaps, that is, two pits side by side. These are to be dug in the rear of my garden, surrounded by shrubbery for screening and protection. The rectangular depressions are to be about 2 feet deep, 2 feet wide, and 4 feet long, with wooden covers to go over them to keep the neighbourhood dogs from scattering the contents, and to keep these receptacles from filling up with snow in the winter season.

In a suburban area as I live in, it would not be acceptable to try to maintain my compost on top of the ground, even with 3 framed sides. The dimensions mentioned would provide relatively small compost heaps, to be sure, but half a loaf is better than none, and I can get away with this size and also get a more rapid turnover than if they were larger.

The main thing to remember is that in just about every garden there *is* space for composting.

Collecting and assembling materials

When it comes to getting materials for your compost heap, the big point is to use imagination and initiative. You'll have a certain amount of waste materials available without moving off your home grounds, such as grass clippings, garden residues, leaves, weeds, kitchen wastes, and so on. If these supply you with enough of the vegetable matter for your composting, that's fine. But don't feel that you are limited to just those sources. If you need more, there are scores of places within a short drive of your home where valuable wastes are available—for the most part *free*.

Speeding up compost making

When made correctly, compost can be prepared by Sir Albert Howard's Indore methods in from 6 to 9 months. The pile is turned after 6 weeks and again at 12 weeks to mix the wastes thoroughly and to allow air to penetrate all parts of the heap.

Few gardeners are content to wait such a long time for much-needed compost and even if power-driven compost-hastening grinders and shredders were on offer in Britain few of us would invest in machinery which ought, though, to appeal to large-scale composters like commercial growers and farmers. From experiments at Organic Park by staff of *Organic Gardening* it has been found that compost can be made quite quickly without the use of special equipment. We used no chemical activators. We consider them absolutely unnecessary to hasten decomposition and to increase the fermentation process. Here is what we suggest for speeding up compost making in your garden:

When making the compost heap, be sure to mix materials such as grass mowings, vegetable tops, weeds, etc., with a little animal manure. Failing horse or poultry—rabbit or hamster will do fine. If you just can't get any manure at all, use dried blood. All material should be moist to start with and the heap should be kept wet. To keep the heap moist water it for the first 3 days after you have completed it.

Turn the heap often. The fastest-working bacteria thrive in the presence of air, and turning the heap is the best way to aerate it. Initially, every 3 or 4 days is not too often. It's best not to make the speed compost heaps too large. Remember, a ton of compost occupies a space only 4 feet square and 4 feet high, and will last the average gardener for quite a while.

Adding some red wrigglers—manure or compost worms—to the compost heap is also an effective way of hastening decomposition.

Compost is plant-food rich

Critics of organic gardening methods often say that back-garden-made compost cannot contain the high amounts of NPK plant foods as are found in animal dung. Therefore, so they contend, your garden compost and mine just isn't as good as, say, farmyard manure or, for that matter, chemical fertilizer mixtures. They forget to take into account that home-made garden compost is made from all sorts of wastes not only from your garden but also from all parts of the world. In it you will incorporate orange skins from South Africa, grapefruit skins from Israel, eggshells from some faraway country or from Denmark, worn-out clothing based on Egyptian or Indian cotton and New Zealand or Australian wool, the daily newspaper (after you have read it!) made from Finnish or Canadian timber, the odd piece of uneaten tomato from

Spain and tea leaves from India or Ceylon.

Perhaps the critics are right; perhaps your sample of garden compost lacks the high amounts of NPK plant foods found in animal dung or in chemical fertilizer mixtures. But what about trace elements? Modern research shows how important it is for the health of our garden plants to have available soil trace elements like iron, manganese, copper, zinc, boron, molybdenum, chlorine, and cobalt. No farmyard manure nor the most expensive chemical fertilizer is likely to contain the mixture of trace elements collected from all parts of the world and contained in the wastes you add to your compost heap and from the compost heap to the garden soil.

Like farmyard manure your garden compost increases the soil's water-holding capacity, improves its tilth and aeration. Unlike farmyard manure there is no forcing action in garden compost so plants grow steadily, naturally. Garden compost also makes plant nutrients already in your soil more available to growing plants.

As for the NPK content of your garden compost. If a critical visitor tries to catch you on that point, just move along to where a heavyweight cabbage or extra-thick long rhubarb stems demonstrate that they are being supplied with sufficient NPK. Your crops are your living soil testers.

If you are starting from scratch and know that your garden soil is on the acid side, don't forget to sprinkle some lime over each layer of wastes as you build your compost heaps.

Mistakes to avoid

Most people get into trouble with their compost heaps by making them of one ingredient. They make a pile of only leaves, or weeds, or grass clippings and are disappointed when nothing happens. Last year we made a test heap consisting only of shredded hay. Although we kept this heap moist and turned it frequently, little decomposition took place. It's essential to add some nitrogen-rich material such as fresh or dried manure, dried blood, or compost previously made, or even a small amount of rich soil, because the nitrogen in these materials is needed food for the decomposing bacteria.

Just as important as not letting the heap dry up, is not keeping it in a perpetually soggy condition.

Difficulties can arise also if the compost heap is too large. Five feet is about the right height, as it allows air to get into every spot, provided that the heap is not too wide either (no more than 10 to 12 feet wide at the bottom, generally not less than 5 feet).

During the winter months, little decomposition usually takes place in the heap because of the cold. Many gardeners get around this by covering the heap with sacking, old sacks, canvas, or tarpaulin sheeting, or even by soil. Newest form of protection is 500-gauge heavyweight black polythene. We'll be having more to say about black polythene later on in this chapter.

How to tell when finished

Some people think the finished product of their composting process should be crumbly like old leaf mould, but generally we're satisfied with a compost in which the straw, grass clippings, and more refractory substances such as cabbage stumps and sweet corn stalks are broken up and have a rich, dark colour.

When we apply compost, the mass is crumbly, not soggy; very often, on close inspection, you can determine its origin. Of course, if you're in no rush to use the compost, there's no harm in letting the compost break down into finer material. For ordinary gardening purposes, this is not necessary though, since the final decay can take place right in the ground. For flower growing, especially potted plants and for starting seedlings, it's good to screen the rougher material or to use the finer material which develops later.

When and how to use compost

Many gardeners schedule their compost applications about a month before planting, when the materials are decomposed and rather fine. Others 'double up' on their composting production by applying it half finished, or notably fibrous, in the autumn, and allowing it to break down right in the soil. In this way, they can make a second compost heap in the same space as the first and have twice as much finished compost by the time spring comes.

For general application the soil should be forked to a depth of around 4 inches and all weeds and weed roots removed. Garden compost may be dug into the top 4 inches of soil but it is more usual to spread it on top of the dug soil as a mulch. When adding garden compost to growing crops it is simply applied as a mulch. This procedure is called a top-dressing of compost.

Compost should be applied annually—and if as a mulch from 1 to 3 inches in thickness. This works out at one large barrow-load per square yard. You can get by with less and if you have a large allotment you will probably well compost a different part of it each season. But most gardeners have such small kitchen gardens nowadays and the amount of compost you will be making each season will permit you to use it generously. As a guide, an average figure of weight for 1 cubic yard of compost is 1,000 pounds.

When composting trees, start about 2 to 3 feet away from the trunk and go to a foot beyond the drip line at the end of the branches. First cultivate the soil under the tree; then work about an inch or more of compost into the upper 2 inches annually.

When adding compost to your lawn, make sure that it is finely ground, so there's no chance of smothering the grass. An excellent way to improve your lawn is to first use an aerator to slice up the sod; then apply a thick covering of fine compost. As an optional final step, you could use a rotary mower to distribute the surface compost into the crevices. In this way, the compost provides the roots with moisture and nutrients and prevents soil from compacting.

3. A Steady Compost Supply for the Small-space Residential Gardener

Want the richest flower beds in town? Want an ever-ready supply of rich humus, and built-in humus beds? Want to stop giving away kitchen garbage to the dustman? If so (and who doesn't), then you should try this simple, but wonderfully efficient, composting method devised by J. J. Bartlett. He combines kitchen garbage, manure, green matter, and earthworms into a neat, workable system, especially suited to the small-space residential gardener.

The first step is to build or find a box (no bottom or top). It can be of any size, but Mr Bartlett has found that a long narrow one is more suited to inconspicuous placement along fences, in front of hedges, in borders, and other small spaces. His boxes are 4 feet long, 1 foot high, and 1 to 2 feet wide.

Next, pick a spot and dig a rectangular hole about 18 inches deep and just slightly smaller in dimensions than the box, so that the box will rest firmly on the ground above the hole. After this is done, you are ready to begin composting. The hole is filled in layer style—kitchen garbage, manure, and green matter, in that order. Mr Bartlett has found kitchen garbage to compost faster when run through a meat grinder, but this is not essential. He keeps a bag of pulverized manure and a pile of shredded green matter at the side of the box, and each time garbage is introduced he follows immediately with the other two layers. After each addition, he covers the pit with a sheet of canvas and wets it down, then places a board on top of the box. In this way there is absolutely no odour, nor any pest problem.

In about 3 weeks' time when the bottom layers have decomposed to a great extent, introduce about 500 earthworms. You'll soon have thousands to use all around the garden. These little composters will work through successive layers, which you add to the pit, mixing and breaking down the heap for you. Be careful, though, not to introduce the worms during the terrific heat of the initial breakdown. Heat of successive layers won't bother them, because they'll remain below until the above layer cools.

Continue this layering process until the pit is filled all the way to the top of the box. Then allow it to decompose for 5 or 6 more weeks, keeping it moist. In the meantime you can start another box.

After the first pit is fully composted, remove the compost down to soil level, place it in several cone-shaped piles on a large board or tarpaulin, and leave it exposed to the sun for 1 to 2 hours. The worms will have balled up at the bottom of each pile, and can be easily removed and introduced to the second pit. The finished compost piles may be sifted and bagged for future use. Meanwhile, you have just created the richest 18-inch-deep flower bed in town, which you can use as it is, or tempered down with soil—any way you like.

Now you may begin pit number three, using the box you have just emptied. Using this system, you'll have a new load of compost each sixth week, you'll be able to make flower beds rich in humus from the worst clay or sand. You'll not only be raising thousands of red wrigglers to deal with your garbage but the richness of your garden soil will lead to the increased breeding of humus-making earthworms, too—and you'll have done it with little trouble or expense in a small space, with no odour or pest problems.

How to make compost in winter

While winter winds and snow may be blowing, your compost heap can still be alive and hot. Many gardeners successfully make compost during the wintertime; following are some ideas they've used:

Pits and earthworms. If compost is made in a pit in winter, the pit sides keep it warm and accelerate the decaying process. Even such resistant materials as bashed cabbage stems and leaves will be ready for soil-building use by late spring with the pit method, especially if earthworms are used to do the mixing. Depth of pit can be 3 feet, length and width about 4 feet. After placing the materials in the pit, cover them with soil, canvas, straw, sacks, or similar materials to retain heat and moisture for faster decomposition.

Insulating heaps. If you do make the heap above ground, choose a protected place, as the south side of a building or wall. Here again, an extra layer of soil on top, or a very heavy hay or straw mulch would help keep the heap warm.

It's even possible to insulate a compost heap outdoors for faster decomposition. You can do this by enclosing the heap with a larger enclosure and filling the space between the two enclosures with leaves, hay, straw, sawdust, or other insulating material.

Greenhouses and cold frames. When compost can be made in a greenhouse, barn, or outbuilding, winter compost making is naturally less of a problem. Some gardeners have had fine results using a cold frame as a winter bin. One Pennsylvania organic gardener reports that the temperature inside the cold frame was as much as 50° warmer than that outside.

In any winter compost project, it's important to use as much manure, tankage, blood bone meal, sludge, or other high nitrogen material as possible. These will aid the heating-up process in spite of the weather.

Compost for starting seedlings

Make a mixture of 2 parts good garden loam, 1 part fine, sharp sand, and 1 part compost. (It's a good idea to let this mixture age for several months before seeding, so January is about the right time to prepare it.) You may want to sift the mixture through a $\frac{1}{4}$-inch-mesh screen, placing the coarser particles in the bottom of the flat to improve drainage.

There is enough plant food in this mixture without adding manure or other organic fertilizers high in nitrogen. Used too soon, these can cause young plants to grow too rapidly, unbalancing their natural growth.

Starter solution

Plant starter solutions made from compost can be a big help in growing plants. According to Ralph Clark, extension horticulturist from Oregon, greenhouse operators have long made use of this method to bring their crops to a rapid and profitable production.

The main benefit received from these solutions is that the plant is provided with immediately available plant food. This stimulates leaf and root growth, giving the plant a thick pick-up after transplanting. These solutions are used especially on young lettuce, tomatoes, celery, peppers, melons, egg plants, cabbages, cauliflower, and all kinds of transplants.

Here is a recommended starter: Fill barrel or other container a quarter full of compost. Continue to fill container with water, stirring several times during next 24 to 48 hours. In using, dilute to a light amber colour with water. Pour 1 pint around each plant when setting out, or later as necessary to encourage growth. Liquid compost can be used at 10-day to 2-week intervals, especially when soils are not high in fertility.

Tests have shown that seeds sprout more than twice as well when soaked in a solution of this kind. In the wild, practically all seeds depend upon the moisture which seeps to them through a layer of nature's compost.

4. BUILDING THE BEST COMPOST BIN

The best compost bin is the one that turns your home's organic wastes into soil fertility quickly, cheaply, and easily.

The materials don't matter, but the results do. For years, organic gardeners have been making compost bins with bits of old wire, scrap wood, discarded lumber, old cement blocks, and battered, secondhand steel drums. They've been using whatever they could lay their hands on (free donations are always appreciated!) to make compost bins that fitted in with their gardening programmes. Here's how they've been doing it for the last 10 or more years.

Three-by-three wire bin cost $4 in 1961

Back in 1961 Lyman Wood built a wire and wood bin using scrap 2-inch-square lumber, which he covered with $\frac{1}{2}$-inch chicken-wire mesh for a total cost of $4. Made of two L-shaped sections held together with screen-door hooks, the cage provided him with 18 to 24 cubic feet of finished compost in 14 days, which was par for the composting course then.

Composter Wood reported that the pile heated up to 140° to 160° in 2 days, and could be turned in 4. He damped down each layer—leaves, grass, garbage, and manure—as he added it, and counted on the well-ventilated cage to encourage complete bacterial action.

Turning was extremely easy. He unhooked the sides, separated each of the L-shaped sections, and then re-assembled them next to the square-sided heap. 'You will be pleasantly surprised at how neatly and firmly the heap stands,' he wrote, adding: 'It is now a simple and satisfying task, using a fork, to peel the layers off the pile and toss them in the now-empty cage.' During the turning operation, he kept a hose handy to wet down the heap as the material was transferred.

'I have used this cage many times, he concludes, 'for 14-day rapid composting, and each time it is a satisfying, successful venture to harvest the cube of dark, moist crumbly humus.'

The same idea—a portable compost bin that can be lifted, leaving a pile ready for turning—was used about 6 years ago by the Peter Seymour Company of Hopkins, Minnesota. The 'Cake-Maker' was made of wood and metal framing and was light enough to be lifted off the pile, leaving a 'cake' of compost, and ready to be filled again.

Bales of hay make a winter compost bin

Alden Stahr once made an all-winter compost bin out of old bales of hay stacked around secondhand storm doors and windows which he put up in the garden. Composter Stahr mixed in garbage and manure to help heat up the pile, while the glass lid—slanted to the south to pick up the long, low, midwinter rays of the sun—also kept out scavenging cats and dogs.

Although he recorded a 50° difference in temperatures between the inside of the bin and the outdoors one cold January morning, he achieved an extra supply of compost, which he had ready for early spring use, 'thanks to the billions of happy bacteria hard at work'.

The New Zealand bin—air from all sides

The classic among compost bins is the wooden New Zealand box which was originally designed by the Auckland Humic Club to admit as much air as possible from all sides. Many variations exist, so don't hesitate to change your design to fit your material and budget.

The important factor is air circulation and ventilation from all sides, so be sure to leave 1-inch spaces between your slabs or boards. It's a good idea to start with a rugged frame work—two-by-fours are excellent—and then nail a lattice of boards over it. The top and bottom are left open, although some composters prefer to cover the top of the pile in rainy weather to prevent leaching. One or two good coats of linseed oil should be allowed to soak into the wood to make it weather- and rot-resistant.

Steel-drum composters for the suburbanite

American West Coast gardener John Meeker reported several years ago how he solved the twin problems of running a compost pile in a congested suburban area without offending his neighbours, while getting enough compost to run his garden. He circulated air into the heap, using a steel drum which cost him $1, and had it raised 6 inches off the ground by setting it up on a circular metal frame with legs. Meeker's frame, worth $15 if done in a commercial shop, cost him nothing. But other readers have set their steel drums on 8-inch cement blocks, which get them up into the air for practically nothing.

Meeker reported that the construction has several advantages over the piles and pits that I used before. *The air can circulate up from the bottom of the barrel.* The six-inch space allows easy removal of the compost. The moisture content of the compost can be carefully regulated by covering the barrel with a lid ... leaching of the compost is perfectly controlled. *By simply covering and uncovering the top, one can regulate the amount of air introduced into the mass.*

There is always a bushel or two of compost ready, Meeker noted, even with so small a composter 'once the cycle has begun'. This includes such seasonal bonuses as lawn mowings, autumn leaves, and crop residues which are 'ready to enrich the garden by the time one gets ready for spring planting'.

As for the neighbours 'who have gladly shared' his bumper harvests while 'turning up their noses at my deposits of leaves, cuttings, manure and—worse—garbage', Meeker reported the solution to the odour problem.

When I have a large amount of lettuce leaves, beet tops, grass cuttings, or kitchen refuse, *I whiten the top of the dampened pile with a sprinkling of lime*, and over that I add a thick layer of dried cow manure. *The lime helps to decrease the smell and lessen the acidity of the green refuse and garbage.*

A more complicated application of the steel-drum composter calls for nesting one drum on the bottom third of a slightly larger container, and installing a metal lattice grate between them to hold the pile up so air can get at it. Built by Ralph Poe of Canton, Illinois, the drum composter also featured a hollow, vertical, 3-inch-wide pipe with $\frac{1}{4}$-inch perforations that was thrust down into the heap's centre and left there for additional ventilation.

Revolving-drum composters mix materials with air

An even more effective way of getting air into the compost pile *by using the drum as a mixing chamber as well as a ventilating device* was reported by Julian Fletcher of California and Frederick J. Barnett, an Australian retired engineer. It is good to be able to report that, while these composters are somewhat complicated, *their cost was very low.*

Although the Australian machine was run by $\frac{1}{4}$-h.p. electric motor, it cost $8.50 because it was made almost completely of discards. The California hand-turned drum cost more—$12.15, of which $7 went for the drum and extra welding. The moral of both composting stories seems plain; you can do almost anything you want to for your home, if you're willing to plan carefully and work hard.

Fletcher spent the extra money for a very tight welding job that secured his 50-gallon drum diagonally to a $1\frac{1}{2}$-inch pipe set 42 inches above the ground, which made 'it easy to get a two-wheel garden cart under it for quick loading'. The supporting pipe was 50 inches long, and measured 47 inches between the two-by-four, 58-inch-long posts that were set 18 inches deep into the ground.

Retired engineer Barnett, who was in his eighties when he perfected his revolving drum, reported that 'as the years went on, it got harder to turn compost in the bins'. So he decided to make 'practically effortless' compost using 'a rotating square container that was easier to make' and producing it economically from materials 'that had been lying about for years'. Cost of materials came to $8.50, including the motor, the pipe on which the box revolves, the wheels from a baby carriage and bicycle, and the pulleys. Although inventor Barnett 'likes' the motor, he concedes that 'a crank-handle may be easily attached to the shaft and do as well'.

Vacuum-cleaner motor blows air into pile

Complete air ventilation of the entire mass has been achieved by the Barnett revolving drum. The fan section of a vacuum cleaner, sealed to one end of a hollow rotating shaft, blew air through it and out into the compost through a series of thirty-two opposing holes.

It is almost impossible to overemphasize the importance of this ideal mixing of air with the layers of grass cuttings, kitchen refuse, sawdust, and fowl manure. Also, each layer is dampened as it is applied, and the box is rotated for 30 minutes. It is then rested for 24 to 48 hours with the lid on top, and covered with three layers of sacking.

The resulting bacterial action caused inside temperatures to reach 160°. After five days, the box is again rotated for 30 minutes, with *the blower again forcing air through the shaft into the centre of the mass*. This time the box rests with its bottom on top to permit air to circulate through twelve $\frac{1}{4}$-inch holes drilled along the bottom. Intermittent turning, the inventor reported, 'seems to produce better heating results'.

Raising pile off ground eases circulation of air

But you don't have to build a revolving drum to get air into the centre of your compost heap. Just raise it off the ground—10 inches is fine—by building a substantial open lattice support right into your bin.

You can also make a wooden base for your compost pile, reinforcing it with $\frac{1}{2}$-inch netting to get it the recommended 10 inches off the ground.

Researchers at Phoenix, Arizona, found that a ton of rapidly decomposing compost uses up 18,000 to 20,000 cubic feet of air daily, and that turning of the pile doesn't always get the job done. But 'forced air' composting—raising the pile off the ground—stimulates uniform decomposition of the the entire pile, not just the top 12 inches.

The 'open-hearth bottom' bin is made of wood with a sturdy grid of 1-inch piping holding the compostable mass 1 foot above the ground. It's 4 feet square, made of sturdy secondhand lumber. A user reports never having to turn the pile, and advises that you don't have to worry about 'mass and bulk as long as you have the open-hearth-bottom, and you'll always have plenty of good compost'.

The compost bin will pay its way

A compost bin will soon pay for itself in reduced garbage disposal expenses. But there is more to composting than that. A compost bin pays for itself in a more productive and beautiful garden, and tastier, more healthful food for the entire family.

The bin shouldn't cost more than £3, and it shouldn't take more than 3 hours to make. Use whatever materials are cheap and abundant in your area, and don't be afraid to accept hand-outs. Put the bin where it will get both sun and air, and is handy both to the garden, where the compost will go, and the path up which much of its material will be barrowed.

Finally, every home—the little ones as well as those in crowded towns—should have its own compost-making bin in this time of widespread and mass pollution of the environment. Remember, composting is the only safe way to handle the family's organic wastes and leftovers.

Better start building that bin—now.

MAURICE FRANZ

The black sheet method

Lots of folk think I invented the Black Sheet Composting Method. I didn't. It was just one of the bright ideas I learnt from reading *Organic Gardening*. I found the method so satisfactory which is why I continue to use it for making my own garden compost and why I write so often about it. You build your compost heap in the way you choose. To prevent any smells and to dissuade your pup and the cat next door from investigating the contents of the pile you keep it covered at all times with a large sheet of 500-gauge black polythene. Whenever you add anything a bit smelly to the heap—droppings from the son and heir's rabbit cage or pressed pulp from the wife's home-winemaking experiments are just two examples—you cover well with some soil and replace the polythene sheeting which you weigh down with anything to hand so that it stays put. When the heap has been constructed, drape it with any old sacks (paper or jute), old rugs, carpets, or discarded clothing and re-cover with the sheet of plastic. I find that sufficient air reaches the heap which, as it is so well protected from the elements, ferments quickly and needs no turning. A heap made within weeks in early spring provides good compost ready for use in early June—just when a supply of compost is needed for brassica, tomato, and vegetable marrow planting. Expect the sacks, rugs, and old clothing to show signs of rot. Use them as long as they will last. When semi-disintegrated tear them in pieces and add them to a heap. Friends and neighbours will be glad to let you have replacements. It will mean less rubbish in their already over-filled dustbins.

BRIAN FURNER

5. MATERIALS FOR COMPOSTING AND SOIL CONDITIONING

Hedge trimmings

Spring, summer, and early autumn hedge trimmings are valuable. They are also soft and lush and help get a compost heap to ferment. Commonest hedge trimmings for gardeners are privet. If you have none watch out for neighbours trimming their garden hedges. I know they'll be so pleased to find a 'home' for what they usually stack and try to burn ... not always successfully in a wet season. If you're like me—ever on the lookout for compost-making material—you'll itch to wheel away the neighbours' loads of hedge trimmings. My advice is don't! They'll expect you to become a sort of odd job man, ever ready—even if you're watching your favourite team on the box or even if you're in the bath—to go into action with the garden wheelbarrow. Instead, guide them with their wheelbarrows to your garden and to your compost heap. Let them make the regular deliveries. Make sure they get a taste of this or that from your kitchen garden. If they go in for any food growing, chances are they'll start composting too. True, you'll lose some supplies of leaves and lawn mowings, but you will have converted yet another gardener to pleasurable, successful gardening.

Hay

In its early stages, all green matter, including hay, contains more nitrogen than when grown to maturity. Therefore, if you can get hay—especially hay containing a high proportion of young clover—it will break down faster in the compost heap. However, it's worth using all the hay you can get—young or old.

Sawdust and wood wastes

Sawdust has excellent properties for building soil, and can be added to the compost heap. You probably can obtain as much sawdust as you want free by checking with a local lumber mill.

Since sawdust does not break down completely unless used in fine sprinklings, it should not be packed too heavily lest it prevent aeration of the heap. Incidentally, sawdust also makes an excellent mulch material around shrubs, flowers, and vegetables.

Garden residues

Tomato and marrow plants, pea bine, flower stems, and all plant remains make a rich harvest for the compost heap. These are among the most available of green matter for your compost.

Weeds

Weeds are a very valuable addition to the compost heap because they belong to different plant families and therefore extract different elements from the soil. All these valuable elements are incorporated and made serviceable to the gardener when properly composted. It is essential to use weeds in green form, so that the nitrogen in them is fully utilized; if the compost is made properly, the bacterial action and heat will destroy live seeds. The more seeds on the weeds, the more manure or other organic nitrogen should be used to insure proper heating. Although it is best to use weeds fresh for compost making, a special weed pile may be started in order to let the seeds drop out. This weed material can be used as the basis of a compost heap.

Grass clippings

Cut grass is almost always sufficiently wilted by the time it is added to the compost heap so that it will soon start heating. The nutrient value depends on the fertility of the soil and the maturity of its growth. A fertile soil produces a grass rich in nitrogen, and grass cut before blooming is richer in nutrients.

Sewage sludge

As a rule, sludge is classified as a source of nitrogen and will act as a bacteria stimulator in the compost heap, even though the nitrogen content may not be above 1 per cent.

Garbage

In using garbage, it is best used as a part of the green matter of the compost heap. Its relatively high nitrogen content produces quicker decay. All kitchen wastes can be used with the exception of soapy water and fat. Soapy water contains dangerous chemicals, especially soda, which is not good for most plants. Only beets like it well. Fat, besides being an attraction to ants, does not break down very well. That leaves us with garbage of all kinds, scraps, bones, etc. But be a good neighbour. Never add cooked wastes to your compost heap if you know there are hungry rats in the neighbourhood. To attract rats is to attract the attention of your neighbours and almost surely a visit from the local pest control officer. Instead of composting kitchen wastes why not bury them on and off at about 1 foot down in the garden soil—somewhere where no crops are growing? The wastes will rot gradually and enrich the garden soil. But here again—make sure that this does not attract rats, the neighbours' cats, or stray dogs—even foxes.

Brewery wastes

Spent hops are not noted for their high plant food content but are an excellent soil conditioner. In their wet state, they have above 75 per cent water, 0·6 per cent nitrogen, 0·2 per cent P205. Moisture content varies considerably, and the analysis expressed on the dry matter is the most satisfactory figure. On this basis, the nitrogen ranges from 2·5 to 3·5 per cent and the phosphoric acid about 1 per cent. Spent hops in their natural condition are to be regarded mainly as a source of nitrogen. In many areas, gardeners and farmers have been successfully using the hops in their natural condition, spreading them in the same way as farmyard manure. Many other growers have been composting the hops before applying to the soil.

Another brewery waste available is the material left over from the mashing process, composed of grain parts.

Leather dust

Leather dust makes an excellent fertilizer material high in nitrogen. The nitrogen content varies from 5·5 to 12 per cent, and it also contains considerable amounts of phosphorus. Available from leather tanneries.

Nut shells

The composition of nut shells varies according to the nuts. Almond shells and pecans decay readily; filberts and walnuts decompose without trouble; Brazil nuts and coconuts could be used only in ground-up form, in the same manner in which cocoa shell meal is utilized. The only analyses refer to the latter product, which is given as 2·5 per cent nitrogen, 1 per cent phosphoric acid, and 2·5 per cent potash.

Peanut hulls

Peanut hulls are rich in nitrogen. Here is an analysis:

	Nitrogen	Phosphoric acid	Potash
Peanut shells	3·6	0·70	0·45
Peanut shell ashes	0·8	0·15	0·50

Coffee wastes

Coffee chaff seems to be an excellent material for use in home gardens as well as farms. Over 2 per cent in both nitrogen and potash, chaff also appears very suitable for use as a mulch material.

Dried blood

Dried blood is the blood collected in the slaughter-houses and afterwards dried and ground. The nitrogen content of dried blood is 12 per cent or over, while the phosphorus content ranges from 1 to 5 per cent. It can be used on the ground but in sound gardening practice is composted. Its high nitrogen content makes a sprinkling of it sufficient to stimulate bacterial growth. Before applying such a sprinkling, it is advisable to soak the plant matter thoroughly or to apply the dried blood in moist form. A relatively fast-working compost can be secured with the use of dried blood.

Manure

The most common domestic animals which are a source of manure are horses, cattle, goats, sheep, pigs, rabbits, and poultry. The dung consists of the un-digested portions of the foods which have been ground into fine bits and saturated with digestive juices in the alimentary tract. It also contains a large population of bacteria which may make up as much as 30 per cent of its mass. Dung contains, as a rule, one third of the total nitrogen, one-fifth of the total potash, and nearly all of the phosphoric acid voided by the animals.

Percentages of Nitrogen, Phosphate, and Potash in Different Manures

Kind of animal manure	% nitrogen	% phosphate	% potash
Rabbit	2·4	1·4	0·6
Hen	1·1	0·8	0·5
Sheep	0·7	0·3	0·9
Steer	0·7	0·3	0·4
Horse	0·7	0·3	0·6
Duck	0·6	1·4	0·5
Cow	0·6	0·2	0·5
Pig	0·5	0·3	0·5

6. HOW TO USE COMPOST

Your compost is finished. After carefully following the recommended steps for turning the year's bounty of organic material into rich, mellow humus, you want to be certain that it's used right—that it benefits your soil most and helps to insure a natural abundance and health in your coming crops.

Let's examine some of the better methods of garden compost application. By doing so, perhaps many people who have recently begun gardening the organic way will find a number of very practical and worthwhile suggestions on making the optimum use of nature's valuable fertilizer. Even those who are 'old hands' at tilling the land and following the recommendations of the organic method may discover some downright helpful ideas and hints.

When to apply

The principal factor in determining when to apply compost is its condition. If it is half finished, or noticeably fibrous, it could well be applied in October or November. By spring it will have completed its decomposition in the soil itself and be ready to supply growth nutrients to the earliest plantings made. Otherwise, for general soil enrichment, the ideal time of application is a month or so before planting. The closer to planting time it is incorporated, the more it should be ground up or worked over thoroughly with a hoe to shred it fine.

If your compost is ready in the autumn and is not intended to be used until the spring, it should be kept covered and stored in a protected place. If it is kept for a long period during the summer, the finished compost should be watered from time to time unless protected by moisture-retaining black polythene sheeting.

How to apply

Apart from what we said earlier on under heading *When and how to use compost*, if you are making a seed bed for vegetables or flowers seed germination will be better and the seedlings stronger if you spread an inch thick mulch of compost over the bed. Pass the compost through a ½-inch sieve first. Coarse material remaining may then be put on to another compost heap in the making.

Orchard composting

To save time, the compost, instead of being made in a separate place and then hauled to each tree, can be made right under the tree. Thus it acts as a mulch also. The reason it is called the *ring method* is that since you start about 3 feet away from the trunk, the material looks like a ring. Apply the raw material under the tree as if you were making compost, but instead of making the heap 5 feet high, make it only about 2 feet high. To hasten the formation of compost, several hundred red manure worms can be placed in the material.

For flowers

All flowers, like any other growing plants, respond well to the organic method and of course to applications of compost. Compost may be safely applied even to acid-loving flowers such as the rhododendron. If a gardener has a considerable number of acid-soil plantings, which include several of the berries as well as many flowers, it would be advisable that he prepare an acid compost. This is done by making the compost without lime or wood ashes, just as it is for those soils that are quite alkaline.

For potted flowers, compost should not be used alone, but should be mixed with soil. Try screening and applying friction to it before using in a flower pot. Then mix about one-third compost and two-thirds rich soil.

Lawns

(a) *Top-dressing*. Where compost is desired to aid a growing crop, there are cautions necessary to avoid injuring plant roots growing near the surface. In order not to disturb these roots of established plants, the compost may be mixed with topsoil and together applied as a mulch. This is the best means of adding what is often termed a top-dressing. It serves a double purpose in that at the same time it is providing plant food, which will gradually work itself down to the plant roots, it also affords an effective mulch to the soil, giving protection from extremes of temperature, hard rains, and so forth.

(b) The organic gardener goes in for lots of food crop growing rather than for large, inedible lawns. But a small lawn is a useful recreation spot and ideal for kiddies to play on in summer. To have a lawn which stays green all summer with little need for watering, use compost liberally when making and maintaining it. You want a thick sod with roots that go down 6 inches, not a thin, weed-infested mat laying on a layer of infertile subsoil.

In building a new lawn, work in copious amounts of compost to a depth of at least 6 inches. If your soil is either sandy or clayey (rather than good loam), you'll need at least a 2-inch depth of compost, mixed in thoroughly, to build it up. The best time to make a new lawn is in the autumn. But if you want to get started in the spring, dig in your compost and sow Italian rye grass or vetches, which will look quite neat all summer. Then dig this green manure in at the end of the summer and make your permanent lawn when cool weather comes.

To renovate an old, patchy lawn, dig up the bare spots about 2 inches deep, work in plenty of finished compost, tamp and rake well, and sow your seed after soaking the patches well.

Feed your lawn regularly every spring. An excellent practice is to use a spike tooth aerator, then spread a mixture of fine finished compost and bone meal. Rake this into the holes made by the aerator. You can use a fairly thick covering of compost—just not so thick it covers the grass. This will feed your lawn efficiently and keep it sending down a dense mass of roots that laugh at drought.

How much to apply

In gardening for best results, compost should be applied liberally, let us say from 1 to 3 inches in thickness per year. Within a few years, your garden will become the wonder and envy of your neighbourhood. Of course, you can get by with as little as $\frac{1}{2}$ inch of compost, but in gardening with small plots, put it on heavy. There is no danger of burning due to over-use, such as is always the case with the chemically concocted fertilizers. You can apply compost either once or twice a year. The amount would depend, of course, on the fertility of your soil originally and on what and how much has been grown in it. Incidentally, an average figure of weight for 1 cubic yard of compost (27 cubic feet) is 1,000 pounds. There would be variations depending on the materials used and the length of time composted.

For orcharding and trees

Compost should be applied under each tree. Start about 2 to 3 feet away from the trunk, and go to about a foot beyond the drip line at the end of the branches. How thick should it be applied? If you are going to apply it every year, $\frac{1}{2}$ to 1 inch will do. First cultivate under the tree, digging in any annual weeds and annual grasses. Dig out all perennials and their roots. Then work in the compost, keeping it in the upper 2 inches or simply spread the compost over the dug ground. To keep the area weed-free, it is a good practice to apply a mulch of old hay or straw. If compost is spread at the rate of about 3 or 4 inches in thickness there would be sufficient plant foods to last the tree 3 or 4 years.

Where there are poisons in the soil from many years of spraying, a 3- or 4-inch layer of compost worked into the soil will tend to counteract somewhat their harmful effects.

MULCH

1. There's More to Mulch Than Meets the Eye!

A gardener who hasn't mulched is like a restaurant gourmet who hasn't tasted organic foods. He just doesn't know what he's missing! But when he finds out, his garden will give forth a bonanza of tasty treats.

Mulch, technically speaking, is a layer of material, preferably organic material, that is placed on the soil surface to conserve moisture, hold down weeds, and ultimately improve soil structure and fertility.

But there's more to mulch than meets the eye. Be it a yellow blanket of straw, a neat brown carpet of sedge peat or a smooth sheet of newsprint disguised with grass mowings, that topping for the vegetable patch and flower bed serves as much more than icing on the garden cake.

Mulch acts. It performs in several wondrous ways. It fills a role as protector of the topsoil, conserver of moisture, guardian against weather extremes, and comfortable, bruise-saving cushioner under ripening produce.

As with composting, mulching is a basic practice in the organic method; it is a practice which nature employs constantly, that of always covering a bare soil. In addition, mulching also protects plants during winter, reducing the dangers of freezing and heaving.

Advantages of mulching

1. We know a mulched plant is not subjected to the extremes of temperature of an exposed plant. Un-

mulched roots are damaged by the heaving of soil brought on by sudden thaws and sudden frosts. The mulch acts as an insulating blanket, keeping the soil warmer in winter and cooler in summer.

2. Certain materials used for a mulch contain rich minerals, and gradually, through the action of rain and time, these work into the soil to feed the roots of the plants. Some of the minerals soak into the ground during the first heavy rain. Therefore, mulch fertilizes the soil while it is on the soil surface as well as after it decays.

3. For the busy gardener, mulching is a boon indeed. Many back-breaking hours of weeding and hoeing are practically eliminated. Weeds do not have a chance to get a foothold, and the few that might manage to come up through the mulch can be hoed out in a jiffy. And since the mulch keeps the soil loose, there is no need to cultivate.

4. The mulch prevents the hot, drying sun and wind from penetrating to the soil, so its moisture does not evaporate quickly. A few good soakings during the growing season will tide plants over a long dry spell. It also prevents erosion from wind and hard rains. Soil underneath a mulch is damp and cool to the touch. Often mulched plants endure a long, dry season with practically no watering at all.

5. At harvest time, vegetables which sprawl on the ground, such as cucumbers, marrows, strawberries, bush tomatoes, etc., often become mildewed, mouldy, or even develop rot. A mulch prevents this damage by keeping the vegetables clean and dry. This is the season when most gardens begin to look unkempt. But the mulched garden always looks neat and trim, no matter what the season. In addition, mud is less of a problem when

walking on mulched rows, and low-growing flowers are not splashed with mud.

Disadvantages of mulching

1. Seedlings planted in very moist soil should not be mulched immediately. The addition of any organic matter which keeps the soil at a high humidity encourages damping-off of young plants. Damping-off is a disease caused by a fungus inhabiting moist, poorly ventilated soil, and can be 90 per cent fatal. Allow seedlings to become established then, before mulching.

2. It is wise, too, to consider the danger of crown rot in perennials. This disease is also caused by a fungus. If there has been especially heavy rains, postpone mulching until the soil is no longer waterlogged. Do not allow mulches composed of peat, manure, or garden compost to touch the base of these plants. Leave a circle several inches in diameter. The idea here is to permit the soil to remain dry and open to the air around the immediate area of the plant.

3. Do not mulch a wet, low-lying soil, or at most, use only a light type of material like straw. Leaves are definitely to be avoided as they may mat down and add to the sogginess.

Where the soil is poor and not well supplied with humus, as it will be when you start dressing it heavily with your home-made garden compost, mulching is pretty valueless. In fact it may be harmful in robbing the soil of what little nitrogen it may still contain. To off-set the possibility of a nitrogen soil deficiency gardeners who do not practise organic methods sprinkle some dried blood or other nitrogen-rich material before mulching with woody subjects like straw, sawdust, or wood shavings.

With the instructions given above, it is simple enough to know when and where not to mulch. Except for these instances, the gardener really can't do without mulching as a wonderful labour-saving helpmate.

2. WHAT MULCHES TO USE

When you set out to mulch a home garden of any considerable size, there are three factors to be considered: (1) how the material will affect the plants most intimately concerned; (2) how the completed mulch will look; and (3) how easily and inexpensively the mulch can be obtained. Following is a list of commonly used mulch materials that have been found beneficial by many organic gardeners.

Lawn mowings

Fairly rich in nitrogen, lawn mowings are useful as a green manure to be worked into the soil, for adding to compost heaps, or for mulching. Mowings from most lawns contain over 1 pound of nitrogen and 2 pounds of potash for every 100 pounds of mowings in the dry state.

Leaves

Leaves are an abundant source of humus and mineral material, including calcium, magnesium, as well as nitrogen, phosphorus, and potassium. They are especially valuable for use around acid-loving plants such as azaleas, rhododendrons, and hollies. They may be applied directly in the soil as a mulch, for leaf mould, and for composting. Leaves mat and seal in moisture, keeping thaws from heaving autumn-planted subjects. They also decay rapidly, giving their benefits more quickly than slower decomposing mulches.

Leaf mould

When stacking autumn leaves apply sprinklings of lime to offset the acidity unless you plan to use the leaf mould around acid-tolerant plants only. Leaf mould from deciduous trees has been found to be somewhat richer in potash and phosphorus than that made from conifers. Nitrogen content varies and is sometimes as high as 5 per cent.

Paper

Newspapers and magazines have excellent moisture-retaining qualities and can be set out in the vegetable garden and nursery. A layer of hay, straw, or wood shavings over the paper will improve the appearance and keep the wind from blowing them away. Paper has a deadly efficiency in preventing weed growth. Because it is dense enough to keep rain from readily passing through to the soil underneath, it is best applied after a heavy rain. Use four to six thicknesses. Paper eventually, though not quickly, decays and adds humus to the soil.

Stones

Stones are one of nature's natural mulches and have all the standard advantages of most mulches plus a few additional ones. Rains and snows leach minerals from the rocks and return them to the soil, creating a valuable fertilizer. Rocks give an added boost of adding warmth to the soil, particularly in the spring and autumn when certain plants have a big need for it. Conditions under stones are ideal for bacteria, earthworms, and other beneficial organisms. Rocks are permanent and rustically attractive to the eye.

Sawdust (well rotted)

Here is a very useful mulch material that should be used more widely. When plants are about 2 inches high, a 1-inch layer can be applied. Prior to spreading the sawdust, many gardeners side-dress with a nitrogen fertilizer like dried blood. A recent survey showed that many sawdust users do not apply a nitrogen supplement and are satisfied with results. The sawdust used by most organic gardeners is left to rot well before use.

Seaweed and kelp

Both are high in potash (about 5 per cent) and trace elements. Many seaweed users apply it fresh from the sea; others prefer washing first to remove salt. It can be used as a mulch, worked directly into the soil, or placed in the compost heap.

Wood shavings

Like sawdust and other wood wastes, wood shavings are useful in the garden. Some people are afraid that the continued application of wood shavings will sour their soil, that is, make it too acid. A very comprehensive study of sawdust and wood shavings made from 1949 to 1954 by the Connecticut Experiment Station, reported no instance of making the soil more acid. The use of sawdust or wood shavings does not attract wireworms as is often said.

Wood shavings are only available if there is a saw mill or possibly a firm using a great deal of wood near your home. In some ways shavings are superior to sawdust particularly if they contain a high percentage of bark.

The general verdict on sawdust and wood shavings is that both materials are safe and effective soil improvers. They do a fine job of aerating the soil and increasing its moisture-holding capacity.

Straw

This is clean, rarely contains many weed seeds, is inexpensive if bought direct from farms, quick, and easy to lay down, and it looks presentable. Once it has been applied, it remains in place an entire season. During the autumn, dig it in, and by spring it will have become an indistinguishable part of the soil. It is estimated that 1 ton will give a 1-inch mulch on an acre of land.

Pine needles

These are good for strawberries the year round. Keep in mind that they can be a fire hazard when dry. Use a 2- to 4-inch mulch and renew every year. Particularly good for acid-loving plants, or to change neutral soil to acid. Pine needles alone are not good on alkaline-loving plants.

Oak tow

Oak tow is like sawdust, but contains coarser wood strings. It is made by tearing the wood lengthwise in sawing stave bolts. If you can get the material from a saw mill, you'll find it does not compact or blow as readily as sawdust.

Rotted pine wood

Like pine needles, these materials are excellent for mulching such acid-loving plants as azaleas, camellias, and rhododendrons. Before being used for plants that require a neutral or slightly alkaline soil, these materials should be composted.

Packing materials

Trees and plants ordered from nurseries usually come packed in sphagnum moss. Breakables shipped from out of town arrive packed in shredded paper. Save these materials and use them as mulches, alone, or mixed with other materials.

Weeds and native grasses

These make an excellent mulch around trees, where it is important to build a deeper covering than we use in the gardens and where this sort of mulch does not look out of place. They should be exposed to the air before applying to prevent rooting. Only young material should be used and it may be mixed with lawn mowings. Old weeds and grasses will drop millions of seeds and are, therefore, not recommended for mulching.

Peat moss

This is particularly decomposed remains of plants accumulated over centuries under relatively airless conditions. Though it doesn't contain any nutrients, peat moss serves to aerate the soil, to improve drainage, ultimately to help plants absorb nutrients from other materials. Established lawns can be top-dressed with a ½-inch layer of peat moss twice a year, and an inch or more can be spread and worked into vegetable gardens and flower beds. Sedge peat is equally effective. Both forms of peat are extremely useful as a mulch.

3. HOW MUCH MULCH IS ENOUGH?

When it comes to getting top garden or farm results, mulch makes a difference. Agreement on that score is just about unanimous, particularly among followers of the organic method. The value of a layer of material placed on the soil surface is pretty well recognized today by gardeners of all shapes, sizes, and sections of the country.

The catch, if really there is one, lies in deciding on the *amount* of mulch to use. Should a good mulch always be the same depth? Must it be measured to slide-rule accuracy to function right? Do any other considerations influence the proper quality? In other words, *how much mulch is enough*?

Generally, gardeners mulch crops that are in the garden for most of the summer. How much? During the growing season, the thickness of the mulch should be sufficient to prevent the growth of weeds. A thin layer of finely shredded plant materials is more effective than unshredded loose material. For example, a 4- to 6-inch layer of sawdust will hold down weeds as well as 8 or more inches of hay, straw, or a similar loose, 'open' material. So will a 2- to 4-inch depth of pine needles. Leaves should be shredded or mixed with a light material like straw to prevent packing into a soggy mass. In a mixture, unshredded leaves can be spread 8 to 12 inches deep for the winter. To offset the nitrogen shortage in sawdust and other low-nitrogen materials, add some compost.

Stout method heaps hay

Speaking of hay leads us to Ruth Stout, America's foremost advocate of year-round mulching. She relies almost exclusively on spoiled hay, which is peeled off in convenient layers, or 'books', from bales standing ready for use, or tossed on by the armful to smother a solitary weed or two that may poke through the existing cover. After years of experience working out the permanent-mulch technique, Ruth has emphatic notions on its proper application.

How much mulch do you need? For her system, Miss Stout replies: 'The answer to this is: more than you would think. You should start with a good 8 inches of it. Then I'm asked: "How can tiny plants survive between 8-inch walls?" And the answer to that is: the mulch is trampled on, rained on and packed down by the time you are ready to plant. It doesn't stay 8 inches high.'

What about specific crops? Such acid-loving plants as strawberries, blueberries, cranberries, raspberries, peanuts, radishes, sweet potatoes, watermelons, azaleas, camellias, mums, rhododendrons, etc., do well with an acid-material mulch—most leaves, pine needles, sawdust, wood shavings, salt hay. According to the Wisconsin Experimental Station, a $1\frac{1}{2}$- to 2-inch layer of salt hay makes the best mulch for strawberries. Pine needles are another excellent topping for this plant, and have been found effective at a 2- to 4-inch depth. Tests at the Ohio Agricultural Experiment Station showed that mulched blueberries yielded more fruit than cultivated plantings, and that sawdust at a rate of 6 to 8 inches gave the most consistent results.

Actually, a mulch programme maintained for several years will let you practically forget about acid or alkaline soil problems. Ample organic matters acts as an effective buffer and helps to neutralize extremes of pH in any soil.

Mulch timing is often important

Some vegetables, like tomato and sweet corn, need a thoroughly warmed soil to encourage ideal growth. A mulch applied too early in the spring, before ground temperatures have had a chance to climb, may slow up such crops. Once plants are well started, though, and the weather levels off, mulch is definitely in order to conserve needed water, stimulate topsoil microorganisms, and generally condition the soil.

Author-gardener John Krill pinpointed the importance of logical mulch timing for tomatoes. His experiments, and the experiences of others, show that early ripe tomatoes cannot be expected if the spring-thawing ground is cloaked to soon. In summing up his findings, Krill writes:

> I have learned this lesson: that if mulch is applied before the earth is thoroughly warmed, it will delay the ripening of tomatoes, I apply mulch now only when the flowers are profuse, or may even wait until the fruit sets before mulching the plants. Then the mulch seals the heat in instead of sealing it out ... For late-ripening tomatoes I mulch my plants heavily when I set them out. For the earliest possible fruit I set out enough to get ripe tomatoes in unmulched soil until the juicier and better-flavoured tomatoes are ripened in the mulched rows. By the wise use of mulch you can prevent tomatoes ripening all at one time.

Sweet corn should not be mulched until the plants are up about a foot high. Other vegetables which do best in well-warmed soils include marrows, cucumbers, and melons.

Potatoes started in mulch

Still another way mulch makes home gardening more rewarding with less work is in growing potatoes. Richard V. Clemence outlines the system:

> Large crops of the highest-quality potatoes can be grown by laying the sprouted seed tubers on top of the remains of last year's mulch. I make double rows, 14 inches apart, with the seed the same distance apart in the rows. The idea of this is not only to get a heavy yield, but to make it easy to inspect the vines from both sides occasionally. Having laid the seed in straight rows with the aid of a string, I cover the rows with 6 or 8 inches of hay,

and do nothing more until several weeks later. After the blossoms fall, I begin moving the hay carefully to see how things are progressing. Small potatoes an inch or two in diameter can be separated from their stems without disturbing the parent plants, and the hay then replaced.

As for the soil-type factor, along with curbing weeds, a carpet of mulch performs yeoman service in a number of less frequently realized directions. USDA horticulturist E. P. Christopher explains that cultivating a hard-packed soil will favour moisture percolation and air penetration, but the dry, bare surface may be completely eroded in a flash storm. Furthermore, he adds, 'continued cultivation may speed up organic matter loss and thus destroy favourable soil structure'.

Mulches, Christopher points out, influence moisture penetration in several ways:

Bulky materials such as wood shavings, sawdust and straw temporarily hold a considerable volume of water, and thus prevent loss by runoff when the rate of application—natural or artificial—is too rapid for soil penetration. This may be more important with a heavy silt than with a porous sand soil. However, maintaining the soil structure loose and open may be the most important factor involved. Rain beating on an exposed soil compacts it and subsequent baking in the sun almost completely eliminates its capacity to absorb water rapidly. The open soil structure found under a mulch is also favourable to rapid air exchange. Roots require oxygen for the respiration process through which energy for growth is released.

Harvest and winter protection

At harvest time, vegetables which sprawl on the ground, such as ridge cucumbers, marrows, strawberries, and self-stopping bush tomatoes, etc., often become mouldy or even develop rot. Others may be damaged by falling on to uncovered soil. A mulch prevents such injury by keeping the vegetables clean and dry, and by providing a cushioned layer on which they can rest or drop.

Besides this aid, a late-summer mulch helps to prolong the growing season. By buffering the effects of early frosts, it allows more time for second plantings or late crops to mature. At both ends of the summer, mulched soil and plants derive a noticeable benefit in this guard against weather extremes.

As autumn makes its mercury-dropping entrance, the usefulness of a mulch follows the season. There's a somewhat different prime purpose in the autumn and winter mulch, though, and it's important to keep this in mind. Protection—especially of bulbs, perennial roots, shrubs, etc.—is the objective now; protection, that is, from sudden temperature changes, from up-and-down thermometer readings which can harm overwintering plants.

The mulch now should be applied *after* the first hard frost to prevent alternate thaws and freezes from heaving soil, roots, or bulbs. Its purpose once winter sets in is to hold the lower temperature *in* the soil, avoid a rise and subsequent refreezing which shifts the earth and plants, often exposing enough to cause winter-killing. To protect young shrubs, and particularly roses, mound several inches of earth around them early in autumn, then mulch after the first freeze with several more inches of leaves, straw, yard trimmings, etc. Young trees can be protected from rabbit or field-mouse damage by wrapping small chicken wire mesh around their base before the circle of mulch is applied.

Of course, the winter carpet of organic matter also helps condition the whole garden area for the next spring.

How much mulch?—the amount that does the best job for you, your soil, and your plants. Working out an ideal mulch programme takes some experimenting, some trials with various materials and depths. It's only common sense to check on the most plentiful free and reasonable sources, to test the effects of different mulches in your climate locale, your own soil type and timing. But the programme more than pays—in handsome dividends of better home-grown foods, a finer soil, and happier gardeners. Get going on your blanket of benefit, no matter where you garden— whether, as I do, in the United States or whether your garden is in Britain, Australia, India, or South Africa— in fact, anywhere in the world.

M. C. GOLDMAN

4. A REPORT ON FOUR MULCHES

One summer we had the opportunity to test four different organic mulches—lawn mowings, rotted sawdust, ground cork, and shredded pine bark. These materials were spread on the richly fertile beds and borders in our garden, and we checked each one for its desirability as a mulch.

Lawn mowings

Our lawn, green, healthy, and practically devoid of weeds, has always provided a more than abundant supply of mowings to cover, thin layer by thin layer, every bed and border in our garden. The pale grey green colour of the drying grass deepens to brown and is not unpleasant. It readily permits raindrops to penetrate to the soil beneath, while its decomposition enriches the soil, and its shady protection keeps the earth beneath it both cooler and damper than cultivated soil exposed to the elements. On a day in July when the air temperature was 98°F and the temperature, in direct sunlight, at the surface of the mulch registered 120°, the surface of the soil beneath the dried grass mulch was 94°.

These lawn mowings, however, require almost weekly

replenishment in order to keep the mulching depth a preferred 3 inches. This rapid decomposition necessitates the constant addition of organic fertilizers, rich in nitrogen, to the soil; and the protected plants, even in a season of fairly normal rainfall, are very often in need of additional moisture. Furthermore, by freeze-up time very little dried grass is ever left for use as a winter mulch.

Rotted sawdust

Another material available to us at the expenditure only of time and physical effort was some *very well-rotted* hardwood sawdust which had been lying in a shady wood for some 20 years, host to centipedes, worms, and beetles, and overgrown with Virginia creeper, honeysuckle, and greenbrier.

This sawdust was, of course, moist and very heavy to handle, but its dark colour was most pleasing to the eye. Even the lightest of rains seemed to go directly through to the garden soil and very little additional water was needed throughout the summer by the herbaceous annuals and perennials protected by it, nor did they show any overt need for additional fertilizers during the growing season. The vegetable garden grew lushly, and strawberries, raspberries, and rhubarb all produced prodigiously, surrounded and protected by this sawdust mulch.

No replenishing of the mulch was necessary from spring to autumn. Not one garden weed penetrated the 3 inches of sawdust, and only an amazing few of the broken roots of the creeping woods plants gave rise to new growth that had to be pulled from the loose, unresisting medium.

On the same July day when the soil beneath the dried grass registered 94°F, that beneath the rotted sawdust registered only 82°. These temperature readings were taken in the same test bed, in the same direct rays of the sun, and within 4 feet of each other.

In early November, checking the decomposition and/or loss of the sawdust, I found approximately 2 inches of loose mulching material, while the first inch or so of soil immediately beneath was so mixed with the sawdust as to be inseparable one from the other. It was, in effect, a rich, black, moist soil, brought about, probably, by the action of rain water, soil bacteria, and little earth animals. Approximately two-thirds of the original material, by bulk, was still available for use as winter mulch or to be raked and stored according to the desires of the gardener.

This particular material, though, as far as this gardener is concerned, is exhausted at the source, and fresh sawdust, while satisfactory in its way, is not to be compared with the well-rotted substance.

Shredded pine bark

The American organic gardener can buy shredded pine bark. When the commercially marketed bags of shredded pine bark are opened and their dark, brown-red contents spread 2 to 3 inches deep around the needled and broad-leaved evergreens of the foundation planting, the woodsy fragrance that rises is so heavenly that the gardener is apt to feel that even if its mulching capabilities are nil, it is worth its price in nostril-tingling value alone. But, fortunately for the garden, it is an excellent mulch. Its pine-woods aroma vanishes after a few weeks' exposure to the elements, but its dark colour remains pleasing to the eye for at least the 2 years I have used it.

It does not rob the soil of moisture and, instead, appears to allow every falling drop to penetrate to the earth. Its fine, dusty particles are, of course, quickly absorbed by the soil, but this is such an extremely small percentage of the mulch that its disappearance is scarcely noted, either in the depth of the mulch on the ground or in the bulk recovered if it is raked up for storage during the winter months. The dust absorbed presumably increases, to a slight degree, the acidity of the soil, but does not noticeably increase the demand for nitrogen.

Possibly because the larger pieces and consequent greater unevenness of the shredded pine bark mulch allow some moisture to escape, but more likely because the foundation planting suffers from being in the rain shadow of the house, a considerable amount of additional moisture was required by these large evergreens. So, too, the smaller-rooted cuttings in the test bed required a great deal of additional water, but this need not necessarily be laid at the door of the pine bark mulch.

When the surface temperature of this mulch was 120°F, the temperature of the soil directly beneath it was 86°, while a temperature of 90° was registered in medium shade with the soil beneath it registering 82°F.

Ground cork

The fourth mulching material tested was ground cork —not yet, to my knowledge, on the open market.

This material was so light and so easy to handle that a 90-pound woman could spread it with ease. It was also so light that I feared the first Howard County breeze would blow it across the countryside and that even the moderate force of an ordinary raindrop would dislodge it from place. But I was wrong.

Scarcely had we spread this mulch when an early-summer thunderstorm raced across the land. Preceded by violent winds, it let loose a volley of pounding, outsize raindrops, and then sluiced down veritable waterfalls upon the earth. The storm passed, the sun shone, and we went out to view the end of a mulch test that had not yet fairly begun; and there lay the ground cork, smoothly and evenly spread upon the ground, completely unruffled by either wind or water. The cork itself was damp, the ground beneath it soaked, and from that moment through the entire growing season that section of the test garden relied on nature for its watering.

This ground cork is reported, authoritatively, to test 1 per cent nitrogen, a fairly negligible amount; but its deterioration is so unbelievably slow that it appears almost to be an inert material, and its effect for good or ill on the nitrogen content of the soil is not observable except probably by highly scientific testing methods. Measured by bulk, there appears to be exactly as much cork in November as there was in May.

Well known for its insulating qualities, there should be no surprise that where its surface registered the same 120°F mentioned before, the temperature of the surface of the soil directly beneath was 82°; and in light shade where the mulch surface showed 94°, the soil beneath showed 78°F.

Dry or wet, it is completely odourless. Its only drawback—and it is no doubt quibbling to mention it in view of its other excellences—is its pale tan colour which does not enhance the beauty of a planting as a darker colour would do.

MARY LEISTER

5. MULCH YOUR WAY THROUGH THE SUMMER

Put mulch to work for you during the hot, parched stretches of summer. Let it stop weeds in their tracks and hold on to needed moisture. Let it keep soil temperature down and garden production up.

Ruth Stout, for example, has roared for years about how a good mulch helps close the 'work gap' between spring planting and autumn harvests. A champion of the year-round hay mulch, Ruth emphasizes in her books and articles that there's less labour, less struggling with watering, wilting, weed competition, insects, or soil conditioning when a constant layer of thick hay blankets the garden. 'The whole thing,' she exclaims, 'can actually almost be said in one sentence: Keep your ground (vegetable patch and flower beds) covered with mulch, and from then on just use your brains.'

Lots of things besides hay make effective mulches. The list of usable materials seems to be growing nearly as fast as the plants in a well-mulched plot. Basically, there are two main divisions of mulch: organic and inorganic.

Experiment pace quickens

Serious interest in mulching has climbed sharply in the last few years and the tempo of mulch experimenting has spurted. At the New Mexico Agricultural Experiment Station, for instance, orchard-management studies showed that apple trees given an alfalfa hay mulch produced larger fruit than trees kept either in permanent sod or under chemical-spray weed control. Grapevines mulched with a layer of straw outyielded cultivated vines by 25 per cent at the Ohio Station, where raspberries mulched with wheat straw also showed a 10 per cent increase over cultivated plants, as well as a boost in berry size. And at the same station, peat moss or sawdust mulches on blueberries brought as much as 80 to 152 per cent higher yields than cultivated berries. Raspberries mulched with lawn mowings, wood shavings, sawdust, newspaper, and maple leaves grew faster and had remarkable flavour improvement for Vermont nurseryman Lewis Hill.

Soil scientists at the Texas Station have worked out a 'mulch recipe' for reclaiming land in the Rio Grande Delta that has been ruined by salt accumulation. The barren clay–loam plots, so saline they produce almost no crops at all, are covered in March with a 5-inch layer of cotton-gin trash (dried bolls, stems, and leaves). The plots are left idle at least 6 months, then ploughed and planted with crops. Within 5 months of applying 30 tons of mulch per acre, researchers found 84 per cent of the salts had been leached from the top 30 inches of soil.

Noted American gardening writer, Cynthia Westcott relates that she's found blackspot of roses 'a disease that can often be reduced in extent by the use of a proper mulch'. She usually mulches her New Jersey rose garden with buckwheat hulls applied 1 inch deep. A 50-pound bag will cover about 60 square feet or more at that depth, she notes. Cocoa bean shells, adds Miss Westcott, seem to be equally effective and attractive, although 50 pounds won't spread quite so far. Ground corncobs, also a recognized preventive of blackspot, she found more conspicuous.

Best mulches for the home garden

For the home gardener, the most practical and popular mulches are those easily available and cleanly handled. Baled hay, usually 'spoiled' for livestock feed, is readily moved and spread by peeling convenient layers or 'books' from the bale. Leaves and leaf mould and lawn mowings are helpful, common mulching choices. So too are a variety of waste or by-products of food processing (if you live near a factory which has them): cocoa and buckwheat hulls, shredded cotton burs and gin trash, ground tree bark, shredded sugar cane (bagasse), and the shells from peanuts, oats, rice, cottonseed, etc. Shore-line dwellers have seaweed, rich in minerals and free of weed seeds; sawdust and wood shavings are often to be obtained at planing mills. Spent hops, the waste product of breweries are quite moist, light coloured, more resistant to fire hazard than straw, and have an odour which persists a few weeks.

Various types of peat, although containing little plant foods, improve soil tilth, aeration, and drainage, ultimately helping plants absorb nutrients from other materials. Peat mulches can be spread an inch or more in vegetable gardens and flower beds, and used as a $\frac{1}{2}$-inch top-dressing twice a year on established lawns.

Sawdust no puzzle

To offset the nitrogen shortage in sawdust and other low-nitrogen materials, add some compost, manure or dried blood to the soil surface before mulching. Actually there is no basis in fact for many of the old accusations tossed at sawdust. Used properly, it's not a 'devil' that sours soil or robs plant food. Weathered or unweathered, from hardwood or softwood, sawdust is not acid, nor is it toxic in any way. It is organic matter, beneficial as both a mulch and soil conditioner. Used about 3 inches thick, it serves efficiently around fruit trees, shrubs, perennials, evergreens, and in border plantings. Like other carbon-rich materials, sawdust will sometimes turn plants yellow if used alone. The reason is that soil bacteria and fungi temporarily use so much nitrogen to decompose sawdust that little is left for the plants. The yellowing is a hunger sign—and the difficulty can be prevented by adding any of the nitrogen-rich organic fertilizers.

Just how effectively a good mulch performs might be

seen in the results that L. Winston Hamm gets in S. Wolfebore, New Hampshire. His half acre of Kennebec potatoes, fertilized in autumn with 500 pounds each of compost and cottonseed meal, has a mixed mulch of 6 to 8 inches deep of hay topped with 6-year-old pine sawdust. Another planting gets cottonseed meal and sawdust in a 4- to 6-inch combination. Fifty- to 60-bushel yields to the half acre of top-quality potatoes are what Mr Hamm harvests. He has no insect troubles, no potato scab, and plenty of customers. His mountainside soil, originally so hard-packed, is now so friable he can poke 8 to 10 inches into it with his finger. As a test, Hamm compared mulched and unmulched plants and found he dug two to three times total yield from the mulched ones.

M. C. GOLDMAN

6. INORGANIC PLASTIC—FOR OR AGAINST?

There are two ways of looking at the use of plastic aids in the garden. You may, as so many Americans do, dislike them intensely because there just seems to be too much plastic and plastic wastes in the United States nowadays, or you may consider their good and their bad points. Take a plastic watering can, for instance. It is lighter than its metal counterpart and won't chip the sink as a metal can does if you aren't all that careful. Plastic greenhouses are pretty fragile and haven't the potential life-span of glass. But if you live where local boys enjoy nothing better than to hear the tinkle of broken glass late at night—rip out the glass and replace with plastic. By and large cold frames with glass lights and cloches made of glass are superior to those with clear plastic parts. But where young children play ball near your kitchen garden or if toddlers are around you when you're digging and tending your crops there's less chance of nasty accidents with plastic.

A compost heap covered with a large sheet of heavy-weight black polythene heats up rapidly and there's no fear of any objectionable smell leading to comments of an unpleasant nature from the neighbours. Remember—even the best-bred compost heap can smell! A pile of autumn leaves covered with a similar plastic sheet will stay put. Even after a March gale there will be no leaves blowing up your garden path or up the neighbours' either. For just how long the sheets will be of service will depend on the treatment you give them.

Metre-wide black plastic sheeting is often recommended for potato growing. If used for the potato crop the sheeting has a life of one season only. Cabbages, tomatoes, Brussels sprouts, and certain other vegetables may be grown weed-free between two sheets of black plastic mulch. If the mulched soil is organically rich it will remain much more moist during dry summer weather than unmulched soil near by. The sheeting may be taken up after use and stored in the garden shed or garage. Squares or circles of 500-gauge black polythene come in handy for keeping the ground beneath fruit trees, currants, and gooseberries free from weeds. Plastic mulches add not a jot of plant food to the ground but for most gardeners in our towns and suburbs they are more or less the only way of controlling summer weeds unless modern weed killers are used. No organic gardener uses them. Some modern weed killers seem pretty harmless when compared, for example, with the old favourite—sodium chlorate. Trouble is we don't know what effect modern weed killers have on the soil and its millions of microscopic inhabitants. Some say we'll know in 20 years time. Willing to use them and wait that long?

BRIAN FURNER

PART III

WHAT TO GROW—AND HOW!

THE BEST-LAID PLANS

1. 'STRETCH THE HARVEST' BY PLANNING

The successful organic vegetable garden will give you and your family a ready and inexpensive supply of fresh, nutritious vegetables throughout the year. With careful planning, you can get a continuous supply of vegetables throughout the year—not just in high summer when most gardeners have supplies. Robert Stevens, extension horticulturist at the University of Delaware, calls this 'stretching the harvest season.'

You'll also be able to double the harvest by interplanting and succession planting. Careful planning will decrease the need to buy fresh or processed vegetables and allow you and your family to have them fresh and uncontaminated by chemical dusts and sprays all year through.

Another advantage of having a definite plan for the garden is that the kind and amount of seed can be determined fairly accurately in advance, and proper amounts purchased. If you have no plan you are likely to get too much of some seeds and not enough of others. These ten points should be considered while drawing the plan, according to Stevens:

1. Perennial crops, such as asparagus, strawberries, and rhubarb, should be located at one side of the garden.

2. Tall-growing crops, such as standard tomatoes and sweet corn, must be kept away from small crops like beets and carrots to avoid shading.

3. Provide for succession crops—ensure that in late summer/early autumn there will be room for sowings and plantings for overwintering and to lead to very early crops in the following season. Have ground prepared early for spring sowings for early and mid-summer vegetables and plan so that there's room for the host of plants which are set out in their growing positions in the garden during June.

4. Early planted, fast-growing, quick-maturing crops should be grouped together. Examples: radishes, lettuce, summer cabbage, salad onions, etc.

5. Grow vegetables like potatoes and carrots for storing. You may also wish to have a go at storing some summer vegetables in a freezer if you have one.

6. Unless you've seen them in a neighbour's garden and are sure they really are fine don't overplant new varieties. Give them a trial in a small way by all means. Most, but not all, may suit your conditions. Never waste space by growing vegetables the family does not like nor too much of any one vegetable so that you have a surplus.

7. If your garden is on a fairly steep slope, rows should be made across the slope—not up and down it.

8. Make sure the plan provides the best spacing between rows so that you can hand weed or hoe without damaging plants near by. If you invest in a motorized cultivator you will have to leave more room.

9. Run rows north and south if possible to prevent plants from shading one another.

10. Long rows save time in care and cultivation. Several crops may be planted in the same row if the distance between rows is the same.

Getting the most out of your garden

Actually, the entire purpose of careful planning is to get the most out of your garden. Managed correctly, a small garden will yield more and certainly satisfy you much more than a poorly run, large plot. Consider the average suburban home with the back garden obviously not large enough to grow all the crops you wish to. Is there anything that can be done about it? Definitely yes! Here's how one Pennsylvania organic gardener, Dr Lewis Theiss, suggests solving the problem:

Production in a restricted garden area can be very largely increased by making a two-storey garden. In a way, such a garden is like a house with two storeys. That type contains twice as many rooms on one plot. Similarly, a two-storey garden greatly increases the productive area.

Some years ago, I had to limit my plantings to an enclosed garden that was just about 50 feet wide. The two-storey garden enabled me to produce a very generous supply of vegetables in this restricted area.

To begin with, I narrowed the space between plant rows. Instead of cultivating, I mulched. That not only did away with a lot of work, but it kept the ground moist in a way that had never happened before. And this generous supply of moisture certainly helped the vegetables to secure more plant food.

But spacing my rows closer did not entirely meet my needs. So I resorted to the two-storey garden. Suppose your garden is 50 by 50 feet. You have 200 feet of fence that ordinarily goes to waste. Yet that fence will hold plants as well as bean poles, trellises, or other supports. Those 200 feet, of course, are the equivalent of four 50-foot rows of vegetables. So the thing to do is to make use of the space along your fence.

What do gardeners usually grow that needs support? There are runner beans, climbing French beans and trailing sorts of vegetable marrow. There are now, too, the hardy trellis kinds of cucumber. So all the gardener has to do is to plant his seeds, or set out young plants, in a long row at the bottom of his fence wire, mulch the ground well, and see that the young plants get hold of the fence wire. The plants will do the climbing.

They do far better on supports than when grown on the flat. In a wet summer not only are bean pods dirtied by mud if the plants are grown dwarfed but slugs nibble at them just as they will nibble at tender young marrows lying on the soil. The new cucumbers of Chinese and Japanese origin do well in southern gardens and replace the older, shorter-fruiting ridge cucumbers which take up far more space in 3-foot-wide beds.

If you want something more attractive in your garden, try scarlet runner beans on the fence. You will not only get some good beans, but the showy sprays of brilliant flowers will make your fence a thing of real beauty. Even beans with inconspicuous flowers add living charm to a fence. The long and sightly pods, hanging in heavy clusters, are also a thing of beauty.

And, when it comes to picking the beans, you never had it so good as you will have it if you put your beans on a fence. There will be no more backbreaking stooping to gather the beans.

You can also tie standard type tomato plants to the fence. Even when green the fruits can be a bit of an attraction to small kiddies next door so consider tomato growing on the fence several times over if your neighbours have any small children. Remember there are not only evenly-shaped, smallish tomatoes as in the shops but golden-coloured and yellows. There are also monster-fruited reds for slicing in salads and decorative small red and yellow cherry, plum and pear tomatoes also noted for their real tomato flavour.

Tall-growing maincrop peas like Alderman were really made for fences. They absolutely *have* to have high support. They will cover the woven wire with their beautiful foliage, and the hanging pods are like striking figures worked into a lovely green fabric.

But you don't need to limit your fence-rows to climbers. A row of sweet corn is a handsome sight hard against the fence. Think of fruit, too. Brambles—and that includes loganberries as well as blackberries—can lead to fruitful fences. For the smallish, modern garden there are now non-prickly blackberries and logans. In many districts of England and Wales and in parts of Ireland garden fences can be clothed with grape vines if hardy Oxted-approved varieties are chosen. And what about the house and garage walls—grapes have long been a favourite for wall-growing.

In earlier days, folks grew many products on the sides of their houses, espalier fashion. They thus grew apples, pears, apricots, and other tree growths.

This is not intended to be a complete list of things you can grow in your two-storey garden. It is meant merely to suggest that, if your garden space is limited, you try two-storey gardening—an excellent plan for you to get the most from any garden.

2. MOTTO FOR MARCH: 'BE READY!'

Here's some advice from Connecticut gardener-mulcher Ruth Stout, author of *How to Have a Green Thumb Without an Aching Back*, on planning your garden:

Are you on the mailing lists of one or more mail order seedsmen? If you aren't, drop a line to one or two so that you get seed catalogues from them early in January each year. Order your seeds as soon as you can. This helps the seedsman who is pretty busy in spring and likes to clear as many orders as he can in winter. Ordering early helps you, too. There's no chance of your order arriving minus certain wanted items shown as 'sold out' with offers to you of second bests.

When preparing your seed order, study the seedsman's catalogue carefully so that you will know exactly what space you can allow for each and what you are going to put where. This done, find a big white sheet of good thick paper, a ruler and soft black lead pencil. Unless you are one of those skillful people who never makes a mistake, you will be better off with an eraser at the end of the pencil.

After outlining the measurements of your vegetable garden, you can settle down to putting your crops on paper.

It's a little unbelievable how much time and space a person can save if he has a complete plan to follow when he is ready to plant.

By about March, your seeds should all be arranged in 3 boxes, marked Early, Middle, Late. They should be in alphabetical order, so it will be easier when planting time comes to pick out the ones you are ready to put into the ground.

I rotate my vegetables because the experts tell us to, and hardly anything makes me feel so virtuous as following the advice of the experts on those rare occasions when I feel it isn't hazardous to do so. Every other year I put sweet corn and tomatoes in the upper half of the garden, the following year in the lower half. Why not?

Maybe you know how many feet of cabbage you want to plant this year. If you don't, figure out how many will be wanted in the kitchen. Ask the wife what she thinks. For goodness sake don't leave her out of your plans. She will be cooking all those tasty garden vegetables you will be growing. Let's say you are going to plant three varieties for summer, autumn and winter heading. Draw lines on the paper for the rows, and put planting dates and name of varieties on each line. It's wonderful when planting time comes just to glance at the diagram and waste no time in figuring where you want to put what.

Next, choose a spot for tomatoes and mark that. Do you plant too many? I do.

You can put autumn- and winter-heading cabbage or sprouting broccoli between the pea rows. This saves a lot of space and peas being an early crop, the two sorts of vegetables don't interfere with each other. Keep the pea plants well supported so they won't steal sunshine from the young cabbage or broccoli plants in June and July.

I plant about the same amount of spinach and onions each year. I always plant these in two rows, the length of the garden, next to the row of strawberries, rotating by putting the onions next to the berries one year, and the spinach there the following year.

If you are like me you are always dashing out for a handful of parsley, so you may want to do as I do: put it at the near end of the garden. Have you ever tried making a border of it around a flower bed?

Most of the other vegetables are a matter of ruling your paper, 1, 2, 3 feet apart as each vegetable requires, and writing the names on the lines. When you choose the rows for cabbage, broccoli and cauliflower you can, if you need the space, put kohlrabi seeds between the plants. I drop a few seeds of the larger plants every 18 inches and put the kohlrabi along the rest of the row. You can also crowd the lettuce and French dwarf beans with any of the later crops; they will mature and be out of the way fairly early. I put lettuce and beets extremely close to each other; neither seems to mind.

Radishes take no space; you can drop their seeds right on top of carrot, parsley and parsnip seeds when sowing these vegetables.

I put poles for beans along one end of the garden and they take up practically no space.

Pumpkins, marrows and gourds are the worst space-grabbers. You might think they were human the way they invade other people's territory. A bush marrow like Zucchini can go right up alongside a row of sweet corn. But if you grow things in the corn which creep between the rows they become a great nuisance. Perhaps you can put these things along one end or one side, or both. I put them all along the asparagus one year; last year I crowded the pole beans with them. They ran outside the garden over the grass and were most prolific.

In planning the garden, you will want to consider the size of the area available, the needs of the family, and their likes and dislikes. Keep these points in mind when you take pencil and paper and start to draw the plan. A rough sketch will do, but it must be fairly accurate to be useful. Make the plan to scale if possible. You can use a scale of $\frac{1}{8}$ inch to 1 foot. Outline the shape of your garden, put down the length and width, space between rows, names of vegetables to be planted in each row, and the names of late vegetables that will follow the early ones.

Suggested specimen seed order for a medium-sized

kitchen garden or allotment. Increase or decrease the potatoes according to the size of your garden:

Quantity			New Pence
1 packet ($\frac{1}{2}$ pint)	Pea		14
1 packet ($\frac{1}{2}$ pint)	Pea	Choose a first early, second early, and a maincrop variety	14
1 packet (1 pint)	Pea		25
1 packet ($\frac{1}{2}$ pint)	Broad Bean		14
1 packet	Dwarf Bean		15
1 packet	Runner Bean		15
1 packet	Beet		5
1 packet	Brussels sprouts		5
1 packet	Sprouting broccoli		7$\frac{1}{2}$
1 packet	Cauliflower		7$\frac{1}{2}$
1 packet	Cauliflower broccoli		6
1 packet	Cabbage	Choose a spring-, a summer-, and a late-heading kind	6
1 packet	Cabbage		6
1 packet	Cabbage		6
1 packet	Carrot		5
1 packet	Cucumber	One variety for under glass and one for outdoors	7$\frac{1}{2}$
1 packet	Cucumber		7$\frac{1}{2}$
1 packet	Kale		6
1 packet	Leek		5
1 packet	Lettuce	Choose a cabbage and a cos variety	5
1 packet	Lettuce		5
1 packet	Melon		7$\frac{1}{2}$
1 packet	Onion (for salad onions)		5
1 packet	Parsnip		5
1 packet	Radish		5
1 packet	Spinach		5
1 packet	Sweet Corn		7$\frac{1}{2}$
1 packet	Tomato	Choose one variety for your greenhouse and a hardier variety for outdoor-growing	5
1 packet	Tomato		5
1 packet	Turnip		5
1 packet	Vegetable marrow		6
1 lb	Onion sets (for maincrop onions)		20
7 lb	Potato	Choose a first early, a second early, and a maincrop variety	40
14 lb	Potato		75
28 lb	Potato		1·45

£5.23

3. MAKE A LITTLE GARDEN DO THE WORK OF A BIG ONE

A tiny garden is the best education that I know.

Each plant is just a few feet from all the others, so you notice things you'd overlook in a large garden. When something goes wrong, you realize it from the start, look for the cause, and take action.

Moreover, the tiny garden can be beautiful. Put to work, every square inch is fruitfully productive. But you must keep its nose to the grindstone. If enough growing season remains, never pull out a vegetable without planting a couple of seeds in its place. Always count of the weather being with you. You lose little if it isn't; and a long shot sometimes pays off, giving you, besides food, that comforting feeling that your judgement is pretty good, after all.

Shade can be greatest problem

In your little garden, the greatest problem may be shade. Raise a light-loving plant a foot or two above the others and in some cases you'll double the light it receives. You can do that by planting it in a bottom-less box on top of the earth. Go around the garden with a light meter (borrowed from your camera-fan neighbour) and test light availability here and there. It will reveal interesting facts.

Space problems

Sweet corn is not impossible in a small garden. True, the leaves should touch for pollination, but they will when planted in triangles of three. Quite a few of these triangles can be wedged in here and there for a vegetable that must be fresh to be real.

The best of all vegetables, asparagus, admittedly is a space-taker. But it makes such a lovely background for the summer flowers and vegetables that I slip one in wherever there are a few inches to spare. Give it room in the tiny garden if only to have a crop when other vegetables are scarce.

My space limitations started me growing tomatoes in large cans. A 2-gallon container with drainage filled with rich earth will hold a well-trained and clipped tomato through its whole bearing period.

DOROTHY BAKER

The gardener who is really cramped for space might take a tip from big city designers. They've learned a long time ago that the best utilization of space is to make things go up. Vertical gardening can be the answer to a highly successful vegetable patch in the modern small garden.

Vertical gardens

Your garden fence can be your most useful garden asset. Each summer sees my fences converted into attractive, fruitful, living walls. I invested in a few rolls of 'Weldmesh', which soon paid for itself and now continues to show a profit. The 6-foot-high fencing has to carry quite a load each season, so I'm glad that I secured it to strong steel poles when setting it up.

Vegetable marrows and cucumbers decorate fences, too

One of the fences is devoted to vegetables. Trailing sorts of vegetable marrow give a remarkable flower display, crop well, and take up no valuable garden space. I give the plants an early start by sowing in peat pots filled with sifted garden compost in mid-April. Germination is good in the cold frame, and I have strong, healthy plants for setting out 15 inches apart along the fence in early June. Although the plants have tendrils, I encourage the main shoots to climb to the top of my fence by tying in regularly until August. Plants of vegetable marrow are greedy feeders and they have a terrible thirst. They find all the nourishment they need in my organically rich soil, and to save precious water, I supply it directly to the roots via a clay flower pot sunk alongside each plant.

Although the flower display is not so gaudy, cucumbers may also be grown on the garden fence. Kaga, Kariha and Baton Vert are rapid climbers. I sow as for vegetable marrow, but when setting out the plants in June I plant them only 12 inches apart. The secret of success with cucumbers is to pick often. This encourages the plants to keep on cropping until temperatures get a bit low around mid-September.

In some summers, most of the 'vegetable fence' is devoted to runner beans; the cucumbers are then trained on a trellis. The bean seeds are sown at 4 inches apart, which some people say is too close, and the plants quickly climb the mesh and make a thick stand of jungle-like greenery and loads of tender pods from late July until October. Here again, regular harvesting is the secret of long cropping. Although I'm a great one for mulching, I do find it necessary to flood the bean plants now and then when they are in full bearing.

Not all neighbours take kindly to 6-foot-high fences, but I see no reason at all why the fruit and vegetables I grow on my own tall fences could not be grown on the more conventional 4-foot fencing, although you'd lose 2 feet of vertical space and yields would be somewhat less. In addition to the crops I have mentioned, I'm sure that tomatoes would do well alongside a 4-foot fence. I know how well my tomato plants crop trained each season to a 4-foot trellis.

Bamboo sticks

Bamboo tepees are a must in vertical gardening—they're so spectacular that you can place them in the flower garden and mingle flowers and vegetables in a startling way. You need four long, strong bamboo canes (tall poles will do). After pushing the supports into the soil a few inches to anchor them, tie them together somewhere near the top. Then link the supports together —from base to apex—with soft wire. You then have an openwork wigwam on which marrows, cucumbers, and climbing beans (French or scarlet runner) can be grown. If the climate permits, muskmelons and watermelons should do fine on tepees, too. It doesn't matter whether you plant inside or outside the tepee. The important thing is to position the plants so that they will be able to climb up the legs of the tepees.

If space is not your problem, pass on these tips to friends and neighbours who say they just can't grow any food crops because of lack of garden space. Make sure, though, that they understand that good, healthy crops like yours and mine aren't produced by waving magic wands or sprinkling chemicals around the garden. Some work has to be done (but not too much), and the soil must get its annual quota of organic matter.

BRIAN FURNER

STARTING PLANTS FROM SEED

1. WHAT SEEDS ARE

Seeds are embryo plants with enough food stored around them to last until they can make their own food. If you soak a bean seed in water for a day or two, then carefully open it along the seam, you can see the young plant at one end of the bean seed. It will be very small and delicate. You'll easily be able to see the first few leaves, as well as the small, round, pointed root.

All seeds are alike in that they have a small plant in them. The rest of the seed contains stored food for the young plant. This little plant needs certain conditions in order for it to grow; these are air, warmth, light, plant food, and moisture. Given these conditions, the plant should become well established.

As soon as the plant has a root and *green* leaves, it can start to make its own food. This usually takes from 10 to 30 days. The root takes up water and minerals from the soil. These *raw materials* are carried in the stream of water or sap up to the *green leaves*, where they are made into plant food. The water and minerals in the soil, carbon dioxide in the air, and light must all come together in a green leaf before they can be used by the plant as food.

The green colour in the leaf is caused by chlorophyll, which has the ability to transform raw materials into starch in the presence of light. Without light, true plants cannot continue to grow because plant foods cannot be manufactured. Both chlorophyll and light are necessary.

Leaves turn green in the light. Seeds germinated and kept dark will have white sprouts which will turn green when brought into the light for a few days.

The leaves and other green parts of the plant are a sort of kitchen or manufacturing plant for preparing plant food. After the green parts have prepared the food, it is sent back to the roots and other parts of the plant and is used for growth. The leaves or 'plant kitchen' must have sunlight in order to work.

On the following pages, you'll learn how to grow your

own plants from seeds and how to provide seedlings with the best growing conditions.

2. GROWING YOUR OWN PLANTS

Plant growing was once an art and a must with gardeners throughout the land. They knew their work, did it well and, as a result, reaped a bountiful harvest.

Today, it is surprising how few gardeners and farmers do grow their own plants. Even those who stand to profit greatly by doing so, turn their backs on the cold frame. They have come to depend upon outside sources for their needs; in turn, they are gambling their entire crop upon another's method of growing the all-important item.

In the opinion of G. J. Raleigh of Cornell University's Department of Horticulture:

Plants of similar quality usually can be grown cheaper than they can be purchased. Moreover, the grower who produces his own plants is much less likely to be troubled by such diseases as clubroot and yellows of cabbage which are commonly introduced by purchasing plants from infested soils. Poor-quality plants may sell at low prices, but too often results with such plants are disappointing.

When early maturity is of importance, as in most market-garden sections, the kind of plants used often determines whether or not the crop will be profitable. Large, sturdy plants with good root systems commence growth quickly after careful transplanting and produce crops earlier than do poorly grown plants.

Another great advantage in raising your own plants in your greenhouse, cold frame, or under cloches—or with hardy subjects—in a seed bed in the open garden —is that you grow just the varieties you want to grow. You will not be tied to just the varieties local nurserymen grow or local shops have for sale. Nurseries usually limit themselves to a few good selling varieties of plants. This is particularly true of tomatoes. Nurserymen know that every gardener in the country knows the variety, Moneymaker. Garden shops know that most of their customers will ask for this variety, too. So it's Moneymaker plants you'll find at your local garden shop and in chain stores each spring. Not that Moneymaker is not a fine variety. It is—and when compost-grown the tomatoes are firm but juicy and of excellent flavour. Trouble is that Moneymaker plants take quite a time to get going outdoors and since Moneymaker was bred around 30 years ago seed breeders have developed other, even better kinds of tomato. For outdoor growing the variety Outdoor Girl is one of the best. Most retail seedsmen and mail order firms offer seeds of this early-to-grow and early-to-ripen tomato.

Another point about raising your own plants is that you will be able to grow vegetables never offered as seedlings in the shops. Examples are the new Asiatic climbing or trellis-type cucumbers, sweet peppers, American green celery and aubergine. Young plants of all of these need to be ready for setting out where they are to grow by late May or early June.

3. The Seed Bed

Crops grown in the kitchen garden are classed as hardy or half-hardy. Among the hardies are all members of the cabbage family (known as brassicae or brassicas) and lettuce. Plants of these vegetables are raised in a seed bed in the open garden. The first week of April sees most gardeners preparing seed beds and there are many ways of doing the job. Plants are made or marred by seed-bed conditions. For strong, healthy seedlings good conditions are so necessary. Here is just one good way of making a seed bed.

First, is the soil drainage good? If you start off with a garden which is badly drained you will rectify this state of affairs over the years by incorporating lots of garden compost and partially rotted autumn leaves into the soil. Is the spot chosen for the seed bed right out in the open? Shade is something seedlings just can't stand. A wall or a fence to the north side won't matter a bit. You will get no shade from that quarter and your seedlings will be protected from cold, north winds.

Have you forked the soil to a depth of around 4 to 6 inches, and removed all weeds and weed roots? If you haven't, do so now. Then rake level to remove any debris and large stones. Break up any clods, using the back of the rake. Firm gently by walking on the dug, raked soil. Then rake once more. Does it look even, flat, neat? Now spread a 1-inch mulch of sifted garden compost over the soil and rake level. If you are new to gardening and have no garden compost ready for use you may, if you wish, invest in a bag of organically-based Levington Compost. This is not cheap and may not contain all the galaxy of plant foods and trace elements which home-made garden compost contains but it does lead to the aerated, porous soil 'skin' which seedlings like so much. After raking level you are ready to start seed sowing.

Use a small hoe to make 1-inch deep seed drills spaced at no more than 9 inches apart. Is the soil below the compost quite wet? If it isn't, flood the shallow seed drills. Wait until the water has drained away before sowing. Do not sow too thinly nor be too heavy-handed. Practice makes perfect. After sowing the seeds draw compost from either side of the seed drills into them so that the seeds are covered. Use your hand to do this. When the drills are filled, firm gently with the palm of your hand. Always label seed rows. It is so easy to forget where different sorts of brassicas were planted. Is there any room available in the seed bed for a couple of short rows of radish? If there is why not make a sowing of French Breakfast now, too? Seed drills are 1 inch deep and again at 9 inches apart but do try to sow very thinly. Each radish plant does best if it has one square inch of surface area to itself. Here and there you may find later you have sown a bit too thickly. Pull out surplus radish seedlings when young. Leave the rest to form into tasty radishes for May salads.

Cabbages and their Kin—What to Sow

CABBAGE
Summer-heading for use between late July and early September
Greyhound, Primo, Summer Monarch

Autumn-heading for use between September and December
Autumn Monarch, Autumn Pride

Winter-heading for use between November and February
Christmas Drumhead, Winter Monarch, January King

BRUSSELS SPROUTS
For December to February use
Irish Elegance, Peer Gynt, Thor

BROCCOLI
For April and May use
Late Purple Sprouting, Late White Sprouting

CAULIFLOWER
For August and September use
All the Year Round
For use in the following April
Reading Giant

SAVOY CABBAGE
For winter use
Ormskirk Late Green, Savoy King

Lettuces

There are many to choose for early April sowing. Unrivalled and Webb's Wonderful are two good cabbage-type lettuces and Giant White Cos or Giant Green Cos are excellent cos lettuces.

In the meantime while you have been busy the roof-top sparrow population has been watching. As soon as you go indoors they'll get down to investigating—and what a mess they will make to your neat seed bed. Stop their nonsense by draping small nylon mesh netting over and around the seed bed. Black cotton stretched across the bed here and there can be effective but only netting provides 100 per cent protection.

4. INVESTING IN A COLD FRAME

A cold frame makes summer longer in your garden. You can start off early seed-bed sowings in March when both soil and climate outside the fames are not right. An earlier sowing means earlier crops—particularly valuable if you think of early summer cabbages and early summer lettuce. With a cold frame you can raise pot plants of vegetable marrow, hardy cucumbers, and sweet corn for moving to their growing sites in early

June. If you live in the south you can even raise your own tomato plants by sowing seeds in the cold frame during the first week of April. By the first week of June there will be stout, strong plants for setting out in the garden and they will be of the variety of your choice.

For midland and northern gardeners a cold frame is just the spot for ridge cucumbers between June and September. The southern gardener often uses a frame for that luxury summer crop, the canteloupe melon.

The comparative warmth and the shelter of the frame make it just the place for overwintering onion and cauliflower seedlings or for protecting a crop of winter lettuces. If you go in for several cold frames they can be used as growing places for earlier lettuces, cabbages, and cauliflowers.

There are various sizes and shapes of cold frame on sale. If you're a handyman you can make your own. You can, if you wish, copy one of the frame designs you see in a shop or a successful frame already in use in a neighbour's garden. Perhaps you'd prefer to design something quite new in frame construction. For the do-it-yourself gardener the type of frame illustrated here may appeal. It has the advantage that fresh frames may be made later on and put in use with the originals for increasing the amount of garden space to receive frame protection. This is a great advantage if, for instance, you wish to get tomato plants growing rapidly for heavier, larger crops or if you wish to have a frame-covered bed for earlier-than-usual June-fruiting strawberries. Frames like this can be moved around the garden easily. They can come in handy for ripening off the outdoor tomato crop in September and October or for the production of October strawberries from a bed of late summer/autumn fruiters.

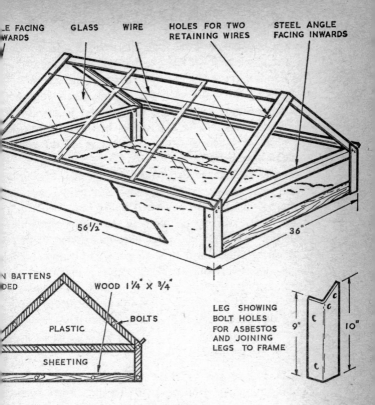

LE FACING WARDS · GLASS · WIRE · HOLES FOR TWO RETAINING WIRES · STEEL ANGLE FACING INWARDS

56½"

36"

N BATTENS DED · WOOD 1¼" × ¾" · BOLTS · PLASTIC · SHEETING

LEG SHOWING BOLT HOLES FOR ASBESTOS AND JOINING LEGS TO FRAME

9" · 10"

5. Cloches

These come in glass or plastic. Glass cloches are considered as being longer-lasting if you treat them with care. Glass cloches vary in shape from a simple tent, consisting of two pieces of glass, to the low barns and large barns made up of four sheets.

Because cloches are not airtight as many commercially manufactured cold frames are, they need far less management as regards ventilation. During very hot weather a top panel on barn cloches may be removed to allow more air to enter or, if you wish, one of the cloches may be removed from the row for greater ventilation. Cloches cover narrow strips of soil surface area. Rain, falling on to the cloches, runs into the soil alongside them. The roots of cloche-grown plants (but not seedlings) extend beyond the cloches and make use of this water. This means that plants beneath cloches do not need so much attention water-wise as do plants growing in cold frames.

Cloches are light to handle and may be moved readily to all parts of the garden for use just where wanted. Glass cloches should be stacked under cover when not in use. There will be no room in the garden shed and the garage is not the place for these breakables. A sheet of thick polythene will provide good protection. Some plastic cloches are quickly taken to pieces and when not in use may be stored in a shed, garage, or even in a cupboard indoors. But try to put your cloches to maximum use. That is the way to make them pay for themselves. Here are just a few ways in which cloches may be used the year long:

Month	Sow or protect seedlings or plants of
January to June	Cabbage, cauliflower, broad beans, dwarf beans, runner beans, onions, lettuce, radish, peas, carrots, Brussels sprouts, leeks, turnips, cucumbers, tomatoes, melons, sweet corn, sweet peppers, vegetable marrows
June to September	Cucumbers, melons, sweet peppers, tomatoes
October to December	Cabbage, broad beans, lettuce, cauliflower, onions, spinach, peas

The use of cloches in home fruit growing is rather restricted. They come in handy for an early crop of

Royal Sovereign or Merton Herald strawberries. Large Barns have been found to be just the sort of protection suited for the production of dessert grapes in the south and smaller-fruited wine grapes in other parts of Britain.

6. YOUR GREENHOUSE

A greenhouse can play an important part in the organic production of home-grown food but you simply must decide when buying one that you will make as much use of it as you can. A greenhouse, whether you build it or buy it, is a capital expense which just has to show dividends year after year. Some people think that a greenhouse is just for growing a crop of tomatoes each summer and for housing a few odd pot plants in winter. A greenhouse programmed like that is not contributing much to the larder.

Here are some hints on greenhouse planning:—

Late March. Make a seed bed in one of the greenhouse borders and sow early summer cabbage and early summer lettuce. In the south of England tomato seeds may also be sown just like cabbage seeds in a greenhouse border, too. No need for artificial heat of any sort.

Late May. Set out lettuce and cabbage plants in the garden. In a cold spring they will benefit a lot from cloche protection for a week to 10 days. Plant tomatoes in the greenhouse and, if the greenhouse is sufficiently large, make room for and set out plants of cucumber, aubergine, or sweet peppers.

October. Clear the greenhouse of all plants from which fine crops were picked all summer. Add all plant remains to the compost heap. Fork over the borders. If you intend keeping the greenhouse slightly warm all winter now is the time to bring in any pot plants.

November. Endive plants may be dug in the garden and replanted for blanching in the greenhouse. The first batch of chicory roots may be planted in the greenhouse for chicon forcing. Rhubarb crowns may be planted beneath the greenhouse staging for an early forced crop. If you have a grape vine in the greenhouse—now is the time to winter prune it.

February. Pot strawberry plants may be taken out of cold frame and placed on the greenhouse staging for a luxury, out-of-season crop. In a heated greenhouse sowings may start now. Suggested sowings are:

Onion   Cabbage   Lettuce   Cauliflower
Tomato

7. COMPOSTS AND POTS

Take note that 'compost' has two very different meanings among gardeners. The organic fraternity chats about the sort of compost each good gardener makes from waste materials. Gardeners who are not completely all-organic may make excellent compost, too. They also use special propagating composts for use in raising plants in seed trays and pots. Some gardeners go to great pains in mixing up all sorts of odd ingredients in order to make what they consider is a first-class propagating compost. Old-time head gardeners sometimes had 'secret' formulae for their own special composts. In comparatively recent years the John Innes Institute recommended two or three successful compost formulae. The composts can be made up by the gardener using a John Innes Base or bought from garden shops up and down the country. John Innes Composts vary a lot—depending on who makes them and with what sort of peat, sand, and loam. John Innes Composts contain minute chemical additions, which is why real organic gardeners don't use them.

The word 'organic' gives a sort of respectability to horticultural aids these days. Fisons claim that their new, soil-less Levington composts are organically based. Most of the compost is peat which is certainly organic. What else is incorporated in the composts is known only to Fisons. Gardeners who have used Levington composts agree that they are excellent. Trouble is that you have to buy them and they are not cheap. For the organic enthusiast the garden compost heap can be utilized for preparing a first-class, home-made propagating compost. Just sift some of your garden compost and you have a natural, porous yet water-retentive, nutritious propagating compost at no cost at all. Never sterilize sifted garden compost before using it. Yes, some weed seeds will germinate in it. Pull them out as soon as they show. Not all that hard work if you are propagating in just a few seed trays and a few dozen pots.

Pot-grown seedlings suffer no check to continued steady growth when you set them out where they are to grow. With our short summer season a check to growth is something our half-hardy plants do not like at all. Some vegetables, particularly marrows and cucumbers, resent any interference to the rooting system when the plants are at the seedling stage and plants should, therefore, always be raised in pots and never in seed trays. Three- and 3½-inch clay flower pots were and still are used by the million. Since World War Two plastic pots have been developed. Peat pots have been around for nigh on 40 years. They are all-organic and are much liked by many. They have one great advantage over clay and plastic pots. If young plants are left too long in clay or plastic pots the roots get horribly twisted and the plants start to grow upwards in an alarming manner. This doesn't happen if you use peat pots and stand them in shallow trenches drawn out in the greenhouse border, in cold frames or under cloches. If because of bad weather you don't wish to move the pot-raised plants to their growing positions outdoors—just wait a week or two. The plants will come to no harm. The roots will pass through the peat pot wall and into the well-composted soil beneath the pots. The plants will just grow on steadily. When about to move them to new positions, dig up the pots so that the new roots beneath them are not damaged. Always tear off any dryish part of a peat pot before planting out. Peat pots are used once only.

Cheapest 'pot' of all is a Soil Block. Soil Block Making Machines may possibly still be on offer. I haven't seen one in a shop for years. If you have one or can get one you may make your own blocks using sifted garden compost.

8. WATERING

When to apply water and how much of it to apply to seed beds, seedlings, and young pot plants are points the gardener has to learn. There are no fixed rules.

A glass- or plastic-protected seed bed may need watering daily with a fine rose on the watering can—or may require no water at all until the seedlings poke through the soil. A seed bed in the open garden may never need watering if spring is wet. In a dry spring such seed beds may, however, need watering fairly frequently. Irrigation sprinklers are excellent for watering seedlings. When to water and how much to apply depends a lot on the texture of the soil. A seed bed in a sandy soil will dry out rapidly. But here again the compost heap comes to the aid of the gardener. With regular heavy dressings of home made compost even the sandiest of soils changes its texture to several inches of spongey, humus-packed goodness.

You need as much common sense when it comes to watering growing plants in summer as you do when it comes to watering seedlings in beds, trays, and pots. Let us go back to your garden soil once more. If there is clay in it there's every chance that you will not have to worry as much about watering as the gardener gardening on gravel. And where do you live? The western half of Britain is noted for its wetter climate; the eastern half for dryness. In fact many gardeners in Kent and East Anglia could probably double their crops and suffer far less from plant pests if more water were applied in summer. This criticism applies particularly to potatoes and peas. A potato plant with dryish roots just dies, leaving the gardener to dig lots of sad-looking marbles instead of a first-class potato crop. Pea plants yellow, the pods seldom swell and get infested with pea maggot grubs where the soil is left to dry out.

Vegetables can be divided into those with a thirst and those which seem to jog along pretty well until rain falls. Not that they like being kept short of water. Here are the really thirsty ones:

Tomato	Vegetable marrow	Broad bean
Runner bean	Cucumber	Sweet corn
Potato	Pea	Cauliflower
Melon	Pumpkin	

BRIAN FURNER

TIMES TO SOW AND PLANT IN THE KITCHEN GARDEN

G = Sow in greenhouse (heated)
C = Sow under cloches or in frames
S = Sow in a seed bed outdoors
X = Sow where plants are to grow
W = Sow outdoors and cover with cloches later on
P = Set out plants, bulbs, crowns, etc.

Vegetable	Feb.	March	Apr.	May	June	July	Aug.	Sept.	Oct.	Nov.
Artichoke, Globe			P							
Artichoke, Jerusalem		P	P							
Asparagus		P	P							
Asparagus Pea				X						
Aubergine (egg plant)		G								
Bean, Broad	CX	CX	X							CX
Bean, Dwarf French			CX	X	X	X				
Bean, Runner			CX	X	X					
Beetroot			X	X	X	X				
Broccoli, heading (see Cauliflower)										
Broccoli, sprouting			S							
Brussels Sprouts	G	C	S							
Cabbage, Chinese			S			X	W			
Cabbage, red		C	S			S	S			
Cabbage, Spring										
Cabbage, Summer		C	CS							
Cabbage, Autumn/Winter			S							
Cabbage, Savoy			S							

Vegetable							
Capsicum (Sweet Pepper)	G		GC				X
Carrots	G	C		X		W	W
Cauliflower, Summer		S	S	X		W	
Cauliflower, Winter/Spring (heading broccoli, cauliflower broccoli)	S			X			
Celery	G	G		X			
Celeriac	G	G		X			
Celtuce	X	X					
Chicory		X	X		W		
Corn Salad (Lamb's Lettuce)	CG		X	X			
Cucumber, ridge and trellis	GC		X	X			
Cucumber, greenhouse or frame	G	GC	X		X		
Endive	X		X	X			
Garlic	X		X				
Horse-radish	X	X					
Kale (Borecole)	X	X	S	X			
Kohlrabi	C	CS	X	X			
Leek	C	CS	X	X		WG	
Lettuce, Summer/Autumn	C	CS	X	X		W	
Lettuce, Spring	X	X			W	WG	
Melon	G	GC	X	X			
Mustard, Chinese	GC		X	X			
Onion, Maincrop from seed	G	GC	SS	X	W		
Onion, Maincrop from sets	X	X	X	P	W		
Onion, salad	C	X					
Onion, Welsh	CP	SP	P				
Parsley	X	X	X				
Parsnip	X	X					
Pea, Early Varieties	C	CX	X	X			

Vegetable	Feb.	March	Apr.	May	June	July	Aug.	Sept.	Oct.	Nov.
Pea, Maincrop		X	X	X						
Pea, Mangetout		X	X	X						
Pea, Asparagus Pea			P	X						
Potato		P	P							
Pumpkin		G	GC							
Radish, Summer		C	CX	X	X	X	X			
Radish, Winter						X	X	W		
Rhubarb	P	P								P
Salsify		X	X							
Scorzonera		X	X							
Seakale	P	SP	s							P
Seakale Beet (Swiss chard)			X	X						
Shallot		P	P							
Spinach, New Zealand		C	C							
Spinach, Summer	C	CX	X	X	X	X				
Spinach, Winter							X	W		
Spinach Beet		X	X	X						
Squash			CG	X						
Swede			CG	X	X					
Sweet Corn		G	CG	X						
Tomato, greenhouse, frame and cloche cultivation	G	G								
Tomato, outdoor cultivation		C	X	X						
Turnip, summer			CG	X		X	X			
Turnip, Winter						X	X			
Vegetable Marrow		CG	CG	X						

SOWING, PLANTING, AND TRANSPLANTING OUTSIDE

Getting plants off to an early start in the garden is an objective of every gardener. All of us want to make the first sowing of each vegetable as soon as it can be safely done—as soon as there's no chance of the seedlings being damaged by cold. There's good reason for sowing early. In many cases it will mean that a second, different crop may be sown or planted later in the season in the same spot.

Many vegetables are so hardy that they can be sown or planted about 6 weeks before the last spring frost is anticipated.

It should also be remembered that most, if not all, of the cold-tolerant crops actually thrive better in cool weather than in hot weather. Cabbage, lettuce, and peas are examples.

For raising plants of quite a lot of vegetables a cold frame or a set of cloches is an invaluable aid.

1. Seed Sowing

Straight rows in the kitchen garden make all the difference between the neat, tidy look you will be aiming for and that muddle you sometimes see in other gardens. Always use a garden line (you can buy one, make one yourself, or suggest that the son and heir make you one in woodwork class). For short, close rows in a seed bed a straight length of wood often replaces a garden line. When using a garden line stretch the string tight enough to lift it above the surface of the soil or the line will not be straight.

Most vegetable seeds should be sown very shallow. The smaller seeds, such as lettuce and radishes, should not be sown more than $\frac{1}{4}$ inch deep. For such small seeds, the hoe or rake handle is an excellent tool for opening the shallow seed furrow. For the larger seeds, such as peas and beans, the proper depth is from $\frac{1}{2}$ to 1 inch. Late plantings may be somewhat deeper than early plantings.

As a general rule, sow seeds somewhat less than the recommended depth if the soil is heavy or the temperature low, and a little deeper in light soil, or during warm weather.

Sow the seed thick enough to get an even stand. Too much seed is wasteful and means twice the work of thinning.

Sow the seed thinly by shaking it from a cut corner of the package or individually dropping the seeds from the fingers. Many gardeners waste seed and make extra work by sowing seed too thick. After sowing, the soil is drawn over the seed, using the corner of the hoe. In case the soil is somewhat cloddy, try to draw in the finer soil to cover the seed.

Sandy soils should be firmed above the seed in order to hasten germination. On heavy soils, where crusting is likely, packing of the soil above the seed increases the danger of crusting. On such soils a shower of rain or sprinkler irrigation may be necessary to facilitate germination, and crusts will be less severe if the soil is not packed.

Late-sown seeds may not germinate unless provision is made to retain moisture. When sowing in summer always water the seed drills unless the soil is quite moist.

The question of how long seeds remain viable often arises. This will depend greatly upon the particular vegetable involved as well as conditions under which the seed is stored. Seed will retain viability much longer when stored under cool, dry conditions as compared with storage that is warm and moist.

Vegetable seeds may be divided into the following general groups:

1. Comparatively short-lived, usually not good after 1 to 2 years: sweet corn, leek, onion, parsley, parsnip, and salsify.

2. Moderately long-lived, often good for 3 to 5 years under favourable conditions: asparagus, bean, Brussels sprouts, cabbage, carrot, cauliflower, celery, chicory, cress, endive, kale, kohlrabi, lettuce, peas, sweet pepper, radish, spinach, and turnip.

3. Comparatively long-lived under favourable conditions, may be good for more than 5 years: beets, cucumber, canteloupe melon, mustard, and tomato.

Most vegetable seeds are sown in seed drills. American gardeners and farmers also sow in 'hills' and by broadcasting. You may find a description of these three methods of interest. It was prepared by members of the Nevada Horticultural Department.

The drill method is usually the best. Using the corner of the hoe, make a straight drill or trench down each row. It should be deep enough to reach into moist ground. The seeds then are dropped into the drill row by hand. Directions usually are found on seed packages indicating the right depth. It is not necessary to fill the drill with soil when covering small seeds. Simply cover the seeds to the right depth and leave the rest of the drill unfilled. Large seeds, such as peas or beans, should be planted from 2 to 4 inches apart. Very small seeds should be mixed with about three times their bulk of dry sand so they will not fall too thickly. This is helpful especially with such small seeds as those of turnips and carrots, which are lost easily out of the hand between the fingers. Seeds should be covered with fine, moist soil, which should be firmly pressed down over the seeds with the back of the hoe. This prevents drying out around the seeds.

Hills frequently are used for plants that spread on the ground. A hole about a foot across and a foot deep is made and a 4- to 6-inch layer of *well-rotted* manure is put in the bottom of the hole. Don't use fresh manure since it injures the plants. The manure is covered with 4 to 6 inches of fine soil, packed down, and the seeds are planted in it. Hills are used because they afford a convenient way to give the plants food material, and because one may know where the roots are after the vines have covered the ground. The distance apart to make the hills will depend upon the size of the vines. Hills for vine squash or pumpkins may be 8 to 12 feet apart, while cucumber hills may be only 3 to 6 feet apart. Unless extra fertilizer is used under the hills, there is little advantage to the hill method. Sweet corn usually is sown in hills because of convenience in planting and because it saves the labour of making a drill.

When the broadcasting method is used, the seeds are scattered thinly over the top of the soil and are then covered by light raking and packing with the back of a hoe. The seed bed should be well prepared first. This method is used with many small seeds, such as those of turnips, lettuce, etc. It is well adapted to use in small vegetable gardens where the sprinkling method of irrigation is to be used. It eliminates the need for irrigation furrows. It makes hand weeding necessary because the plants are not in rows and cannot be cultivated with power equipment or tools.

2. THINNING

Most gardeners sow too much seed. Consequently, plants are too close if seed has good germination. The natural tendency is to sow crops like beets, carrots, radishes, lettuce, turnips, and endive too thickly. This is because it is difficult to sow small seeds thinly enough to eliminate hand thinning, says E. C. Wittmeyer, Ohio State University extension horticulturist. Beet seeds, for example, are actually fruits containing several seeds. If root crops are not thinned, poorly shaped roots will result.

The easiest time to do the thinning job is when the plants are small and the soil is moist. Turnips should be thinned before their taproots become fleshy. They need 3 inches between plants for best development. Radishes, on the other hand, can be left in the ground until those that are to be thinned are large enough to eat unless they were sown very thickly. If this is the situation, thinning should be done early.

Surplus beet plants can be pulled when they are 4 to 5 inches tall and used for greens. Beets should have 3 inches between plants. Carrots should be thinned early and allowed to stand 1 inch apart. Later, alternate carrots can be pulled and used.

Lettuce, Swiss chard, endive, kohlrabi, and similar crops almost always need thinning.

Here are some general rules regarding thinning:

1. Thinning should be done while plants are small and when the soil is moist, so they can be pulled out easily without injuring those that are left.

2. Root crops should be thinned before their taproots become fleshy. Onions from seeds and radishes can be left in the ground until those that are thinned out are large enough to eat.

3. Carrots should be thinned first when they are 2 to 3 inches tall, so as to stand about 1 inch apart. They can then be left to develop until large enough to

be eaten, when alternate plants can be pulled and used, leaving more room for those that are left.

4. Where seeds of cucumber, sweet corn, and vegetable marrow are sown directly into the garden soil in May it is the practice to sow two or even three at each 'station'. The seedlings are thinned when small to leave just one strong one at each station.

5. Thinning is rarely practised with beans, peas, and some other large-seeded plants which produce vigorous seedlings, for a good stand usually is obtained by planting only a few more seeds than the number of plants required.

Pelleted seeds

Some vegetable seeds are now being offered in pellet form. Seedsmen so far are using just clay—no chemical fertilizers or pest-killing additives. Benefit of pelleted seeds is that you can sow at just the right spacing in the seed drill. This means little or no thinning of seedlings at all. But seeds need a fair amount of moisture before they can germinate—and the clay pellet is dry. This means that seed drills must invariably be wetted well with water before you start sowing these so easy to handle pellet seeds.

3. TRANSPLANTING VEGETABLES

The few minutes spent transplanting are the most important minutes in the life of the plant.

Some plants are more resistant to shock than others, but all react to some degree. Among the easiest plants to transplant are broccoli, cabbage, cauliflower, lettuce, and onions. Box-grown and outdoor-raised bean seedlings transplant fairly well. Pea seedlings do not, nor do tap-rooted vegetables like carrot, beetroot, and parsnip.

Young plants of cucumber, sweet corn, melon, pumpkin, and vegetable marrow do not take to being moved at all. But they are usually propagated in pots and, as pot plants, there is no root disturbance during transplanting. It is root disturbance which so many vegetable seedlings just don't like at all.

The idea in transplanting, of course, is to lessen the shock as much as possible. The plant is an amazingly well-integrated mechanism in which each function of each cell is interdependent on the actions of other cells. Water and soil materials are moving constantly through the roots, stems, and leaves, feeding the cells of the leaves which manufacture the plant food. When transplanted, some of the vital roots and tiny root hairs are almost always torn away, the entire water-chain system may be disrupted, and changed light conditions and temperature may disrupt other normal plant functions. It's up to you to help the seedling make as smooth an adjustment as possible.

If possible, try to transplant on a cloudy, moist day, when light and heat shock will be small. Before beginning to transplant, loosen soil in the new location, and about an hour or two before removing seedlings, thoroughly water soil in the frame, cloche, or open garden seed bed. Boxes containing seedlings also need a thorough watering. The watering tends to make loosening of the roots easier.

When taking up seedlings, take plenty of soil along. Some root damage is almost inevitable, but it can be kept to a minimum by special care in handling.

When transplanting seedlings in the garden always water planting holes unless the ground seems quite wet. Firm well after planting so that roots are in good firm contact with the soil. A great deal depends on this as roots depend on firm contact for absorption of essential soil ingredients. It is usually necessary to water well after planting. When planting out pot-grown seedlings the procedure is the same but, of course, handle the soil balls carefully so that roots are not damaged after you have removed the plants from the pots. With peat pots don't forget to tear off any parts of the pot which are not sodden and show signs of disintegration. A second watering on the evening of the day after transplanting is beneficial in hot, dry weather.

If tender seedlings were to be transplanted from their protected quarters—greenhouse, cloches, frames— directly into the open ground, the inevitable result would be serious injury, often fatal. Therefore, to lessen the shock of temperature, wind, and sun, a hardening-off process is used, in which seedlings are gradually exposed to the natural elements.

Usually, the hardening-off process takes about 2 weeks, and should be timed so that the young seedlings end the 2 weeks in a period warm enough for them to be planted outside safely. The best way to harden off greenhouse-raised seedlings (or cuttings for that matter) is to move them in their boxes or pots to a cold frame.

The frame should be closed for the first 2 days of the period. On the third day, the top should be opened just a crack, and over the remainder of the period the air space should be widened more each day until, on the last day, the top is removed.

Cloches come in handy, too, for hardening off greenhouse-raised subjects. If you have raised plants in a cold frame or under cloches the plants will need hardening off if you wish to transplant them to an outdoor position. To harden off frame-grown seedlings the technique is similar to that already explained. Just open the light more and more for a period of about a week. On the first three or four days always keep the light closed at night. Providing you feel sure there will be no chance of one of those unexpected late spring frosts, leave the light off at night towards the end of the hardening-off period. To harden off cloche-raised plants stand all the cloches an inch or so apart at first. Then a day or two later remove the end pieces, too. On the third or fourth day remove one or more of the cloches—depending on the weather. Finally remove all of the cloches. Replace the cloches each evening at the start. Here again always replace cloches even later on if you fear a night frost. Television and radio reports are sometimes helpful in warning of late spring frosts which can blacken and kill tender, unprotected seedlings during the hardening-off process.

SOME BASIC VEGETABLE-GROWING ADVICE

1. TABLES FOR ROTATION PLANTING—GETTING THE MOST FROM THE SPACE AVAILABLE

   Plants Occupying the Ground All of the Growing Season

   Perennial

Artichoke Globe	Horse-radish
Artichoke Jerusalem	Onion Welsh
Asparagus	Rhubarb

   Annual

Garlic	Seakale beet (Swiss chard)
Onion	Salsify
Parsley	Scorzonera
Potato (second earlies and maincrop)	

Plants Occupying Ground Part of Season May be Followed by Others

Bean, broad	Kohlrabi
Bean, French dwarf	Lettuce
Beetroot	Onion, salad
Broccoli, sprouting	Pea
Brussels sprouts	Potato (first earlies)
Cabbage, spring	Radish
Cauliflower, winter/spring	Spinach
Kale	Turnip, summer

Plants Which May Follow Others

Bean, French dwarf	Lettuce
Beetroot	Endive
Cabbage	Mustard, Chinese
Cabbage, Chinese	Onion, salad
Carrot	Radish
Celery	Spinach
Chicory	Swede
Corn, salad	Turnip, winter
Kale	

Plants Which May be Utilized in Interplanting Early, Quick-Maturing, Narrow-spaced

Bean, French dwarf	Pea, early
Beet, early	Radish
Carrot, early	Kohlrabi
Lettuce	Turnip, summer
Onion, salad	Spinach

Later, Slower-growing, Wider-spaced Plants

Broccoli	Spinach, New Zealand
Brussels sprouts	Squash
Cabbage	Tomato
Cucumber	Vegetable marrow
Pumpkin	

Plants Which May be planted Together in the Same Row

Quick Germinating and Maturing

Non-hearting lettuce such as Salad Bowl } with
Parsnip } summer
Spinach } radish

Slower Germinating and Maturing Plants

Beet (maincrop)	Salsify
Carrot (maincrop)	Scorzonera
Leek	Seakale beet
Parsley	Spinach, New Zealand
Parsnip	Onion, (maincrop)

Plants Which Can be Cut More than Once

Asparagus	Rhubarb
Broccoli, sprouting	Seakale beet
Kale	Spinach
Mustard, Chinese	Spinach, New Zealand
Parsley	

Plants of Which Only a Few Are Needed for Average Family

Artichoke, globe	Horse-radish
Artichoke, Jerusalem	Rhubarb
Asparagus	Sweet peppers
Herbs, various	Vegetable marrow

Plants Which Can be Staked or Trellised

Bean, French climbing	Pumpkin
Bean, runner	Squash
Cucumber	Tomato
Peas	Vegetable marrow

Sun-loving Plants

Aubergine (egg plant)	Squash
Cucumber	Sweet corn
Melon	Tomato
Pumpkin	Sweet pepper

Shade-tolerant Plants

Lettuce is a cool weather crop and will thrive in partial shade where sowings are made from May to July.

Summer-sown garden peas will thrive in partial shade.

Cucumbers often require shading when grown in a greenhouse, a cold frame or under cloches. Melons, too, benefit from shade in hot, sunny weather.

Kohlrabi needs well-drained soil and need not be grown where there is bright summer sun all day.

Mint will grow in shade providing there is also much moisture.

2. ARTICHOKE, GLOBE

Soil. Fertile, well drained but not one which dries out rapidly in summer.

Location. Sunny position.

Fertilizer. Apply a mulch of garden compost after planting and renew each autumn.

Width apart in the row. 3 feet.

Date of planting. April.

Varieties. Vert de Laon is about the best.

Harvesting. Cut flower buds when still quite tight.

Note. Best to start with young plants. May also be raised from seed, but resultant plants vary a lot, and the edible buds are not as large and tight as on a named variety. Stems are from 4 to 6 feet high, with large, silvery leaves. Useful for planting in the flower garden. In cold parts protect crowns in winter with a straw mulch. Water often in summer. Mulch, too. After 4 years propagate by taking rooted shoots from around base of plants.

3. ARTICHOKE, JERUSALEM

Soil. Almost any sort of soil.

Location. Anywhere but not in dense shade. Excellent for use as a windbreak. Grow where the tall, spreading plants do not interfere with good growth of other garden plants.

Fertilizer. Best results are forthcoming where this vegetable is grown in soil to which garden compost is applied regularly.

Depth of planting. Tubers at 6 inches deep.

Width apart in the row. Allow 1 to 2 feet between tubers when planting.

Date of planting. February, March.

Varieties. The French variety Fuseau is considered to be the best.

Harvesting. Tubers are usually left in the ground until wanted. Some of them—or the total crop—may be lifted in November and stored in boxes of sand in a shed or garage.

Note. Select a few tubers for replanting elsewhere in the garden. When harvesting make sure all pieces of root are dug up. This artichoke can be an invasive garden weed if pieces of tubers are left in the ground. Plants may reach a height of 10 to 12 feet. They may be pruned back in August or tied securely to stakes and wires. Yield is between 2 and 4 pounds per root.

4. ASPARAGUS

Soil. Rich, deep loam, preferably free from stones.

Location. Asparagus should be planted along one side of the garden where its continued existence does not interfere with the cultivation of the garden.

Fertilizer. Just as soon as it is possible to work the ground a heavy application of lime should be made over a 2-foot-wide strip along each side of the rows. This should be well raked into the surface. An inch deep layer of compost should then be well worked in over the same area. Well-rotted horse or farmyard manure may be used instead of garden compost.

Soil type. Asparagus is rank-growing, it demands an adequate supply of lime to assist in making available plant nutrients.

Depth of planting. Crowns at 5 inches beneath the surface and sited on a ridge in a 10-inch-deep trench so that the spider-leg roots hang downwards.

Width apart in the row. 18 inches.

Distance between rows. 3 feet.

Planting instructions. Dig a trench along the side of the garden about 2 feet from its edge. The trench should be 14 inches wide and 14 inches deep. In the bottom of the trench, place mature compost to a depth of around 4 inches. Water thoroughly. Then prepare a ridge with soil on which crowns may be set. After planting fill in the trench with soil and firm gently.

Date of planting. Late March, early April.

Types. Connover's Colossal, Lorella.

Harvesting. Do not harvest until plants have settled down for 1 or 2 years and are well established. Top-dress each spring with garden compost. Cut shoots below soil level and when they are about 4 inches long. Better-blanched shoots may be obtained by mulching the bed with leaf mould, clean hay, or straw during the period of bearing. Cease cutting after mid-June. If the surface of the ground is given a light dusting of salt, surface weeds will be kept under control without damage to the asparagus plants.

5. ASPARAGUS PEA

Soil. Light, well drained.

Location. Open, sunny site.

Fertilizer. Choose a spot which had a compost application in the previous season.

Depth of sowing. 1 to $1\frac{1}{2}$ inches.

Distance between seeds in the row. 9 inches to 1 foot.

Distance between rows. $2\frac{1}{2}$ feet.

Date of sowing. Late April, May.

Harvesting. Pick the pods when 1 inch long. Go over the plants every second day and pick more. Longer pods are stringy.

Note. May be raised under glass and seedlings set out in the garden in late May or early June. In colder parts of the country plants need cloche protection. Also known as 'Winged Pea'. It is not a pea nor is it related to asparagus.

6. AUBERGINE (EGG PLANT)

Soil. Light, well drained.

Location. Greenhouse.

Fertilizer. Set out plants in bed mulched with 1-inch layer of garden compost.

Depth of sowing. $\frac{1}{4}$ to $\frac{1}{2}$ inch in pots.

Distance between plants in the row. 15 to 18 inches.

Date of sowing. Early March in gentle heat.

Plant out in greenhouse border. May.

Cultivation. When plants are 6 inches high, pinch off central growing point of each plant so that branching is induced. Keep well watered. Spray with clean water to prevent Red Spider on the plants.

Harvesting. Pick in August.

7. BEAN, BROAD

Soil. Good rich loam.

Location. Open, unshaded site.

Fertilizer. Preferably sown in soil which received a heavy dressing of garden compost in the previous season or dressed with compost in the autumn where the sowing is being made in spring.

Depth of sowing. 1 to 2 inches.

Distance between plants in the row. 6 to 9 inches.

Distance between rows. 2 to $2\frac{1}{2}$ feet.

Sowing instructions. Sow as early as possible or in autumn and overwinter the row of seedlings beneath cloches. Early sowings are less liable to Bean Aphis infestation. Seeds may also be sown in pots and overwintered in an unheated greenhouse or in a cold frame.

Date of sowing. Early spring or in November.

Varieties. Green Windsor, Colossal, The Sutton, Seville, Aquadulce Claudia.

Cultivation. Spray with pyrethrum in May to ward off

Bean Aphis. Pinch out growing points of plants when flowers have set. Keep plants watered in dry weather.

Harvesting. Pick pods when seeds inside are of fair size but still young. Old broad bean seeds have a leathery skin.

Roots of all bean and pea plants may be dug into the ground. They are a source of nitrogen. They may also be composted.

8. BEAN, DWARF FRENCH

Soil. Rich loam and well drained.

Location. Open, unshaded.

Fertilizer. Sow in soil which was dressed with garden compost in the previous season.

Depth of sowing. 1 to 2 inches.

Distance between plants in the row. Double staggered row with plants at 9 inches apart.

Distance between rows. 2½ feet.

Sowing instructions. Make flat-bottomed, 9-inch-wide seed drills.

Date of sowing. April (under cloches), May (outdoors). Can be sown too in June and early July. Plants may be raised in pots in a greenhouse or frame from a sowing made in early to mid-April. Set out plants under cloches or outdoors. Outdoor plantings should be made after last spring frost is anticipated.

Varieties. Canadian Wonder, Masterpiece, The Prince, Cherokee, Golden Butter, Glamis.

Cultivation. Remove weeds, water, and mulch. If plants topple under weight of crop provide supports—twiggy branches or strings.

Harvesting. Pick often when pods are young.

Haricots are grown in the same manner but all pods are left on the plants to ripen and dry before being harvested.

9. BEAN, FRENCH CLIMBING

Sow and grow as runner beans.
Varieties. Blue Coco, Blue Lake, Kentucky Wonder.

10. BEAN, RUNNER

Soil. Rich loam and well drained.
Location. Open, unshaded.
Fertilizer. Soil best dressed with compost for another crop in the previous season and mulched in July with garden compost.
Depth of sowing. 1 to 2 inches.
Distance between plants in the row. 6 to 8 inches where plants are trained upwards on supports; 9 inches apart in staggered rows if plants are grown dwarfed.
Distance between rows. 5 feet for plants on supports; 3 feet for plants grown dwarfed.
Sowing instructions. For dwarfed plants make flat-bottomed 9-inch-wide seed drills. For plants on supports make drills quite narrow or sow with cabbage dibber.
Date of sowing. For early crops sow in pots, trays, or boxes in greenhouse or cold frame in April. Set out plants under cloches in May or in open garden in June. Outdoor sowing may be made in late April in warmer parts and during May and June elsewhere.
Varieties. Streamline, Prizewinner Enorma, As Long as Your Arm and many others.
Cultivation. Allow plants to climb to top of supports. Then pinch out growing point of each plant. For dwarfed plants nip off growing points of plants at 12 inches. Shorten the branching stems now and then until low bushes form. Remove weeds, water well and often in dry weather, and mulch. Plants growing in organically rich soil are unlikely to be troubled with Bean Aphis unless plants are short of water at the roots.

Where Bean Aphis is feared spray with pyrethrum. Ladybirds are able to cope with a mild attack of Bean Aphis on the plants.

Harvesting. Pick often when pods are still young and tender. Regular pickings ensure a continued supply.

11. BEETROOT

Soil. Loose and slightly sandy but water-retentive in hot weather.

Location. Beets require an open, well-drained site, free from shade.

Fertilizer. Sow in a part of the garden which was dressed with garden compost for a crop in the previous summer. Well-rotted—but never raw or semi-decomposed—manure may be dug into the bed during winter or early spring digging. If the garden soil is short of lime, apply ground chalk to the soil surface during winter digging; $\frac{1}{4}$ pound to the square yard is a suitable rate of application.

Depth of sowing. 1 to 2 inches.

Distance between plants in the row. 4 to 6 inches.

Distance between rows. 12 to 15 inches.

Sowing instructions. Sow thinly because each 'seed' in the packet is really a cluster of seeds.

Date of sowing. April and May. May also be sown again in June and July.

Succession planting. Early beets may be followed by sprouting broccoli, cauliflower broccoli, autumn radish, autumn lettuce, or kale.

Thinning. Thin when the seedlings are small so that those left to grow on are spaced at about 2 inches apart. Pull some of these later when the beets are still tiny. They are delicious. The leaves may also be cooked as spinach. Finally plants in the rows should be left spaced at from 4 to 6 inches apart.

Varieties. Boltardy, Housewives' Choice, Crimson Ball, Cylindrica, Suttons Green-top.

Harvesting. Early beets are usually gathered and used at or before maturity. Winter storage kinds are allowed to remain in the ground until lifted for storing in late September/early October.

Storage. After lifting the foliage is twisted off, leaving about an inch of the leaf stalks to remain. Take care not to break the skin. Store beets, sandwich fashion, in dry ashes or dry peat in boxes. House the boxes in a garden shed or garage.

12. BROCCOLI, HEADING (see CAULIFLOWER)

13. BROCCOLI, SPROUTING

Soil. Fertile, well-drained loam.

Location. Open, unshaded.

Fertilizer. Sow in specially enriched brassica seed bed. Grow plants on in ground recently dressed with compost or in soil which received a compost dressing for the previous crop.

Soil type. Broccoli succeeds only in soils rich in natural calcium. Soils deficient in this element are usually dressed with lime in winter or early spring. If you add lime when making garden compost your soil will not need liming, too.

Depth of sowing. $\frac{1}{2}$ to 1 inch.

Distance between plants in the row. 18 inches.

Distance between rows. 24 to 30 inches.

Sowing instructions. Sow reasonably thickly in a prepared seed bed for cabbages in April. Keep down weeds and water often in dry weather.

Planting instructions. Water the seed bed on the evening of the day previous to planting out. At planting out time use the garden line to ensure that rows are straight and a cabbage dibber to make planting holes. Fill these holes with water unless the soil is already very moist. Plant to the lowest leaf of the plants. Firm well, using the dibber. Then water again. Water the next day, too, if weather is dry.

Date of planting. June.

Succession planting. Broccoli plants may be set out in areas from which early peas have been harvested.

Companion cropping. Plants may be interplanted between rows of peas, broad beans, and dwarf French beans. By planting between these rows valuable garden space is put to work. The broccoli plants will have lots of room in which to grow well after the pea and bean plants have been removed in July or August.

Varieties. Purple Sprouting, White Sprouting. The purple sort is the hardier.

Harvesting. Start picking shoots in late March/early April and continue to pick until May. Cut the loose central head when shoots in it are well developed.

14. CABBAGE

Soil. Rich, moist, friable loam.

Location. Open, unshaded, well drained.

Fertilizer. All cabbages do best when plants are set out in ground over which a 1-inch-thick mulch of garden compost has just been spread.

Soil Type. Cabbages thrive only in soil which has its full quota of natural calcium. If you feel your soil is short of this element, apply lime to the proposed sites for cabbages after winter or early spring digging.

Depth of sowing. $\frac{1}{2}$ to 1 inch.

Distance between plants in the row. Spring, summer, and compact autumn cabbages, 15 to 18 inches. Winter cabbage, 18 to 24 inches.

Distance between rows. Compact cabbages, 18 inches. More spreading, leafy sorts, 24 to 30 inches.

Sowing instructions. Sow in the seed bed prepared for brassicas. Sow fairly thickly. Keep down weeds and water in dry weather.

Planting instructions (as for Broccoli). Cabbage and broccoli seedlings may be transferred to a nursery bed if you have no ground prepared where they may be planted out. Use a cabbage dibber to plant seedlings in nursery bed at 2 to 3 inches apart. Water well and move plants to their final growing positions before they get too large.

Watering. It is important that cabbage plants are kept well watered after being planted out should the weather be hot and dry. It is not customary to water plants after they have become established. Mulching summer, autumn, and winter cabbages after rain has wetted the soil in July is most helpful to the good growth of the plants. Spring-heading cabbages mature between mid May to early July. In dry periods during May and June the bed should be soaked with water unless the plants are being grown in a moisture-retaining mulch.

Dates of sowing. Summer—March in protected seed bed. April in outdoor seed bed. Autumn/winter—April. Spring—Late July/early August.

Succession planting. Autumn and winter cabbages may be set out in ground from which broad beans or early peas have been cleared.

Companion cropping. Cabbage plants may be set between rows of lettuce, broad beans, dwarf French beans, and peas.

Varieties. Summer—Primo, June Star, Greyhound, Summer Monarch. *Autumn*—Autumn Pride, Autumn Monarch, Christmas Drumhead. *Winter*—Christmas Drumhead, January King, Winter Monarch. *Spring*—

Flower of Spring, Harbinger, Ellams Dwarf Early Spring, Suttons April.

Note. Cabbage plants benefit by a sprinkling of salt water before they form heads. The salt water hinders the growth of cabbage caterpillars.

Red Cabbage. Although served cooked on the Continent red cabbage is usually grown only for pickling in this country. Better results are obtained by sowing in autumn, overwintering the plants in a frame or under cloches and setting out at 2 feet between plants in the row and 2 feet between rows in early spring. But seed can be sown in spring provided that the gardener knows that smaller, later-maturing cabbages will result. There are not many varieties.

Savoy Cabbage. Sow and grow as a winter cabbage. Not so popular as it used to be. Because the leaves are so crinkled they are fine feeding grounds for caterpillars of cabbage white butterflies—and spotting these pests is no easy job on savoys.

15. CABBAGE, CHINESE

Soil. Rich, moist loam.

Location. Open with a tendency towards coolness, as on a northern slope of slight elevation.

Fertilizer. Chinese cabbage requires an abundance of available plant food, the moisture to make the food easily assimilated and coolness. If the soil is not reasonably rich a 3-inch layer of mature compost should be lightly dug in along the line where the rows are to be. Well-rotted farmyard manure may be substituted (where available) for garden compost.

Soil type. Like all brassicas good results are only to be expected where the soil contains lime.

Depth of sowing. $\frac{1}{2}$ to 1 inch.

Distance between plants in the row. 12 inches.

Distance between rows. 2 feet.

Sowing instructions. Sow where the plants are to grow. Use a garden line to have straight rows and make shallow drills with a hoe. Sow thinly, then cover seeds with soil and firm lightly. If the soil is dry, flood the seed drills with water and sow after this has drained away.

Date of sowing. Late July. Earlier sowings usually run to seed or 'bolt'—in gardener's jargon.

Succession planting. Chinese cabbage may follow a July-harvested crop of lettuce, broad beans, or peas.

Thinning. Seedlings must be thinned when quite small to leave one strong plant at 1 foot apart all along the rows.

Watering. Chinese cabbage requires an abundance of moisture. This is most easily supplied by giving the area where the plants grow a thorough drenching every evening during hot weather.

Varieties. Chihli, Pe-Tsai, Wong Bok. Look for new hybrid varieties in seed catalogues.

Harvesting. When the heads reach maturity, cut them. The outer leaves are customarily removed, although these may contain very valuable vitamins. The young and tender blanched heart may be used in salads or cooked.

Storage. Do not trim the heads of outer leaves before placing the cabbages in a refrigerator where they will remain in good condition for about a month.

16. CALABRESE

Also known as Italian Sprouting Broccoli. Sow and plant as for Broccoli, Sprouting (page 154).

Varieties. Green Comet, Green Sprouting, Late Corona.

Harvesting. Cut the central, green head when it is

formed in high summer. Cook as cauliflower. Wait for thick side shoots to follow. Cut these when stems are 6 inches long. Discard leaves on the side shoots, peel the stems, and cook as asparagus.

17. CAPSICUM (SWEET PEPPER)

Soil. Mellow, not over-rich.

Location. Greenhouse, garden frame, cloches in very sunny position.

Fertilizer. Peppers do best in a soil which does not contain an excess of nitrogen. Too much plant nutrient favours the excessive formation of leaf growth detrimental to the proper forming of the fruits. Mature compost should be supplied moderately, a 1-inch layer being lightly dug in if the soil is very poor. Never apply raw manure.

Soil type. A loose, well-matured loam, containing some gravel and having a gravel rather than a clay subsoil is best. It should not be acid.

Depth of sowing. $\frac{1}{2}$ inch in $3\frac{1}{2}$-inch pots.

Width apart in the row. 18 inches.

Distance between rows. 30 inches.

Sowing instructions. Sow in pots during late April to early May. If the plants are to be grown on in a greenhouse the sowing may be made in March at a temperature of 55° to 60°F.

Planting instructions. Set out plants in greenhouse border when they are about 6 inches tall. Wait until late May/early June before planting out in frames or beneath cloches. Always water planting holes well before planting, unless ground is quite moist.

Varieties. Yolo Wonder, Bull-Nosed Red. Outdoor Pepper, offered by Dobies of Chester, is sufficiently hardy for outdoor growing in the south of England.

Plants should be raised under glass and planted out in early June at 1 foot apart.

Cultivation. Weed, water, and mulch. Spray greenhouse, frame, and clothed plants with clean water in July and August to prevent an attack of red spider.

Harvesting. Pick peppers when still green, of full size and with shiny, unwrinkled skin.

18. CARROTS

Soil. Well-prepared, fertile loam, preferably one rich and sandy.

Location. Open, sunny, well drained.

Fertilizer. Carrots require an abundance of well-broken-down material. A 2-inch layer of mature compost should be placed along the line where the row is to be before the shallow seed drill is made. If your compost is lumpy, sift it and use the sieved material. Never use raw manures. Their use leads to forked, often valueless carrots.

Soil type. Carrots succeed in almost any reasonably good garden soil. However, it should be well dug and pulverized and free from large stones. Generous additions of garden compost improve all soils for good carrot production.

Depth of sowing. $\frac{1}{2}$ to 1 inch. Carrot seed is very fine. Mix the seeds with some fine, dry sand. Budgie sand is ideal. Sow the mixture of sand/seed and sow thinly.

Width apart in the row. 2 to 4 inches.

Distance between rows. 12 inches.

Watering. Root crops require adequate moisture for their proper growth. During dry spells use sprinkler irrigation. Alternatively place the hose on the ground and flood the area.

Dates of sowings. Early March, April and August. Maincrop.

May/early June.

Succession cropping—Carrots may be sown between rows of lettuce, radish, etc.

Companion cropping. Where early carrots have reached maturity it is practicable to set plants of broccoli and kale between the carrot rows.

Thinning. Where sowing has been made correctly, that is to say neither too thinly nor too thickly there will be useful thinnings of maincrop carrots in July and early August. Pull thinnings so that carrots left in the ground have from 2 to 4 inches of row space in which to develop. If the ground is dry, always water it well before pulling carrot thinnings.

Varieties. Amsterdam Forcing, Nantes Improved, Intermediate, Scarlet Perfection, Carters Autumn King.

Harvesting. Early carrots and carrot thinnings are pulled for use just as soon as sufficiently large for salads or for cooking. Dig maincrop in early October.

Storage. Cut off the leaves of maincrop carrots as near to the crown as you can but do not cut the crown. Store sandwich fashion in boxes of moist sand, leaf mould, peat, or dampish ashes. House storage boxes in a garage or garden shed. Ask the local greengrocer or supermarket for unwanted apple and orange boxes. These are ideal for use as storage containers.

19. CAULIFLOWER

Soil. Rich, moist loam.

Location. Open, well drained, free from shade.

Fertilizer. Cauliflowers require a plentiful supply of organic matter. Fertile humus may be supplied by adding a heavy layer of compost on to the soil just before plants are set out in their growing positions. If available, well-rotted manure may be dug into the ground during winter/early spring digging.

Soil type. Soil even slightly lacking in its natural amount of calcium should be corrected by liming in winter or early spring.

Depth of sowing. ½ to 1 inch.

Width apart in the row. 18 inches between plants.

Distance between rows. 24 to 30 inches.

Sowing instructions. For cauliflowers in summer, autumn and in the following spring sow seeds in the special brassica seed bed in April. Earlier summer supplies are obtained by sowing under glass in March. In the south it is also possible to sow in August and to overwinter plants in frames or in a greenhouse for setting outdoors under cloches in early March.

Planting instructions. Summer cauliflower plants must be planted at the same depth as they were growing in the seed bed. Winter cauliflowers (cauliflower broccoli, heading broccoli) are planted an inch or so deeper.

Watering. Cauliflowers are rapid growers and demand abundance of plant food and the moisture to make this food available. Seedlings, when transplanted, should be watered liberally. In hot, sunny weather transplanting should be carried out as quickly as possible, and evening is by far the best time to do the job. Apply water again on the second and third evenings after transplanting unless rain falls. Summer cauliflowers should never be permitted to suffer from lack of water. Always water thoroughly each evening during dry spells.

Succession planting. Late cauliflowers may be planted to follow early lettuce, early peas, radishes, etc.

Companion cropping. Cauliflower plants may be set alongside maturing lettuces during June and early July.

Varieties. There are many and success with cauliflowers depends greatly on choosing the correct variety. 'All the Year Round' is a popular summer cauliflower. For autumn Veitch's Self-Protecting is often grown. For

April cutting Sutton's Reading Giant is dependable. New Australian cauliflowers are now being offered by leading British seedsmen.

Harvesting. Always harvest cauliflowers when the curds are white. Never leave them to become yellow. Frost damage to late autumn- and to spring-heading cauliflowers may be prevented by breaking a leaf over the developing head. This action is advisable, too, to prevent bright sunlight from yellowing developing heads of cauliflowers in high summer.

20. CELERY

Soil. Very fertile with abundant moisture.

Location. Level, well drained, and open.

Fertilizer. Celery requires an abundance of plant food and the moisture to make this material available. Mature compost should be dug into the soil or spread as a mulch. There are three types of celery. Self-blanching and American Green are grown on level ground. Celery which needs blanching is grown in a 1-foot-deep, 15-inches-wide trench. Make the trench 14 inches deep and spread compost over it to a depth of 2 inches, and water copiously before planting. Self-blanching is best grown in a garden frame from which the light is removed in June and straw tucked around the plants in mid-July to assist the blanching. American Green is harvested and eaten green. Try it. It's delicious and the green sticks probably have much greater food value than blanched celery.

Soil type. Celery will not thrive in a very acid soil. If rotted manure is being used to fertilize the soil for celery lime should have been applied earlier to correct acidity.

Depth of planting. Not deeper than the plants stood before being transplanted.

Width apart in the row. 9 inches.

Distance between rows. Trenches at least a yard apart. Self-blanching 9 inches in frames and American Green 12 inches outdoors.

Sowing instructions. Sow in seed trays in a heated greenhouse during March.

Planting instructions. Harden off plants to set outdoors; frame-grown self-blanching celery does not have to be hardened off. Plant out in late May or early June.

Watering. Celery is a marsh plant and must always be kept well supplied with moisture.

Blanching. Varieties which need blanching require your help. About mid-August is the right time to start this operation. Hold each plant tightly to prevent soil entering the heart and heap about 4 inches of earth around all of the plants. Water well and a fortnight later, earth up again, using the soil you excavated when making the trench. Two or 3 weeks later, tie the foliage of each plant together and earth up finally to just below the green leaves. Firm the banked-up soil around the plants using a spade.

Varieties. American Winter Green, Golden Self-Blanching, Solid White.

Harvesting. Self-blanching celery is ready for use in August and September and American Green in early autumn. Blanched celery is dug between November and January. Spread straw over the foliage of trench celery during November to protect plants from severe frost damage.

Celeriac is also known as Turnip-rooted celery. This celery makes a large, edible root instead of edible stems. Sow and grow as American Green celery. Celeriac may be eaten sliced as a substitute for stick celery in salads or used in soups and stews.

21. CELTUCE

Sow and grow as summer lettuce. The young leaves may be used as a substitute for lettuce in salads or cooked as spring greens. The plants are grown, however, for their tall, thick stems. Peels these and slice for eating as celery.

22. CHICORY

Soil. Free from large stones, water-retentive.

Location. Open, well drained.

Fertilizer. Grow in ground which was dressed with garden compost for a crop in the previous summer.

Depth of sowing. ½ inch to 1 inch.

Width apart in the row. 9 inches.

Distance between rows. 12 inches.

Sowing instructions. Wait until mid-June in the south, early June in the north before sowing the seeds rather thinly in 7-inch-deep seed drills. If the soil is dry fill the drills with water before you sow.

Cultural instructions. Thin seedlings to 9 inches apart when they are 2 inches or so tall. If you mulch the plants with peat or straw in late July there will be no weeding to worry about.

Harvesting. Dig all of the parsnip-like roots in November. Discard any roots which are thin or fanged. Plant the rest close together in a trench. Pack soil around the roots and spread straw over the foliage.

Blanching. Take a few roots from the trench as and when wanted for blanching. Reduce the length of the roots by an inch or two and cut back foliage to an inch above the crown. Use a cabbage dibber to make planting holes in moist soil in a greenhouse or garden frame. Plant a root in each hole. Then spread straw quite thickly over the bed and weigh down with some *dry* soil. In a warm greenhouse chicons will form within a month; in an unheated house or in a frame, longer.

Harvesting. Inspect the bed occasionally to see if any chicons are ready. When they are, remove the straw and soil and cut chicons with a sharp knife. Compare their flavour with that of imported chicory!

23. Corn Salad

Also known as Lamb's Lettuce. A useful substitute for lettuce during winter.

Soil. Well drained.

Location. Open and preferably facing south-west.

Depth of sowing. $\frac{1}{2}$ to 1 inch.

Width apart in the row. 4 to 6 inches.

Distance between rows. 9 to 12 inches.

Sowing instructions. Sow between July and early September. Sow thinly and reduce seedlings to about 6 inches apart when they are tiny.

Cultural instructions. Give plants cloche protection from November onwards.

Harvesting. Start pulling a leaf here and there when plants have made four leaves and continue plucking leaves on and off as and when wanted.

24. Cucumber

Soil. Rich, well drained.

Location. Open and sunny.

Fertilizer. An abundant supply of easily available food is essential. This is best supplied by spreading a 1- to 2-inch layer of garden compost over the ground before planting or by mulching young plants with a similar amount of compost.

Soil type. Cucumbers thrive in a moderately acid soil but will not do well if conditions are too acidic.

Depth of sowing. $\frac{1}{2}$ to 1 inch.

Sowing instructions. Although plants of hardy kinds may be raised from seeds sown where the plants are to grow in the garden it is the practice to give the plants an early start by sowing under glass. Unless your greenhouse is to be heated until quite late in the spring wait until mid- or late April before sowing cucumber seeds. If you live in the north slight heat will be necessary for good, quick germination.

Sow two or three seeds in each $3\frac{1}{2}$-inch pot filled with a suitable compost. Sifted compost from the garden heap is ideal. Keep pots moist but not wet. Thin seedlings to leave just one in each pot.

Planting instructions. Set out plants in a single row at 2 feet apart in a greenhouse border. Hardy ridge cucumbers may be spaced at 18 inches apart and open garden trellis sorts at 1 foot. Never plant cucumbers deeply. Always leave from $\frac{1}{4}$ to $\frac{1}{2}$ inch of the soil ball above ground level.

Cultural instructions. Greenhouse and open garden trellis cucumbers need a framework of wires and canes to which the plants may be tied. Stop the plants when they reach the top of the supports. Trellis cucumbers need no further pruning. Greenhouse cucumbers do. Pinch out all sideshoots at the second leaf beyond the small cucumber on each of them. The side-shoots will then begin to make lots of weaker shoots. Stop these in the same way. Remove all flowers on the main stem and pinch out as many male flowers as you can. Never remove male flowers on trellis- or ridge-type cucumbers. Ridge cucumber plants are 'stopped' by pinching out the growing point of each plant when seven leaves have been made. To prevent water from splashing cucumber stems sink a clay pot alongside each plant and apply water to the roots via the pots. Cucumber plants need a lot of water. Mulch the plants with a 1-inch layer of rotted manure or garden compost in July or give liquid manure feeds as soon as the cucumbers start to form and swell. If you intend growing newer all-female flowering greenhouse cucumbers, follow special instructions on pruning as recommended by seedsmen.

Varieties. For greenhouse—Telegraph, Conqueror and all-female flowering kinds. For frames—Conqueror. Trellis—Kaga, Kariha, Baton Vert. Ridge—Burpee Hybrid, Nadir.

Harvesting. Cut from plants when cucumbers are dark green and are obviously of full size. The more often you harvest the more cucumbers you will pick.

Pickling. Surplus cucumbers may be pickled in vinegar.

25. ENDIVE

Soil. Good, rich, fertile loam.

Location. Open, well drained.

Fertilizer. Endive demands an adequate supply of natural plant food located near the surface. If 2 inches of mature compost is dug in over the area where the plants are to grow results are bound to be good. Well-rotted manure may be substituted.

Soil type. Any reasonably good garden soil will suffice.

Depth of sowing. $\frac{1}{2}$ to 1 inch.

Width apart in the row. 1 foot.

Distance between rows. 18 inches.

Sowing instructions. Sow in straight seed drills. Do not be too heavy-handed when sowing. Thin small seedlings to stand 12 inches apart in the row.

Date of sowing. Endive is usually grown as an autumn crop. Stands up to moderate frost but if grown in a frame or given cloche protection in late October endive is a useful substitute for lettuce in late autumn/early winter salads. Mid- to late June is a recommended sowing time.

Watering. Being largely composed of water, sufficient moisture should be available to the plants. If considerable garden compost has been applied to the soil its water-holding capacity will favour the steady growth of endive. During excessively dry spells it is sometimes necessary to flood the area where the plants grow for several hours during the evening.

Succession planting. Endive may follow spring cabbage, lettuce, early peas, etc.

Varieties. Improved Green Curled, French Moss Curled Green, Ruffec, Batavian Broad Leaved.

Blanching. Green endive is bitter. Blanching reduces the pungent bitterness of the leaves and improves the flavour. Partial blanching—aimed at leading to a creamy yellow heart—is achieved by tying the outer leaves together in a bunch at the top of the plant when plants are two-thirds grown. Partially blanched heads are cut for use 2 weeks later. For fully blanched endive dig plants when wanted and replant under large pots or boxes. Tie the outer leaves together and ensure that all light is excluded.

26. GARLIC

Soil. Light but water-retentive in hot weather.

Location. Open, sunny.

Fertilizer. Succeeds only in fairly rich soil. One which was well-composted for crops in the previous summer is ideal.

Depth of planting. 1 inch.

Width apart in the row. 6 inches.

Distance between rows. 1 foot.

Date of planting. March.

Planting instructions. Plant cloves in straight 1-inch deep drills. Then cover with soil.

Watering. Water often in June and July during dry weather if the garden soil is a light type.

Harvesting. Harvest bulbs in July or August when the foliage begins to yellow.

Storage. Lay out or hang so that the bulbs are quite dry. This will take about 10 days. Then rub off dead roots, dead foliage, and any adhering dry soil. Hang garlic in a string bag somewhere in the kitchen.

27. HORSE-RADISH

Soil. Sandy or clay but also very rich.

Location. Preferably open and unshaded.

Fertilizer. Plant in ground known to be well supplied with humus from heavy dressings of garden compost made over the years.

Planting instructions. Plant short thongs at 12 inches apart in a yard-wide bed.

Date of planting. Winter.

Harvesting. Wait 2 years, then dig up all roots in the autumn. Choose 4-inch thongs for replanting elsewhere.

Storage. Store thick roots in boxes of sand, ash, or peat in a garden shed or garage, or shred and pickle straight away.

28. KALE (BORECOLE)

Soil. Rich, fertile loam, preferably one in which cabbages or related plants have not been grown the previous year.

Location. Sunny, well drained. If possible with some shelter from north winds.

Fertilizer. Kale requires a reasonably large amount of plant food. This is best supplied at planting time.

Soil type. Lime is essential for the good growth of all members of the cabbage family. Where the soil has been dressed with regular applications of neutral garden compost for some years conditions should be ideal for this vegetable. An acidic soil needs an application of lime in winter or early spring before kale is planted.

Depth of sowing. $\frac{1}{2}$ to 1 inch.

Width apart in the row. Plants at 18 inches.

Distance between rows. 24 inches.

Sowing instructions. Sow as for cabbage on prepared seed bed for brassicas.

Planting instructions. Use a cabbage dibber to make planting holes and set plants to the lowest leaf. Water after planting. In hot, sunny weather repeat water application during the following two evenings.

Date of sowing. April.

Date of planting out. June or early July.

Succession planting. Kale may be very conveniently used to follow almost any crop which matures by midsummer.

Companion cropping. Kale plants may be set out alongside rows of early peas and dwarf French beans.

Thinning. There may be no plot prepared or ground free for planting out kale in the earlier part of June. To leave the seedlings crowded together in the seed bed would lead to long, weak 'leggy' plants. Pull up all of the seedlings, choose large strong ones, and plant them in a nursery bed. Use the dibber to do the job and plant at from 1 to 2 inches apart. Water well and keep well watered in dry weather until planting out in their growing positions during July.

Varieties. Dwarf Green Curled, Tall Green Curled.

Harvesting. Kale is hardy and is seldom harvested until late winter. First cut and use the central, loose rosette of young leaves at the top of the plants. Side-shoots will then develop in the leaf axils. Pick these when still young. Delicious!

29. KOHLRABI

Soil. Rich, moist, friable loam.

Location. Well drained, open position.

Fertilizer. Does well in ground which received a generous application of garden compost for some other crop (not a member of the cabbage family) in the previous summer.

Soil type. Kohlrabi is a brassica and thrives only in soil in which the natural calcium is present in quantity. calcium is chalk or lime. Where it is known that the soil is acidic spread lime (ground chalk) on the dug surface in winter or early spring; $\frac{1}{2}$ pound per square yard is a reasonable quantity to apply. Gardens which have been fertilized with garden compost for some years seldom need liming.

Depth of sowing. $\frac{1}{2}$ to 1 inch.

Width apart in the row. 4 to 6 inches.

Between rows. 15 inches.

Sowing instructions. Sow fairly thinly in straight, shallow seed drills which have been flooded with water beforehand if the ground is dry.

Thinning. Thin small seedlings to between 4 and 6 inches apart.

Date of sowing. March (under cloches), April to June.

Water. Like all members of the cabbage family, kohlrabi is a gross feeder and demands plenty of water for its rapid growth. If sufficient water is lacking, the enlarged root stalk which it forms will be small, hard, and woody.

Successive planting. Kohlrabi may be sown in ground

from which earlier non-brassica crops have been harvested.

Varieties. Early Purple Vienna, Early White Vienna.

Harvesting. Pull for use when the turnip-like kohlrabi is of cricket-ball size. When larger kohlrabi is tough.

30. LEEK

Soil. Rich, deep loam.

Location. Well drained, open, and reasonably free from stones.

Fertilizer. Leeks will respond to heavy applications of garden compost. Well-rotted farmyard manure may be substituted, but avoid the use of raw manure.

Soil type. Leeks will tolerate a moderately acid soil but it must be one rich in nitrogen. This is especially essential during early growth.

Depth of sowing. $\frac{1}{2}$ to 1 inch.

Width apart in the row. 8 inches.

Distance between rows. 12 inches.

Sowing instructions. Sow quite thickly in a prepared seed bed under cloches in March or outdoors in April. If you wish you may sow in boxes in a slightly heated greenhouse in February. Keep seedlings well watered if conditions are dry.

Transplanting. Dig up all of the seedlings in June or early July. Discard small seedlings. Use a dibber to make 6-inch deep holes alongside the garden line and at 8 inches apart. Drop one strong seedling in each hole. After doing this fill the holes with water.

Cultivation. Keep weed free. Water in summer if necessary. Mulch.

Varieties. Marble Pillar, Musselburgh.

Harvesting. Leeks are customarily dug at maturity or when required in the kitchen, sometimes slightly before they reach maturity. For most people the leek comes into its own in the lean time in the garden—late winter/early spring—when freshly dug leeks are welcomed by the cook and the family.

31. LETTUCE

Soil. Loose, rich loam.

Location. Cool, temperate. Lettuce is a cool weather crop, and high summer sowings benefit from partial shade.

Fertilizer. Lettuce is very shallow rooted. An inch of mature compost raked into the surface of the garden before planting time greatly benefits the plants.

Soil type. Lettuce will thrive in almost any type of well-drained garden soil.

Depth of sowing. $\frac{1}{2}$ to 1 inch.

Distance between rows. 12 to 15 inches.

Width apart in the row. 8 to 12 inches.

Sowing instructions. For early summer supplies sow in a frame or beneath cloches in March or early April. A sowing may be made outdoors in mid-April. A very suitable spot for this sowing is in the special seed bed prepared for brassicas. Sow fairly thinly.

Watering. For its rapid growth, lettuce requires the addition of water in dry summer weather.

Date of sowing. Early crop—March–April. Late crop —July.

Successional sowings. Sow, too, in May and June and where the plants are to grow instead of in a seed bed.

Thinning. Seedlings in a seed bed need digging up and the strongest 2- to 3-inch plants selected for planting out in their growing positions. Water generously and do any thinning and transplanting late in the day to avoid heat.

Varieties. There are very many and care should be taken to choose correct varieties for the season and the method of growing. Among cabbage lettuces are: Unrivalled and Fortune for early summer supplies, Webbs Wonderful and Peson for high summer lettuces, and Avondefiance for early autumn. Little Gem and Lobjoits Green Cos are fine cos sorts.

Note. Lettuce from sowings made in summer do not do well if exposed to much hot, bright sunlight. Better results are achieved by sowing in a cooler, partially shaded spot.

32. MELON

Soil. Light, rich, fertile, warm.

Location. Sunny, well drained, preferably where considerable humus is found mixed with sandy soil.

Fertilizer. A liberal supply of plant food should be provided. A 1- to 2-inch mulch of garden compost spread all over the melon bed does so.

Soil type. Melons will not tolerate a heavy, acid soil. Even though a light soil may be slightly acid, they will thrive.

Depth of sowing. $\frac{1}{2}$ inch.

Sowing instructions. Raise plants for greenhouse growing by sowing seeds in $3\frac{1}{2}$-inch-size pots in heat during March. For frame and cloche melons delay sowing in a greenhouse until April.

Planting instructions. Set out plants in greenhouse border during May at 18 inches to 2 feet apart. Do not plant deeply. Leave $\frac{1}{4}$ inch or so of the soil ball protruding above soil level. Set out plants in frames or under cloches in late May or early June. Frame plants need 2 square feet of surface area; under barn cloches allow 2 feet of row space per plant.

Cultivation. Provide greenhouse plants with supports and tie in shoots regularly as plants grow upwards. Pinch out the growing point of each plant when the top of the supports is reached. When four fruits have set on each plant, cut off all surplus growths and start feeding with liquid manure. A top-dressing of garden compost in July is beneficial. A week after planting frame and cloched melon plants pinch out the central growing point of each of them. Side-shoots will be produced. Leave four side-shoots on frame plants and only two on plants under cloches. Later, prune back these side-shoots to leave just four leaves. Raise young melons on to pieces of wood, tile, or slate to prevent slug damage. In very bright summer weather provide the plants with temporary shade. Laying some old nylon curtaining over the frame light or over the cloches is a good way.

Watering. Cantaloupe melons contain a very large percentage of water, both in the fruit and in the vine. Plenty of water is urgently needed for their proper growth. The supply is best given by filling small flower pots sunk on either side of each plant. The water will run straight to the roots and not gather around the stem where a disease known as Stem Rot can occur if this happens.

Varieties. Dutch Net, Tiger, No Name, Milky, Sweetheart.

Harvesting. To determine when a melon is ripe just follow your nose. There really is nothing quite like the sweet scent emitted from a ripe melon.

33. MINT

Soil. Moist, fairly rich loam, having plenty of moisture.

Location. Mint will grow almost anywhere if much moisture and a little shade are available.

Fertilizer. For best results, mint should be supplied with a very moderate amount of mature compost. This is best done by placing a 1-inch layer on the surface of the area where the mint is to be planted and raking in. Raw manure is not recommended.

Soil type. Mint will thrive on a moderately acid soil. One type of mint known as Water Mint grows in its natural state in the very acid soil which borders small streams of water.

Depth of planting. Mint is propagated by cuttings. Cuttings are easily made to form roots by setting them in water and later planted $\frac{1}{2}$ inch deeper than the roots which have formed.

Width apart in the row. Mint is grown in a special bed. Planting at 12 inches apart is suitable in the square yard of ground chosen for this herb. Mint is invasive. It can be controlled by (*a*) digging a trench a foot deep around the bed and filling the trench with house bricks, (*b*) making slits with a spade around the bed and pushing 500-gauge polythene sheeting into the slits, or (*c*) dig a trench around the bed and fill it with wood ashes. Mint just can't stand potash contained in wood ash and the roots will not pass through this barrier.

Watering. Mint requires much moisture. It will thrive in a damp shady place but in the open it is best to give the bed a good soaking now and then in dry summer weather.

Date of planting. April–May or August–September.

Varieties. Spearmint is most popular but Apple Mint is considered superior by herb specialists.

Harvesting. Mint should be picked when required. It is used in the kitchen for enhancing the flavour of new potatoes and peas, for jellies, and as a flavouring for drinks apart from traditional mint sauce with roast lamb.

Storage. Mint is seldom stored except in the form of mint jellies and the like. Mint may also be dried by hanging the leafy stems in a shady place where there is good air circulation. Mint dried in the open may be later crushed or ground and stored safely in tight cans or jars.

Note. For the best flavour, the tips of the tall stalks are picked before the plant has bolted, that is, run up a seed stalk. When the plant goes to seed much of its aromatic value is lost.

34. MUSTARD, CHINESE

Sow and grow as Chinese Cabbage (page 157). The leaves may be used raw in salads or cooked as spinach.

35. ONIONS

Soil. Rich, moist loam, preferably with a subsoil of clay.

Location. Onions thrive in a moist (not wet) location which is also well drained. Any place in the garden where rain tends to form a pool instead of passing into the soil immediately is not well drained.

Fertilizer. Onions demand an abundance of moisture and plant nutrients especially during the early stages of their development. They require much nitrogen and this is best supplied by a heavy layer of mature garden compost laid down over the area where they are to grow. Well-rotted farmyard manure may be substituted if available.

Soil type. Onions prefer a moderately acid soil.

Depth of sowing and planting. Seed: ½ inch; sets (small onions): 1 inch; plants: slightly deeper than they grew in seed box, pot, or seed bed.

Width apart in the row. 9 inches.

Distance between rows. 12 to 15 inches.

Sowing instructions. Space seeds 1 inch apart if plants are being grown in a greenhouse and in boxes or pots. Outdoors, sow quite thickly in shallow, straight drills.

Planting instructions. When setting out onion plants

water the holes if the soil is dry. Cover sets with soil—better still with a 1-inch layer of sifted garden compost. Cheap onion sets are not worth planting. Sets from such specialists as Samuel Dobie & Son Ltd., Chester, and S. E. Marshall & Co. Ltd., Wisbech, are strongly recommended.

Watering. If you have no irrigation sprinkler it is a good plan to lay the hose down on the ground near a bed of onions and allow the water to flood them during dry spells in July and August. If the subsoil is of clay, this has a tendency to prevent the too rapid passing away of the water.

Varieties. For sowing in August and overwintering beneath cloches for plants to set out in the garden in March—Giant Zittau, Suttons A.1. For spring sowings James's Keeping, Bedfordshire Champion, Superba.

Harvesting. As the plants mature, the tops will fall to the ground. Those still standing should be pushed down gently by hand so that bulbs are encouraged to mature. When the green leaves have shrivelled and are brown in colour lift the bulbs off the soil and spread them on the ground or tie them in bunches and hang them in a sunny spot. A week later the onions will be ready for storing.

Storage. The ripe bulbs may be roped or stored in Dutch trays or net bags. Suitable storage places are the attic, the garden shed, a garage, or an unheated greenhouse.

Other onions

During the cultivation of maincrop onions raised from seeds sown in the open ground many seedlings have to be removed in June and July so that the onion plants left to grow on have 9 inches of row space. These thinnings are excellent for salad use. The variety White

Lisbon is grown solely for salad use. Seeds are sown quite thickly in ½-inch seed drills in August or at any time between March and June. The immature onions are pulled as and when wanted for salads and before they become large and 'hot'.

The Welsh Onion is a perennial grown for salad use and the Tree Onion for small onions for cooking. Seeds of both of these onions are offered by Laxton & Bunyard Nurseries Ltd., Sealand, Chester.

For cocktail picklers grow Paris Silver Skinned. Sow seeds fairly thickly in shallow drills during early May. Do not thin the seedlings. Harvest the bulbs immediately after the foliage dies down in late summer.

The Shallot is grown by countless gardeners for pickling but it may also be used as a substitute for ordinary maincrop onions in cooking. Buy shallot bulbs in early spring and press them at 9 inches apart in loose soil. Allow 12 inches between rows. Keep down weeds and dig the clumps of shallots when the foliage starts to die in July. Dry the plants in the sun. Then remove any soil and loose, dry foliage when separating the bulbs for storing in a cool, frost-proof place.

36. PARSLEY

Soil. Fertile, rich loam.

Location. Open, well drained, and not shaded excessively by tall-growing plants.

Fertilizer. Parsley requires large quantities of nitrogen for its successful growth. This is best supplied by a heavy dressing of garden compost forked into the soil during autumn or winter digging.

Soil type. Any ordinary garden soil, preferable one that does not dry out too rapidly and is not excessively alkaline.

Depth of sowing. Sow seeds fairly thickly in a ½- to

1-inch deep seed drill. It is a good idea to mix the seeds in a cup with some sharp sand and to sow the mixture. This leads to an even sowing.

Date of sowing. March/April, July.

Companion cropping. Parsley may be grown successfully between rows of such tall-growing plants as staked tomatoes or sweet corn. It does well either in open sun or partial shade.

Thinning. Thin seedlings to 2 inches apart in the row.

Varieties. Dwarf Perfection, Moss-Curled.

Harvesting. Just pick a few of the largest leaves from each plant. Pull them with a sideways movement.

Storage. The leaves may be picked and spread out in the shade until partially dry. They should then be moved to a very dry place and completely dried. When the dried leaves crumble easily, the flakes may be stored in sealed cans. A few plants carefully dug up in September may be replanted in 5-inch pots and moved indoors to a sunny windowsill or to a slightly heated greenhouse for parsley in winter. In the south parsley plants need no protection to get through the winter. In exposed, cold parts give the row frame or cloche protection. During its second year of growth parsley goes to seed and arrangements should be made for a replacement row in the following spring.

Note. Parsley is a herb. Hamburgh Parsley is a vegetable providing the cook with roots for boiling and with foliage as a substitute for real parsley. Seed is seldom seen in shops. A supplier is Thompson & Morgan Ltd., London Road, Ipswich. Sow and grow Hamburgh Parsley as PARSNIP. Lift roots for use in the autumn.

37. PARSNIP

Soil. Good, rich, very deeply dug unless light and sandy.

Location. Open, sunny, preferably with clay subsoil.

Fertilizer. Parsnips demand plenty of food for the formation of their roots. Raw Manure should be avoided as should semi-decomposed compost. Parsnips are best grown in soil which received a heavy dressing of garden compost for some other crop grown in the previous season. An excessive amount of stones will lead to malformed roots.

Soil type. Parsnips will grow in any reasonably good soil not excessively acid.

Depth of sowing. Sow quite thickly in 1-inch-deep, straight seed drills.

Width apart in the row. 8 inches between plants after final thinning.

Distance between rows. 12 to 15 inches.

Sowing instructions. Because parsnip seed is so light and apt to be blown away water the seed drills before sowing. Then hold the packet close to the ground, tip out a few seeds on to the palm of one hand and sprinkle the seeds on to the mud and cover with a sprinkling of dry soil at once. After sowing use a rake to fill the seed drills with soil. Do not firm the soil after sowing parsnip seeds.

Date of sowing. February/March/early April.

Thinning. Thin small seedlings to from 2 to 3 inches apart. Thin again in June to leave plants at 8 inches apart all along the rows.

Watering. Parsnips are seldom watered. In the drier south-east of England applying water copiously in a very dry summer can lead to a first-class crop. In such a summer parsnips short of water lead to no crops. Parsnip plants also benefit from being mulched after the final thinning in June.

Varieties. Tender and True, Improved Hollow Crown, Avonresister. Tender and True and Avonresister show some resistance to Parsnip Canker, a disorder common to this vegetable. Brown patches of canker occur on the roots and may lead to rotting of the parsnips if the outbreak is severe.

Harvesting. Parsnips are dug as and when required between November and March. Frost improves their flavour and leads to a higher sugar content.

38. PEAS

Soil. Light, rich, sandy.

Location. Enjoy moderate temperatures and will thrive in partial shade.

Fertilizer. Sow in soil which received a heavy dressing of garden compost for a crop grown in the previous season.

Soil type. Peas prefer a neutral soil which is not over-rich in nitrogen.

Depth of sowing. 1 to 2 inches.

Width apart in the row. 2 to 4 inches.

Distance between rows. 30 to 48 inches.

Sowing instructions. Sow fairly thickly in 9-inch-wide, 1- to 2-inch flat-bottomed seed drills. Always flood seed drills with water before sowing unless the soil is really moist. Use a garden rake to cover in drills after sowing. Do not firm.

Watering. Peas suffer most from heat and drought. They require adequate moisture during dry weather. Unless the roots have sufficient moisture pods do not swell and the plants yellow. Pea Moth maggot trouble is to be expected in pods on plants short of water at the roots.

Special care. Pea plants have tendrils for use in climbing. Even dwarf varieties like supports of some sort. Provide supports—brushwood, garden netting, chicken wire, strings.

Date of sowing. If cloche protection can be given sow First Earlies in February or March. First Earlies may also be sown without protection in March if the weather and the ground are favourable. Most First Earlies and Second Earlies are sown, though, in April. A First Early may also be sown in late June. Maincrop peas are sown in late April/early May.

Succession planting. Winter cabbage, broccoli, and kale may be planted just as soon as the peas are out of the way.

Companion cropping. Young plants of cabbage, cauliflower, lettuce, broccoli, and kale may be planted between rows of peas.

Varieties. First Early—Forward, Early Bird, Histon Mini. Second Early—Onward, Histon Kingsize, Chieftain. Maincrop—Histon Maincrop, Alderman, Senator.

Harvesting. Pods should be harvested daily before they are drum-tight and while they are young and the peas inside sugary-sweet. When you taste peas organically grown you'll find out just how peas ought to taste. Delicious!

Mangetout (Sugar Peas) are grown in just the same way. Harvest pods when still quite flat and before peas inside start to swell. Cook pods whole.

39. POTATOES

Soil. Fertile garden soil, preferably a sandy loam.

Location. Well drained, moist. Potatoes thrive best during mild, cloudy weather. They are very sensitive to frost.

Fertilizer. After planting the sprouted tubers cover the whole bed with from 1 to 2 inches of garden compost. Avoid the use of raw manure and the use of lime.

Soil type. Neutral to acid. If the soil contains lime

expect to have potatoes having scab marks on the skin. Common Scab is a harmless disease but disfigures the tubers.

Depth of planting. Tops of tubers 3 inches below ground surface.

Width apart in the row. First Earlies, 12 inches; Second Earlies and Maincrop, 15 inches.

Distance between rows. First Earlies, 24 inches; Second Earlies and Maincrop, 30 inches.

How much seed. This depends on the size of the garden and on how much space you can allow. Because of the lack of space problem many gardeners plant just 7 pounds of a First Early. Buy seed tubers in winter and stand them upright in seed trays, Dutch trays, or egg cartons in a frost-proof, light, cool place indoors. The tubers will have sprouted by Easter.

Planting instructions. Reject any tubers which have not made at least one short sprout. During planting take care that sprouts are not damaged. Make 8-inch-deep trenches with a draw hoe or with a spade. Plant tubers with sprouts uppermost. Cover in carefully with soil. Then spread garden compost all over the bed.

Watering. Potatoes enjoy moist, temperate conditions. They should be soaked with water, if necessary, during excessively hot, dry spells.

Date of planting. Easter or thereabouts.

Succession planting. Lettuce and radish may be sown in soil from which First Earlies were lifted in June and July. Spring cabbage plants may be set out after Second Earlies and Maincrop have been harvested in September.

Companion cropping. Trailing sorts of vegetable marrow may be planted at the end of the rows and the vines allowed to grow between rows of First Earlies.

Varieties. First Early—Arran Pilot, Home Guard, Duke of York, Sharpe's Express. Second Early—Arran

Banner, Great Scot. Maincrop—King Edward, Arran Chief, Arran Peak, Majestic, Golden Wonder.

Harvesting. First Early potatoes are dug during the summer for use in the kitchen. Second Earlies may be dug as and when wanted in August or left to ripen off and be dug with Maincrop in September by which time all potato plants will have died down.

Storage. When lifting the crop for storage in early autumn choose a fine, sunny day for the job. Leave the potatoes on top of the ground for an hour or so after lifting so that they are quite dry before storing. Store in boxes or trays in a dry, cool but frost-proof place. Drape black polythene sheeting over the containers to prevent the tubers from greening.

40. Pumpkin

Soil. Sandy loam, rich in natural humus.

Location. Well-drained, open, sunny site.

Fertilizer. An abundance of moisture and plant nutrients are essential. Well-rotted manure was traditionally used in large quantities for pumpkin growing. Large quantities of garden compost are equally good. Grow in soil which has been well fed over the years with garden compost and covered, too, at sowing or planting time with a 2-inch mulch of compost.

Soil type. Do not lime before pumpkin growing. Soil texture is all-important. Heavy soils and sandy soils may be brought up to scratch for pumpkin growing by incorporating large quantities of garden compost during digging.

Depth of sowing. Although plants may be raised from seeds sown 1 inch deep in the garden during late May far better results are obtained if plants are given an early start. Sow in small pots in a greenhouse, a frame or under a cloche in late April/early May.

Width apart in the row. Each plant requires almost 2 square yards of surface area.

Planting instructions. Unless cloche protection is given it is unwise to set out pumpkin plants before early to mid-June. An unexpected spring frost at night kills pumpkin plants. Water planting holes. Do not plant deeply but firm well. Pumpkin vines may be pinned to the ground to prevent them from wandering over rows of other plants or into your neighbour's garden.

Watering. Seedlings should receive adequate moisture during their stay in pots. The plants need a great deal of water in summer—especially when swelling their gourds. Liquid manure or liquid compost water feeds can lead to larger pumpkins.

Varieties. King of the Mammoths.

Harvesting. Wait until the skin is firm before harvesting in September or early October.

Storage. Store on a shelf in a moderately cool place.

41. RADISH

Soil. Light, sandy loam, one that drains rapidly.

Location. Open or fairly open.

Fertilizer. Radishes thrive with little plant food. Soil which was composted for a different crop in the previous season is very suitable.

Soil type. Radishes do well if sown in any reasonably good garden soil.

Depth of planting. $\frac{1}{2}$ to 1 inch.

Width apart in the row. Fifteen seeds per foot of row.

Distance between rows. 12 inches.

Sowing instructions. Rake soil level and remove any large stones and clods. Then make shallow seed drills. Flood these with water before sowing if the soil is dry. Cover with fine soil and firm gently. The brassica seed bed is a good spot for sowing the first batch of radish seeds.

Watering. For rapid growth radishes demand adequate moisture. Much of their fine flavour and crisp quality depends upon a good supply of moisture.

Date of sowing. March (in frames and under cloches), outdoor sowings start in April and continue on and off until July. For late autumn/early winter use sow in late June and sow very thinly because each large plant requires 9 inches of row space.

Succession planting. Sow on and off during spring and summer as and when ground is free for this crop.

Varieties. Summer radish—French Breakfast, Icicle, Sparkler, Scarlet Globe. Autumn/winter radish—Black Spanish, China Rose.

Storage. Summer radishes are never stored. They are harvested when young and succulent and not left to become woody and 'hot'. Autumn/winter radishes may be dug as and when wanted for September and October salads. Those remaining should be dug and stored in a box of moist sand in a shed, garage, or unheated greenhouse. Grate these large radishes for salads and sandwiches.

42. RHUBARB

Soil. Deep, rich loam.

Location. Rhubarb should be grown along one side of the garden and preferably where it will receive plenty of moisture and sunshine.

Fertilizer. Being a gross feeder, rhubarb should be treated to a mulch of garden compost each autumn and be planted in land already brought up to a high state of fertility.

Soil type. Rhubarb will tolerate a moderately acid soil.

Depth of planting. Plant so that the crown of the plant is at soil level.

Width apart in the row. 48 inches.

Distance between rows. 48 inches.

Planting instructions. Make planting holes sufficiently large to take the roots comfortably. Firm very well after planting.

Watering. Rhubarb plants require great quantities of moisture but few gardeners give their rhubarb clumps a flooding in hot, sunny weather. Keep your rhubarb plants moist and healthy in summer. The annual compost mulch is of great help in keeping the roots moist and cool as well as supplying much-needed plants foods.

Date of planting. Late autumn.

Varieties. Timperley Early, Hawkes Champagne.

Harvesting. In the spring pull sticks on and off and never too many from one plant. Careful harvesting encourages the growth of more sticks. Never pull rhubarb in the first spring after planting and harvest but a few sticks in the second spring. Do all you can to build up strong, fruitful plants. Rhubarb harvesting stops when gooseberries are around.

Note. Never try forcing your rhubarb plants by placing pails, boxes, and baskets over the crowns in winter. Doing this leads to weakened plants.

43. SALSIFY

Soil. Light, mellow loam, fairly free from stones.

Location. Open, sunny, well drained.

Fertilizer. Grow this and other root crops in ground which was heavily fertilized with garden compost for different crops in the previous season.

Soil type. A soil known to be acidic should have been dressed with lime after digging in autumn or early spring.

Depth of sowing. 1 inch.

Width apart in the row. 8 inches after final thinning.

Distance between rows. 15 inches.

Sowing instructions. Sow seed fairly thinly in shallow, straight drills.

Watering. Flood seed drills before sowing if considered necessary. Apply water in summer if weather is hot and dry.

Date of sowing. April. May be sown in late March if soil conditions and weather permit.

Varieties. Most seedsmen simply offer packets labelled 'Salsify'.

Harvesting. Roots may be dug as required from October onwards. Freezing is said to improve the flavour.

44. SCORZONERA

Also referred to as 'Black Salsify'. Sow, cultivate, and harvest as SALSIFY.

45. SEAKALE

Soil. Sandy or medium loams with a good lime content.

Location. Open, sunny.

Soil type. Soil must never get really dry but waterlogging proves fatal. Organic matter in quantity must be present.

Depth of planting. Top of the prepared root cutting is 2 inches below ground level.

Width apart in the row. 15 inches.

Distance between rows. 24 inches.

Planting instructions. Although this vegetable can be raised from seed the popular method is to start off with root cuttings known as 'thongs' or 'sets'. Plant thongs with a cabbage dibber. After planting mulch with a 1-inch layer of garden compost.

Watering. If allowed to become dry in summer the roots are likely to be weakened and crowns for forcing will be small. So, in long dry spells water copiously and mulch.

Special care. Remove all flower stems.

Date of planting. February, March.

Forcing. After the foliage has died down fork the bed lightly and remove all plant debris. In November cover a few plants with large pots or boxes and pack horse manure (if you can get some) or use decaying leaves as the alternative over the containers. Another way is to surround several of the plants with boards and then to spread autumn leaves within the boarded area to a depth of 1 foot. Snow-white shoots will be produced rather slowly. Always cut the shoots with 1 inch of stem attached. If you don't, your blanched seakale shoots will come apart. After harvesting the blanched seakale cover the crowns with some leaves and wait until late March or early April. Then, rake off the leaves, cut off any small blanched seakale pieces and fork garden compost over the entire bed.

46. SEAKALE BEET (SWISS CHARD)

Soil. Seakale beet thrives in any garden soil containing plenty of natural humus.

Location. Open, sunny, well drained.

Fertilizer. This vegetable belongs to the beet family. It responds to the use of lime (where necessary). Sow in soil fed with garden compost for a different crop in the previous summer or in soil to which garden compost was added during autumn or winter digging.

Depth of sowing. 1 inch.

Width apart in the row. 8 to 12 inches.

Distance between rows. 15 inches.

Sowing instructions. Make straight, shallow seed drills with a draw hoe. Sow seeds thinly.

Date of sowing. March to May.

Thinning. Thin seedlings when tiny to 4 inches apart. Thin again later so that a strong plant is left at between 8 and 12 inches all along the row.

Varieties. Usually packeted as Swiss Chard, Seakale Beet, Silver Beet.

Harvesting. Only the outer, mature leaves should be gathered. Never over-pick from any one plant. The inner, younger leaves should be allowed to remain so that the plant will continue to grow and thus form a steady supply of valuable greens both in summer and in autumn.

Note. To have tasty Seakale Beet leaves in winter cover the plants with a deep layer of straw in late October or set cloches over a row.

47. SPINACH

Soil. Spinach requires an abundance of plant food, especially nitrogen.

Location. In summer a northern exposure is suitable because the plant enjoys low temperatures.

Fertilizer. Because this plant requires plenty of nitrogen it is a good plan to dig in a heavy layer of mature garden compost where the plants are to be grown. Rotted manure, where available, may be used instead.

Soil type. Spinach thrives in any reasonably good garden soil.

Depth of sowing. $\frac{1}{2}$ to 1 inch.

Width apart in the row. 3 to 4 inches.

Distance between rows. 12 to 15 inches.

Sowing instructions. Sow reasonably thickly. After covering the seed with soil firm lightly.

Watering. Spinach is a quick-growing leafy plant. It requires adequate moisture. Thoroughly soak the rows late in the day in dry, summer weather.

Date of sowing. Summer Spinach—February (under cloches), March (under cloches or outdoors). From then on sow until July as and when space is available. Winter (Prickly-seeded) Spinach—July, August, September.

Succession sowings. Spinach is a cool weather crop. It is not damaged by late spring frosts. Cover plants from an August sowing with cloches in October.

Succession planting. Early spinach may be followed by broccoli or kale.

Thinning. Thin seedlings to leave plants at from 3 to 4 inches apart in the rows. Thinnings removed may be used to make another row.

Varieties. Longstanding Round or Summer, Longstanding Prickly or Winter.

Harvesting. The outer leaves are gathered and the centre of the plants left intact to continue growth and the production of new leaves. When harvesting take no more than one or two leaves from each plant to prevent plants from being weakened.

New Zealand Spinach. This is a substitute for true spinach. The plants tolerate the heat of high summer and will thrive in temperatures which do not suit cool weather spinach. It is best raised from a sowing made under glass in March or April and the plants set out at a yard apart in May somewhere where they may ramble at will over the ground. *Perpetual Spinach* (*Spinach Beet*)—sow in March or early April and thin seedlings to 8 inches apart.

48. SQUASH

Sow, grow, and harvest summer squash as VEGETABLE MARROW and winter squash as PUMPKIN.

Varieties. Summer Squash—Zucchini, Cocozelle, South African Marrow (Little Gem), Custard (Patty Pan), Gold Nugget. Winter Squash—Hubbard. Gold Nugget is also grown as winter squash for storing.

49. Swede

Soil. Deep, moist, fertile, sandy.

Location. Well drained, open, preferably with a sub-soil of clay.

Fertilizer. Swedes require a rich, mellow soil containing a maximum of easily available plant nutrients. May be grown in ground heavily fertilized with garden compost for a different crop in the previous summer or in soil enriched with compost during autumn/winter digging. Lime should be supplied to correct any soil acidity.

Depth of sowing. 1 inch.

Width apart in the row. 12 inches.

Distance between rows. 18 inches.

Sowing instructions. Sow in straight drills made with a draw hoe during late May/early June. Thin seedlings to 12 inches apart.

Watering. During the early stages of its growth the swede should be supplied with adequate moisture. To offset the lack of rainfall during July and August it may often be necessary to water the seedlings well during the evening. Sprinkler irrigation is ideal but make sure that the soil is really wetted—not just the soil surface.

Succession planting. Swedes may be sown in ground from which very early lettuce or radishes have been cleared.

Companion cropping. Radish seeds may be mixed and sown with swede. The radishes will be ready for pulling 4 to 5 weeks later, leaving the thinned swede plants all the room they need.

Varieties. Purple Top Garden, Suttons Bronze-Top, Chignecto.

Harvesting. Lift swedes as and when wanted in the kitchen during the winter.

Storage. Swedes are usually left in the garden but the quality is better if the roots are stored in November. Store in boxes of moist sand or peat. House containers in a shed, outhouse, or garage.

50. SWEET CORN (CORN ON THE COB)

Soil. Fertile, medium loam.

Location. Well drained, sunny.

Fertilizer. Sweet corn demands sufficient natural humus for its speedy, heavy growth. Spreading a 1- to 2-inch layer of garden compost over the ground provides all plant nutrients needed for good, quick growth.

Soil type. The soil should not be acidic. An acid sort of soil should have been limed after winter digging.

Depth of sowing. $\frac{1}{2}$ inch (in pots), 1 inch (outdoors).

Width apart in rows in the block. 12 to 15 inches.

Distance between rows in the block. 15 to 18 inches.

Sowing instructions. Sow in $3\frac{1}{2}$-inch pots under glass during late April or early May. Seeds may be sown outdoors where the plants are to grow in southern England. Wait till mid-May before doing so.

Planting instructions. Sweet corn plants are set out in blocks. Four or five short rows make a good block. Plant in early June after all danger from frost has passed. In the midlands and northerly areas give cloche protection until late June.

Companion cropping. Trailing kinds of vegetable marrow may be grown alongside the sweet corn block and the marrow vines encouraged to grow between the corn plants.

Varieties. Suttons First of All, Earliking, Kelvedon Glory, North Star.

Harvesting. During August or early September the silks hanging from the cobs change in colour from yellow to blackish brown. The silks also shrivel. At this stage check if a cob is ready for picking. Strip back a part of the green sheath and press a grain with your thumbnail. If the juice exuded is watery, the cob is not ready; if milky-cream it is just right; if starchy mush it is past its prime and fit only for hens! Always harvest corn cobs just before the wife intends to cook them. Deterioration is rapid after harvesting with the sugars turning to starch. Children just love a raw cob to chew.

51. TOMATOES

Soil. Light, porous, and well drained.

Location. Sunny and open.

Fertilizer. Set out greenhouse or outdoor tomatoes in ground over which a thick mulch of garden compost has just been spread.

Soil type. Almost any garden soil providing drainage is good.

Depth of sowing. $\frac{1}{4}$ to $\frac{1}{2}$ inch in trays or pots.

Width apart in the row. Greenhouse, 18 inches; cloche, frame, and outdoors, 15 inches.

Distance between rows. Greenhouse, 20 to 24 inches; cloche, 3 to 4 feet; frame, 18 inches in the frames; outdoors, 30 to 36 inches.

Sowing instructions. It is the practice to raise tomato plants by sowing in seed trays and to transfer the seedlings to $3\frac{1}{2}$-inch pots. For early greenhouse crops the sowing is made in a heated greenhouse during February or early March. For late summer/autumn tomatoes seed may be sown in a heated greenhouse in the north and in an unheated greenhouse or in a frame or beneath a cloche in the south. This sowing should be made during the first week of April.

Planting instructions. Make planting holes with a trowel and fill planting holes with water before planting. Do not disturb the soil ball. Tear off mulch, card, or polythene pots and remove all dry parts of peat pots before planting. Do not plant deeply. Plants set out in the garden may be protected from an unexpected night frost by being covered with paper 'dunce caps'.

Date of planting. Set out plants when they are about 7 inches high in greenhouse border, in frames, and under cloches. Wait until early to mid-June before setting out plants in the open. Young tomato plants can be killed by frost.

Varieties. Many. For the greenhouse Eurocross A, Supercross, and Sioux are suggested. These are also suitable for frame and cloche growing in the south of England. For outdoor growing in the south and for frames and cloches in cooler areas the variety Outdoor Girl is strongly recommended.

Cultivation. Remove all side-shoots in the leaf axils and tie plants regularly to strong supports. Greenhouse-grown plants need a great deal of water and daily watering is the rule when the plants settle down and get going. Lights may be taken off frames and cloches removed from plants in early July. Water these and plants set out in the open frequently in hot, dry, weather. Mulching with straw stops weeds, saves water.

Harvesting. Pick ripe fruits on and off until all have been harvested from plants in a greenhouse. Pick ripe tomatoes from plants in the garden from early August until mid September.

Storage. Between mid to late September pick all tomatoes remaining on outdoor plants. Green tomatoes of good-size store and ripen well in trays in a warmish room. Small, hard green tomatoes are excellent for chutney-making.

52. TURNIPS

Soil. Sandy and not too rich in nitrogen.

Location. Cool weather plant requiring a temperate climate, adequate moisture, and good drainage.

Fertilizer. Early turnips should be sown in ground into which garden compost was incorporated during autumn or winter digging. Where winter turnips or turnips for 'turnip tops' are being grown there is sufficient plant food left in the soil from which another, different crop has just been harvested. Acidity in a soil must be rectified by liming before turnips are sown.

Depth of sowing. $\frac{1}{2}$ to 1 inch.

Width apart in the row. Summer turnips, 6 inches; winter turnips, 12 inches; 'turnip tops', 1 to 2 inches.

Distance between rows. In frames and cloches, 8 inches; outdoors, 12 to 15 inches.

Sowing instructions. Sow fairly thinly in straight, shallow furrows. Cover with fine soil and firm gently. When sowing in summer always flood seed drills with water before sowing unless the ground is quite moist.

Watering. Turnips require a lot of water. Summer turnips which have been grown without sufficient moisture are hard and unpalatable.

Date of sowing. Summer turnips—March (under cloches or in frames), April and May (outdoors). Winter turnips—July, August. Turnips for 'turnip tops'—late July or early August.

Succession planting. Winter turnips and turnips for tops are sown in ground from which another crop such as early peas or broad beans has been cleared. A very good plan is to look over the garden in late July and August and see how many rows are vacant and then sow turnips to use plant nutrients left over by the crops which occupied the rows and to provide the family with more and more home-grown vegetables.

Varieties. Summer—Early Snowball, Sprinter, Early White Milan. Winter—Golden Ball, Green Globe, Manchester Market. Turnip tops—Hardy Green Round.

Harvesting. Pull summer turnips when fully grown but still young and tender. Winter turnips may be left in the ground or lifted in early November and stored in boxes of sand in a shed or garage. Gather foliage for turnip tops as and when wanted in the kitchen.

53. VEGETABLE MARROW

Soil. Sandy loam, rich in natural humus.

Location. The plants thrive in well-drained sandy locations and in full sun.

Fertilizer. An abundance of moisture and plant nutrients is essential. An easy way of supplying adequate plant foods is to spread a 1-inch-thick mulch over the ground but only 18 inches if trained upwards on a wire tions or before sowing seeds in the open garden.

Soil type. Texture is of great importance. It is possible to improve the condition of very heavy soils by the incorporation of large quantities of a 50–50 mixture of garden compost and sharp sand.

Depth of sowing. In pot, $\frac{1}{2}$ inch; outdoors, 1 inch.

Width apart in the row. Bush types, $2\frac{1}{2}$ feet. Trailers 4 feet, or even more if plants are to roam all over the ground but only 18 inches if trained upwards on a wire fence or on bean netting.

Distance between rows. 6 to 8 feet.

Sowing instructions. For an early start sow marrow

seeds in $3\frac{1}{2}$-inch pots in a greenhouse or a cold frame during late April or early May. Seeds may be sown outdoors where plants are to grow but wait until mid May at least before doing so.

Planting instructions. Set out pot-raised plants in early June when all danger of a night frost has passed. Do not plant deeply and if the soil is not wet fill planting holes with water before planting. Each bush-type plant requires $2\frac{1}{2}$ square feet of surface area. Trailing kinds take up a great deal of garden space unless planted alongside supports. They may also be planted at the ends of rows of early potatoes and the main lateral shoots of the marrow plants be guided between the rows. When the potato crop is being lifted between late June to mid-August the marrow plants will take over the whole patch.

Watering. Seedlings should receive adequate moisture and the plants a great deal, especially after they have flowered and are swelling fruits.

Varieties. Long Green, Long White, Green Bush, White Bush, Zucchini.

Harvesting. Cut vegetable marrows when between 1 foot and 18 inches long and when the thumbnail pierces the skin with ease. Cut often so that production continues into September.

Courgettes. If you wish to have lots of tasty courgettes reserve two plants of Zucchini just for this purpose. Cut courgettes when they are no more than 3 inches or so in length. Try them sliced and fried in bacon fat.

Part IV

*PROTECTION AGAINST BUGS—SOME
ALTERNATIVES TO INSECTICIDES*

Hundreds of thousands of gardeners in this country
have made up their minds to grow fruits and vegetables,
flowers, and lawns *without* using pesticides and weed
killers. They realize the danger of poison spray residues
—how the problem can eventually be more serious to
mankind than fallout. They have read about the death of
children from playing with pesticide containers; they
know how bird populations and wildlife have been killed
by indiscriminate use of sprays. They understand the
futility of having to make continually more lethal substances in order to kill the new insect generations which
have built up a resistance to the older types. They have
no desire to pollute the portion of the earth which they
own. They have made their decision *not to use poison
sprays*.

In the next section, we will set forth some of the
methods used by organic gardeners to control insect
damage. We do not include all methods for the simple
reason that new ones are being devised daily, as often
as one careful observer of insects gets an idea. You will
learn the methods used by people who have successfully
made the transition from the separate gardening worlds
of artificial and organic. While the way at times may
have been confusing, their path has led them to a
method compatible with their goals.

You'll learn about some strange ideas that work; the
sceptics will scoff—but that's the role of sceptics, and
we expect it. Organic gardeners and farmers are very
sceptical themselves about the majority view on insect

control methods, so we're not sensitive when the roles are reversed.

The only thing we do hope is that the variety of control methods described in the following pages will show without doubt that poison sprays are not the answer to preventing plant damage by insects. Consider the warning of Nobel Prize Winner Joshua Lederberg of Stanford University: 'Every mouthful of food any American eats in the next century,' he explains, 'will contain at least one molecule of DDT—even if DDT were never used again!' Put another way, the gardener or farmer who blithely sprayed this highly promoted poison back in 1942 (when it was first applied to food crops and entered water, soil, air, and all living things) had half of the DDT remaining in his own polluted environment in 1956, and one-quarter of it is still there today. What's more, in 1984, one-eighth of that poison will be right there causing trouble.

Since the mid-1940s when large-scale use of 'hard' pesticides began, 'something of the order of a million metric tons of DDT have been distributed over the earth', estimates Dr Goran Lofroth of the Institute of Biochemistry, Stockholm, Sweden. Because of its persistence, much of this poison remains in the environment and in the tissues of living things. The concentration increases on the way up the natural food chain—amphipods (tiny sand fleas) contain approximately 0·014 ppm, the small fish that feed on them contain 3·6 ppm, and coho salmon as much as 20 ppm.

When accumulated poison reaches high proportions, damage to the organism results. Persistent pesticide residues present serious hazards to consumers. They simply do not deteriorate or disappear from our food, and neither washing nor cooking destroys them. Taken into our bodies, they are stored in fatty tissue—and evidence of their danger to both man and beast continues to mount. There is a close link between pesticides and cancer; reproduction is disrupted in birds and wildlife; mother's milk is now found laced with about four times as much DDT as is permitted in milk sold to the public; and residues discovered in stillborn and unborn babies are capable of doubling the mutation rate in man, according to famed British geneticist Dr Osny G. Fahmy.

Turning to stronger and stronger insecticides certainly isn't the answer. Pests quickly develop resistance, then immunity to the chemical compounds used to clobber them indiscriminately. Look at it the way Dr Robert van den Bosch, head of the University of California's Division of Biological Control at Albany, puts it: 'Modern agricultural chemicals,' he says, 'are ecologically crude in their effect on insect components in the environment.' These chemicals are designed to kill off 100 to 1,000 species, including the beneficial insects. (Remember, there are nearly 700,000 known species of insects—and one of people.) 'Chemical sprays as they are used today create an insect vacuum for a time. Then, all the old pests come roaring back at a level increased 15 times. It's a disruption of the natural balance—and it's happening all over the world.'

One final thought: some people have trouble adjusting themselves mentally to the idea of working with nature instead of trying to dominate her. Insect control, as described here, requires that the gardener must put more trust in nature and disabuse himself of the notion that science has the answer for every problem. We must realize that man has yet to make nature knuckle under to his will. We must adjust ourselves to working with nature. Once that is done, the decisions, methods, and problems no longer seem so difficult to solve.

RECOGNITION AND QUARANTINE

A big step in any control programme is knowing who the culprit is. With a little practice, you can learn to recognize at a glance the signs and symptoms of common pests.

The various chewing insects make their own patterns. Flea beetles make tiny round perforations; weevils produce rather typical angular openings; beetle larvae (grubs) 'skeletonize' leaves, chewing everything but the epidermis and veins.

Sucking insects cause leaves to be yellowish, stippled white or grey. These insects, as well as their brownish eggs or excrement, can often be seen on the underside of foliage. Red spider can be spotted by yellowed leaves that are cobwebby or mealy underneath; whitish streaks mean thrips. When leaves are curled up or cupped down, look out for aphides. Deformed leaves may be caused by cyclamen mite; blotches or tunnels by leaf miners; round or conical protrusions by aphids, midges, or gall wasps.

The partial collapse and dying of a plant, termed *wilt*, may result from a number of causes—very often nematodes or grubs.

Quarantine for Plants

No one would think of going out of his way to visit someone who has a contagious disease. Yet this phenomenon occurs daily in gardens everywhere. The amusing hobby of keeping a 'pet' diseased plant for anyone to handle should not be tolerated; it is very dangerous. Everyone who enters the garden is shown it and asked if he or she knows what the trouble is. While giving an opinion, the visitor does the natural thing—turns up the leaves to see the disease underneath and later examines plant after plant in similar manner, thereby infecting the entire garden.

There is a strong case for isolation and destruction of diseased and insect-ridden plants. Recent experiences show that it is not a good practice to use such plants as a mulch or, in fact, in sheet composting. It's risky trying to use infected plants, except in the compost heap, and even then you must be careful. When in doubt, it's better to destroy such material and to make certain of not spreading the trouble.

All gardeners should become health-minded and not worry too much about disease. If it comes, act promptly and destroy the first specimen. Feed the soil so that plants are in sturdy health, because all the remedies in the world are useless if the underlying cause is repeatedly neglected,

writes E. R. Janes, V.M.H., in his book *The Vegetable Garden.*

SAFE INSECTICIDES

The early pioneers of organic gardening methods made the astounding claim that plants growing in a soil dressed liberally with home-made garden compost have a built-in pest resistance. Few gardeners at the time could swallow that one and we don't expect you to, either. But wait until you've gardened for a year or two by methods outlined in this book. By then you'll have proof of the pudding and you'll wonder why other gardeners consider your claim for built-in pest resistance as pretty crazy. But let's consider this crazy claim calmly. If you're already an organic gardener chances are that you never get a cold. But you know plenty of folk who catch colds quickly. In fact, the common cold must surely be the top, common disease in Britain and a disease which causes more loss of man hours per year than all of the many strikes do. Next time you have a cold (if you get the nasty things) ask your doctor who is most likely to catch a cold—the chap who is fighting fit, bursting with energy and eating good, nourishing food or the run-down, over-worked type on an unbalanced, poor diet. I know what your doctor will say.

Now almost every plant in the garden, apart from weeds, is man-developed. But although man may develop what to him are superior fruits, vegetables, and flowers they are weaklings when compared with the originals of creation. Without man around his superior fruits, vegetables, and flowers would quickly disappear from the face of the earth. The plants of creation fit in with the environment and with the soil type. Man's plants fit in nowhere except in gardens, farms, and parks. Some of these plants need special soil conditions; they also demand certain sorts of climate just as wild plants do. Wild plants grow in the climate and in the soil conditions which suit them best and they are usually tough and healthy. If they were not, they would not last long in the competitive world of wildlife.

Man selects a few of the hundreds of thousands of wild plants and develops them to his taste and to foster them he does all kinds of odd things—chopping off bits of some of them (pruning), moving them from place to place (transplanting), changing their colour (blanching), giving them an artificial environment (in greenhouses and frames), and moving them around the world to places in which the original undeveloped wild plant could not thrive. Above all, man learnt that *his* plants need good soil and can't abide competition from wildings so man cultivates *his* plants and rids them of weeds.

All gardeners get rid of weeds; not all give their garden plants the best soil conditions. It is the condition of the soil which is the most important factor in plant growing providing, of course, plants which suit the climate are chosen. Thus, a man-developed weakling if grown in a plant-food-rich soil has the tolerance to resist insect pests and plant diseases because the plant itself is well fed and healthy.

In his plant breeding man never paid any attention at all to immunity. Only in comparative recent years has this aspect of plant health been studied and immune varieties bred. Wart Disease, caused by a soil fungus, was a serious disease of the potato. All modern potato introductions are immune from Wart Disease. Resistance of a variety to a disease does not mean that the plant is immune but that it resists it. Thus Avonresister parsnips resist Parsnip Canker under soil conditions which would ruin a crop of most other parsnips. Most of the new hybrid tomatoes are resistant to the common fungal disease of greenhouse tomato plants, Tomato Leaf Mould. Among new lettuces, Avoncrisp and Avondefiance resist downy mildew and grey mould.

Virus diseases are extremely common. The symptoms vary from one kind of plant to another but most virus troubles may be recognized from the distortion of the foliage, a mottling of the leaves and poor crops from dwarfed plants. It is believed that most viruses are transmitted from plant to plant by sap-sucking insects like aphides (black fly, green fly). Virus-free stocks of some tree, bush, and cane fruits are offered by nurserymen nowadays and there are also stocks of virus-free strawberries. Starting off in the garden with clean (virus-free) trees, bushes, and plants is most desirable. But for how long what you have planted will remain free from a virus disease depends a great deal on the healthy environment. If, for example, you plant a bed of virus-free strawberries in your garden and your neighbours harbour plants of virus-sick plants in theirs, there is every chance that your strawberries will be infected within 2 years. Now and then a claim is made that plants badly virused have been cured of the disease after they had been transplanted to a soil richly fed with garden compost. In gardening strange things can happen but stories of this sort should be accepted with reserve. Only a trained specialist would be able to recognize many specific virus diseases and would be able to judge whether the disease could be cured at all. In fact, some virus troubles closely resemble plant troubles caused by the absence in the soil of a mineral trace element. This means that the plant may not have been suffering from a virus disorder at all and after having been moved into different soil containing the missing trace element the plant cured itself. There is little we can do to protect our garden plants from weakening virus troubles and, from my own experience, nothing the gardener can do to cure them. But as many virus disorders are supposed to be transmitted by aphides we can go on now to considering insect pests.

It stands to reason that if you deliberately foster aphides by providing them with the conditions they enjoy you are going to have more of them and therefore a greater possibility of their moving from plant to plant or tree to tree to carry on their personal job of virus-infection. This all fits in with nature's pattern. The insects we call pests are scavengers. Their work is to seek out the weaklings of the plant world and to destroy them so that they do not propagate themselves and populate the earth with weaklings. In the wild the insect pests of our gardens lead a tough existence. Not only must they come across likely weaklings but they themselves are the live food of other insects and of many animals and birds. Nature is not interested in man's plant breeding plans for bigger strawberries and fat cabbages. To her man's plants are weaklings from the start and are unwanted. Somehow she looks with a pretty favourable eye on the healthy plants we organic gardeners grow—but only up to a point. Try to cross nature and see what happens! Do your best to work with her and she's pretty kind. That's my experience over the past 25 years. Watch nature at work in late June. You've left a few surplus spring cabbages in the bed from which you've cut so many tight-hearted tasty heads. Time to go—says nature—and along come cabbage white butterflies, flying over your newly set young cabbage plants, making a bee-line for the old cabbages you should have either eaten, given to that old lady up the road or added to the compost heap. Then comes August and you've had enough Primo cabbage and are tucking into runner beans and marrows. Out—says nature and more butterflies appear along with every slug in the garden. Take fruit this time. You have a fruitful clump of raspberries and one or two blackberries on the garden fence. Both of these fruits suffer from a pest called the Raspberry Beetle which appears in a bowl of fruit as white maggots crawling out of the berries. I've never seen them on my fruit, you say. Perhaps you will meet a fruit farmer one day—one who grows raspberries in a big way. He has to spray his raspberry canes with insecticide. Why? Because he is practising monoculture—meaning too much of one particular crop. Nature is all against monoculture. She likes to mix plants not have a few acres of one sort.

Let's move on to the commonest garden pest—the slug. Somebody somewhere—and not all that time ago —and I quite forget who—carried out some research work on slugs. I got quite a shock when I read part of the report. It said that in any garden there are hundreds (or was it thousands?) of slugs going about their business and generally unnoticed by the gardener but much sought for by friend thrush and friend hedgehog. It's when the gardener does something odd that a build up of the slug population occurs. Take what I did some years ago. I sowed runner bean seeds alongside my fence which was right up against a wilderness of a garden next door. As soon as my runner plants appeared above ground every slug next door moved in to take a bite at what, I suppose, is a real delicacy to a hungry slug. The cure? Slug bait? Slug pellets? No, I took over the weedy next-door garden for growing more and more fruit and vegetables. Trouble with most slug baits and slug pellets is that although they probably kill off slugs they leave their dead bodies on the ground. Dead slugs must be food for something and the eating of poisoned slugs would poison or weaken the eater. If the eater also eats live slugs then by using poison pellets you kill off a useful friend and invite more slugs to lead longer lives in your garden and possibly build up a thriving, dangerous colony well above the average. Sweetened beer is what gardeners used to give to their slugs—according to Lawrence D. Hills in his very much-worth-having booklet *Pest Control without Poisons*. Apparently the beer (you can use sweetened milk if you're teetotal) was placed in a dish, sunk in the ground. The sweet beer or milk, so says Mr Hills, attracts the slugs. They fall in and drown. A final point about slugs—Remember, they and their relative the snail, need daytime hiding-places. Likely spots are beneath rocks, bricks, large stones, rubbish ... so keep the garden clean and free from these oddments.

A few creepy crawlies here and there should never be considered as pests. They have as much right to live as man ... and do far less damage to the world generally.

Until a year or two back the chemical industry thought it could defeat pests and plant diseases by manufacturing and beguiling farmers and gardeners to dust and spray with killer-potions. They didn't give a thought to the fact that chemical killer-potions do not fit in with nature's plan. It didn't take nature long to deal with the problem and answer it. New, killer-potion resistant strains of insects appeared. Let's use stronger poisons—preached the pseudo-scientist in the chemical lab. And they did. Bet your life nature is developing another legion of chemically immune plant pests. Some of the pseudo-scientists think this, too. That is why naturally poisonous-to-insect life products like derris and pyrethrum are being included in manufacturers' pesticides.

If you are changing over from artificial inorganic gardening methods to saner, organic ways be prepared for a continuation of some pest troubles during the transition period of around two summers. If you feel forced to use anti-pest products choose derris and pyrethrum —both derived from plants. But keep derris away from the garden pool. It poisons fish.

Natural history may not be your strong point but it pays the organic gardener to know the difference between the helpful centipede and the less friendly wireworm and millipede. The ichneumon fly is our special cabbage caterpillar controller and it is in our interest to note what its cocoons look like when we come across them on cabbage leaves. Hover flies which look like wasps are stingless and friendly. The wasp is an ally in spring and early summer when it cleans the garden of potentially pesty insects. Wasps are not so welcome when plums are ripening. The hive bee and its more attractive relative the bumble bee are not anxious to sting man because the sting and a part of the bee's anatomy usually get left behind leading to the bee's death. Make sure your kiddies respect the bee. Without bees most plant life would disappear from the earth. The bumble bee is the pet insect of the runner bean grower. The more bumble bees around—the heavier the set of pods. Hive bees just haven't the sort of long tongue needed to reach into runner bean flowers so it's the long-tongued bumble bee who effects their pollination.

The home remedies our grandparents used—a little salt water to defeat cabbage caterpillars, a soapy spray against aphides and trapping wireworms with skewered potatoes buried in the ground—worked then and work today. Why buy if the remedy is in the cupboard?

Count your blessings when friend frog jumps out of the strawberry patch and the wife declares she has a heart attack—and count your blessings again on a summer evening when friend hedgehog sniffs and snorts through the cabbage patch towards that saucer of milk you left for him, her and the growing family. These are the simple pleasures of life which the flame gunner and the poison-spraying inorganic-minded gardener doesn't know about.

If the garden is big enough keep a large clump of stinging nettles on which caterpillars of some of our most handsome butterflies feed. What a treat in summer and autumn to have tortoiseshells, red admirals, and peacocks flitting around the garden.

COMPANION PLANTING

Companion plantings—mixing one kind of plant with another kind in the vegetable row or flower bed—is a novel way of trying to beat insect pests. Here are a few examples of this practice.

Chives chase aphides from roses

An old-timer once said to me, 'If you want to keep aphides off your rose bushes, just plant clumps of chives between the plants.'

'How ridiculous,' I thought at the time. But the more I thought of it, the more I figured, 'These old-timers are often so right; why not try it?'

So 3 years ago, I purchased a few clumps of chives which I planted in the rose bed. As they developed, I separated them and spread more clumps through the bed and also beside my rose climbers. I found that what he told me is absolutely true—I never have aphides on the rose bushes. Furthermore the neighbours on both sides of me are also using chives between their roses. When the plants grow too big and begin to blossom, you can cut them down, and they will come up again from the roots. However the purple blossoms are quite attractive in the garden.

The chives serve a double purpose. Besides keeping the aphides away, the tops are really delicious cut up in salads and soups. However, to have them tender and young, you must keep the old growths and blossoms cut off.

HELEN W. KORTZ

Nasturtiums between fruit trees

Although the nasturtium is plagued with its own fleas

—in the form of a black aphis, Beatrice Trum Hunter recommends the growing of nasturtiums between fruit trees and vegetables to repel aphides—in her book *Gardening without Poisons*. Other suggestions are plant tomatoes near asparagus to fight off asparagus beetles and keep ants out of the kitchenette by growing mint just outside the door—just the place where the cook likes mint to be!

Marigolds, asters, and chrysanthemums are, so some gardeners claim, good insect pest repellents. Very attractive, too, to grow among the vegetables. Herbs like basil, anise, and coriander have been found to be especially effective.

Of course, basic to any insect control programme is a sound rotation schedule as well as good cultural practices.

CHOOSE RESISTANT VARIETIES

By planting a variety with high resistance to a specific disease you can prevent a great deal of trouble right at the start. Much progress has already been made in this work, so when you're looking through nurserymen and seedsmen's catalogues be sure to look for such terms as virus free clone, immune, resistant, or slightly susceptible in the descriptions of plants and seeds.

Dr Byron T. Shaw, American Agriculture Research Service Administrator, rates the importance of resistant varieties as follows: 'The ultimate answer (to the chemical residue problem—meaning the residues of chemical sprays and powders which occur so often on crops grown by faulty, inorganic methods) is the breeding of plants that have natural resistance to insect attack.... Once you get to that stage, you just sow one kind of seed instead of another.'

Sometimes a plant is more likely to escape infection when it matures before the season of disease infection occurs. First Early potato plants are likely to escape Potato Blight which arrives on the scene when the haulm of First Earlies is dying or dead. Second Earlies and Maincrop still have lush green foliage then and are more possible victims. Other times, the fact that a plant stands up well to drought—better than most other varieties of the same plant—can help increase its defences against pest attacks. The list of vegetable varieties resistant to one or another disease or pest is growing all the time. But always keep in your mind the true belief that healthy growth is one of the best natural deterrents against both disease and bugs. Here are several recommended garden practices which should keep disease either completely out of the garden or hold it to an absolute minimum.

Work with resistant varieties

Study catalogues carefully and, where possible, choose virus-free or disease-resistant varieties. You'll notice that this information is included in plant descriptions and general information.

Fertilize and compost vigorously and thoroughly

Build up your compost and mulching programme until it is a real factor in your gardening. While we admittedly don't know all about the many and sometimes obscure diseases we are fighting, we do know that soils with a humus content encourage the soil microorganisms which keep disease bacteria from flourishing and establishing colonies.

Use care in watering

When watering plants try not to do it late in the day. Give enough time for the foliage to dry out completely by nightfall. Sprinkling in the late afternoon and in the evening is believed to spread foliage diseases more readily.

Touch wet plants as little as possible

Stay out of the garden when plants are wet. Bacteria or fungus spores can be present in the moisture on the leaves. You can be the prime infective agent by merely going down the row—spreading the disease by touching the plants as you go.

Good garden sanitation and residue disposal

Clean up the garden at the end of the season and get all vegetable wastes into the compost pile where the heating-up process will destroy disease spores and bacteria.

Rotate your crops

If possible, don't grow the same crop twice in the same spot or row. Many troublesome diseases and pests such as nematodes and Club Root can be checked by a good rotation of crops around the kitchen garden.

KNOW YOUR FRIENDS

Get to recognize ladybirds and their larvae, centipedes, violet ground beetles, devil's coach-horse, hover flies, lacewing flies—they're on your side. Welcome the arrival of that lovely innocent—the dragon fly. Welcome, too, all butterflies apart from the cabbage whites and, if you have sufficient soft fruits, be thankful, and share the surplus with your garden birds. Encourage birds to visit and to know your garden as home ... providing you don't stock a cat. Construct nesting boxes for them and enjoy their song and watch them clear your garden of all sorts of bugs. Hang up fat and suet in winter and a string bag of peanuts—on sale in most pet shops.

Frogs and toads

Most gardeners think of the toad with its appetite for ants, moths, caterpillars, flies, and slugs as being more helpful than the frog. True a toad may well gobble up thousands of insects but the frog is equally hungry. Toads are stay-at-homes and possess a certain amount of homing instinct. Frogs are inclined to wander and to do their good work in the neighbours' gardens. Both of these amphibians are night workers and do their good deeds when the sun goes down. They are active between March and November and then hibernate. Frogs and toads need a pool in which they can spawn in spring. If you have no garden pool, why not construct one so that local frogs and toads gravitate towards your garden each spring? Garden frogs and toads soon get to know you and accept you as part of the gardening scene.

WHAT TO DO IF THE BUGS ARE ALREADY THERE

1. ANTS

The ant is beneficial in being a scavenger and in making some fine soil which the gardener may wish to use for some special purpose. Ants are a nuisance in lawn and in the kitchen. They also transfer aphides from plant to plant. Steamed bone meal has been found to discourage ants. If ants persist a pepper spray makes them think twice. Tansy and mint have been found to discourage ants from entering the kitchen by the open door. Tansy is also recommended to prevent flies in the house. Grow both near the back door. The dried leaves of tansy sprinkled about in cellar or attic are a harmless indoor 'insecticide'. Use paraffin or boiling water on nests between crevices of crazy pavement; boiling water only on nests in lawns.

2. APHIDES

Enrich your soil organically as aphides detest plants grown in organically rich soil. Some gardeners have had success by growing nasturtiums, which repel most aphides, between the vegetable rows and around fruit trees. However, often the nasturtiums themselves are plagued with Black Bean Aphis. One of the best controls for aphides of any kind is the ladybird which eats many times its own weight of aphides.

The gardener working to chemicalized methods kills helpful ladybirds when he sprays or dusts with poisons. Try to trap aphides. Paint a small tin bright yellow and fill it with detergent water. The aphides will become attracted to the bright yellow colour, alight on the water surface and trap themselves. You can also trick aphides by placing some shiny aluminium foil around your plants so that it reflects the heat and brilliance of the sun. Aphides normally shy away from foil-mulched plants. For aphis-free broad beans—sow seeds in November.

3. CABBAGE ROOT FLY

The fly lays eggs just below the soil near the roots of cabbages and cauliflowers; less often near other brassicas. The maggot hatches and enters the roots. Cabbage Root Fly damage shows as stunting, flagging, and with foliage taking on a bluish tinge. Plants usually die. Preventive measures are (*a*) plant out seedlings firmly and (*b*) always in a mulch of garden compost. The odour of the compost camouflages the brassica smell and the female flies are not attracted to the transplants.

4. CARROT FLY

Eggs are laid in the soil near plants in May and June and again in August and September. The maggots tunnel into carrot roots. They can also attack celery, parsnip, and parsley. Damage shows when the foliage of carrots take on a rusty hue. Camouflaging the odour of carrots, etc., is a good way of preventing this pest. Grow onions next to carrots and, in areas where Carrot Fly damage is the norm, grow onions alongside celery, parsnip, and parsley. Try garlic, too. When cultivating carrots try not to break any foliage and bury any unwanted carrot thinnings *inside* the compost heap. Sow in May instead of April. This later sowing may miss the trouble entirely. Not a usual trouble in an organic garden. Possibly with so much garden compost around with its own specific odour female Carrot Flies just don't notice any carroty smell to attract them to our plants.

5. CLUB ROOT

Do not confuse this most unpleasant disease of brassicas with the root galls of the pretty harmless Turnip

Gall Weevil. Galls of this insect are near the surface end of the roots of cabbages and their kin. Cut open a gall and there, snug as a bug in a rug, is the white grub of the Turnip Gall Weevil. Don't worry about him. Club Root, also known as Finger-and-Toe, makes huge swellings on brassica roots. The roots become knotted, gnarled, swollen, and rot. The smell is pretty vile at that stage. Never buy brassica plants from him-down-the-road or that-shop-in-the-high street unless you're sure plants are free from the disease. Just one good reason for raising your own cabbage plants! Specialists in inorganic gardening say the use of acid fertilizers should be avoided. That's pretty difficult as most chemical fertilizers are acidic. Some specialists advocate liming. Liming is very necessary if you start off with an acidy soil but don't overdo it. The inorganic people sometimes regularly dose their soil with lots of hydrated lime and probably give the soil a bad attack of indigestion. Use the less concentrated Carbonate of Lime (Ground Chalk) at $\frac{1}{2}$ pound to the square yard at first and then drop down to $\frac{1}{4}$ pound after two seasons. Lots of organic gardeners sprinkle lime over wastes when they add them to the compost pile. Egg shells contain lots of lime. Where Club Root damage is severe stop growing cabbages and their kin, if possible. Give the soil a rest and feed with lots of garden compost and lime well for three seasons before trying cabbages again. If roots show mild Club Root infection with some brassicas quite free from the disease keep on composting and apply heavy dressings to the soil. The disease will disappear. This is not a disease of organic gardens but, if offered brassica stumps for your compost heaps, examine the roots for Club Root and chop off and burn infected roots—then add the stems and leaves to the compost heap. Remember this is a disease of acidic soils. Rather oddly chunks of acidic rhubarb sticks placed in planting holes when brassica transplants are being set out are, so many organic gardeners claim, able to ward off Club Root fungi. By all means try rhubarb. Do not try the inorganic preventive—Calomel Dust. Its pleasant name hides the fact that it is mercurous chloride. The Henry Doubleday Research Association has done some excellent research work on Club Root.

6. CABBAGE CATERPILLARS

Excellent food for fish in the garden pond but, except where fish are whoppers, need squashing (as do slugs) before the fish take them. The female cabbage white butterfly has a predilection for weakly cabbage and Brussels plants. She is also keen on cauliflower but with little appetite for sprouting broccoli and kale. A favourite is the savoy cabbage with those wrinkled leaves which make a perfectly safe home for young cabbage caterpillars. Quick-growing, organically-fed cabbage plants do not usually attract this destroyer of weaklings during the stage when the plants are in robust health. But if the cabbages have reached their prime and should have been cut for use earlier on they then seem to emit a scent pleasing to cabbage whites which then turn up in droves to lay eggs on the foliage. But we all make mistakes and female cabbage whites are no exception. Here and there in an organically-run garden a few cabbage caterpillars may be seen grazing contentedly on plants where mum butterfly made a mistake. If the caterpillars worry you, pick them off. If you don't then expect to find holed and gnawed outer leaves when you cut your cabbages. Bear in mind you are not going to eat the outer leaves. In areas where the cabbage white is a real menace sprinkling a little salt or salt water over cabbages before they start hearting up is a good precautionary measure. The salt kills hatching caterpillars. Any small caterpillars will also die. They are not keen on salted cabbage! Caterpillars of the Cabbage Moth are also seldom a pest in the organic garden. When present they burrow into the hearts of growing cabbages —and the heart is the part you want to eat. If present— spray or dust with caterpillar-killing derris.

7. Celery Leaf Miner

The maggots burrow into the leaves. In bad cases this leads to leaves browning and dying leading to a poor crop. Can, but rarely, attacks parsnip foliage. If you have had this trouble in the past prevent it from recurring by spraying young plants with derris in early May. Spray again 2 weeks later. In areas where this pest is a regular, spray with derris regularly until August. Not normally a pest of organic gardens. A mild attack may occur and the blistered leaves containing the maggots should be picked off and placed inside the compost heap where heat will kill the maggots. Always do this too, or burn tops of infested celery plants when digging up celery for use.

8. Leatherjackets

Not a pest of organic gardens but are frequently encountered when the inedible green lawn is reduced for food crop growing and when weed-covered ground is first dug. These, the larvae of the Crane Fly or Daddy Longlegs, are brownish-grey, tough-skinned, and legless, and about 1 inch long. They feed on roots, bulbs, and corms. The Cutworm, a yellow to grey-brown, $1\frac{1}{2}$-inch-

long, soil-inhabiting caterpillar has similar habits. They
also gnaw through plant stems at soil level—thus their
name of cutworms. Remove any leatherjackets and cutworms found when initially digging new ground, squash
them and feed them to the pool fish. Keep the hoe going
in summer to expose the pests to birds. As the organic
content of the soil rises and good cultivation maintained
these larvae will no longer be pests.

9. MILLIPEDES

Chocolate brown, many-legged, thin 'watch springs'
which uncurl and wander off slowly. If you live in Lin-
colnshire your garden millipedes may have red spots.
Not a pest of organic gardens but will be met there.
Female millipedes are particularly fond of converting
rotting bean seeds (your fault for sowing the seeds in
such cold ground!) into nurseries with a store of rich
food for the progeny. Millipedes will be found if you
dig grassland to make a vegetable garden. To trap them
take a small tin, punch lots of holes in it through which
millipedes can enter, fill with potato peelings or cut-up
carrot. Bury the tin about 6 inches below soil level.
You'll forget where you buried it—so attach it to a
length of wire with its end poking out of the ground.
Dig up the tin or tins once weekly, take out trapped
millipedes, refill with more fresh potato or carrot, and
rebury.

10. FLEA BEETLES

Small, blackish beetles seldom seen but riddle leaves
of seedlings with small circular holes. Not a pest in the
organic garden but inhabit it. Should they get out of
hand dust leaves of seedlings with derris. They are par-

ticularly keen on brassica seedlings—including the radish. Hoeing disturbs the beetles (and their eggs) and makes life pretty uncomfortable for them.

11. Onion Fly

Rarely a nuisance to the organic gardener. After hatching grubs of this small fly burrow into the below-ground part of onion seedlings and feed. The foliage of the seedlings turns yellow and the below-ground part rots. Female onion flies do not lay eggs on plants growing from onion sets nor (even if eggs are laid) can the grubs eat into the stems of autumn-sown onion seedlings. With spring-sown onion seedlings take care not to damage foliage when hoeing or hand weeding. Thin seedlings only when soil is quite wet so that the seedlings may be pulled out with ease and are not damaged or broken. Idea behind all this is to prevent the oniony smell of the damaged seedlings being noted by every female onion fly in the next parish and making a bee-line for your onion bed. Bury unwanted seedlings immediately inside the compost heap. To prevent fungal rotting diseases of onions always grow the plants in a different part of the garden and never use fresh manure to try to get monster bulbs.

12. Parsnip Canker

Can occur in an organic garden but the trouble is seldom severe. A peculiar disorder suffered by the parsnip. Parsnip Canker is not a disease. Cracks in the skin of the root occur and fungi and bacteria obtain an entry and brown patches show on the root. In bad cases there is also internal decay. Cracks usually occur if parsnips have insufficient moisture. A deluge follows and cracking takes place. Keep parsnips watered in very dry summer weather. Mulch in July with peat or straw after rain has penetrated the soil well. Where this disorder has occurred often change over to Tender and True or Avonresister. Both varieties resist the trouble but neither is immune to it.

13. TOMATO LEAF MOULD

This is a common fungal disease of tomato plants in greenhouses. It is very rare on plants grown outdoors. The trouble usually starts in June or July. Yellowish spots appear on the upper surfaces of the foliage and on the undersides a pale greyish mould develops. In severe cases the leaves become completely discoloured and shrivel. The flowers are also attacked by the fungus and plants become very weak and crops are poor.

The cause is due to the gardener not understanding that the tomato plant does not like very hot temperatures and a very moist atmosphere. Ample ventilation is of the greatest importance where tomatoes are being cultivated in a greenhouse. Between July and mid-September the lights and the greenhouse door should be left open all day. At night one or more lights should be left open so that there is always a current of air. Too much water or too little water applied to the plants is another contributory factor. The gardener who bears these points in mind is unlikely to meet this trouble. Some new tomato varieties resistant to Leaf Mould are around —Kingley Cross, Amberley Cross, Eurocross A, Findon Cross.

14. POTATO BLIGHT

A fungal disease which attacks the foliage of potato plants. Spores fall from the foliage to the soil and pass through it on to the tubers. In its early stages small brown or black spots show on the leaves. These enlarge and become a smelly, black mass. The stems are also affected and the rotting tubers develop sunken, dark-coloured patches. Finally the tubers are just an evil-smelling, black pulpy mess. There is no cure. Wet summer weather favours the disease which is more common in the western half of Britain than in the drier east. The preventive chemical method is to spray and keep on spraying with a copper salt solution throughout the summer. This is expensive and time consuming and as the spray must cover the undersides of the leaves as well as the upper surfaces the appliance used must provide a very strong jet. The organic way of beating this unpleasant disease is quite different. Where the disease was endemic the thoughtful gardener grew only First Early potatoes. Many of the roots had been dug and the potatoes eaten before the disease was at its height. At that time, too, the haulm of First Earlies was dying so the crop could be dug and stored before the fungal spores reached the tubers. The First Early variety, Arran Pilot, is excellent for defeating Blight in this manner. In recent years plant breeding stations in Ulster and Scotland have produced potato varieties which resist many races of the fungi which cause Blight. Among Second Earlies are Maris Peer, Ulster Classic, and Pentland Ace. Ulster Viscount, Pentland Ivory, and Pentland Hawk show resistance to Blight. They are maincrop varieties. Pentland Crown, the best early maincrop potato bred in Britain in recent years has no immunity from Blight but rather oddly the fungus seldom causes severe damage. The gardener with the Blight problem is advised to plant these new varieties instead of the older, susceptible-to-blight kinds.

15. MOLES

The mole eats leatherjackets, wireworms, millipedes as well as earthworms which form its basic diet. That the mole can lead to improved soil drainage does not endear him to the gardener when choice plants are uprooted as friend mole delves around the garden. The organic gardener is unlikely to favour the use of poisonous gases or of steel-jawed spring traps. Moles hunt by scent and the placing of some cut pieces of onion in the runs is advised if you simply wish to drive the moles out of your garden—and, of course, into neighbouring gardens! The Mole Plant (*Euphorbia lathyrus*), the Caper Spurge, emits something unpleasant from its roots—unpleasant to moles that is—and gardeners not wishing to welcome moles sometimes ring the garden with Mole Plants. If moles are your problem and you wish to try Mole Plants as a preventive but can't buy the plants, drop a line to Thompson & Morgan, Ipswich. A much-advised way of dealing with moles is to place thorny rose or blackberry stems in the mole's runs. Moles, it is said, tear their skin on the thorns and bleed to death. No wonder moles avoid anything that smells of human beings. You can't blame them. In our opinion it always seems a great pity to kill the little gentleman in black velvet!

16. SLUGS AND SNAILS

Snails and slugs tend to be nocturnal. Take advantage of their night-time habits by placing planks, boards, or other similar covers in the garden to serve as traps. Each morning destroy snails and slugs which have hidden away there for the day. The bodies of snails and slugs are soft and highly sensitive to sharp objects such as sand and to dry, slightly corrosive substances as slaked lime and wood ashes. A narrow strip of sharp sand or cinders around a bed or border will serve as an effective barrier against them as will a sprinkling of slaked lime or wood ashes. Many gardeners have found that setting out saucers of beer, sunk to ground level, attracts slugs by the droves so that they can easily be destroyed. Never use slug pellets—unless the manufacturer assures you on the packet that they are harmless to birds and wild-life. Song-birds and hedgehogs may eat the poisoned slugs and snails and be your unexpected victims.

17. WIREWORMS

Yellow-brown grubs with short legs and a dark head. They measure from $\frac{1}{4}$ to $\frac{3}{4}$ inch in length and live from 4 to 5 years in the soil chewing away at roots. Their favourite diet appears to be the roots of grasses. The grubs are unlikely to be met with in an organic garden unless the garden contains a lawn or abuts on to a grassed area. A very common pest of wasteland being converted into a garden or allotment. During the initial preparation of weedy/grassy soils all wireworms met with should be killed. During the first summer many more will be exposed during hoeing. These should also be killed. Baiting wireworms by burying pieces of carrot or potato in the ground is usually very effective. Fix skewers into the cut pieces of vegetable so that you do not forget where they are buried. Remove daily and pick off and kill the wireworms, then rebury the vegetable pieces. The Henry Doubleday Research Association reports on first-class results with *Tagetes minuta* as a killer or repellent of wireworms and also of the Keeled Slug which can damage potato tubers badly in a wet summer and in gardens where conditions suit a build-up of this pest.

The organically minded gardener eager to learn more about pest-control methods which do not depend at all on poisonous chemical preparations will find the booklet *Pest Control without Poisons* a most useful and interesting work. The booklet costs 15p plus postage and may be obtained from the Henry Doubleday Research Association.

Part V

WHEN TO HARVEST

Vegetables must be picked at the psychological moment, at that stage in their development when they *taste best to you*. This is usually just before they go through chemical changes that convert sugar to starch and fibre to cellulose (wood). *Many vegetables are picked too late.*

How can you know the right time? Taste them again and again until you recognize the size and appearance at which they reach their peak of flavour and aroma (which has a lot to do with the flavour of things). You will never know what thrills you have been missing until you systematically test your own garden products from the earliest stages of maturity to the latest. They vary in quality and flavour far more than you might believe possible.

SOME HARVESTING HINTS *

Vegetable	Time of harvest
Asparagus	Not until third year after planting when spears are 6 to 10 inches above ground, while head is still tight. Harvest only 6 to 8 weeks to allow for sufficient top growth.

* Based on information prepared by the University of Minnesota Agricultural Extension Service.

Beans, broad	Don't wait until pods are full of large seeds with leathery skins. Pick pods when young and enjoy a vegetable lots of folk dislike. Why? They have never sampled organically-grown, young broad beans.
Beans, dwarf	Pick pods when young and when they are stringless. The 'string' is similar to a thread along the edge of the pod. Older sorts made this string as the pods aged. There are now, newer stringless kinds. American gardeners call them Snap Beans. A useful term for us to adopt, too.
Beans, runner	There are no stringless varieties. Always pick runner beans when quite young and free from string. Never leave pods to swell seeds. Swollen pods are inedible being tough and stringy.
Beets	When 1¼ to 2 inches in diameter.
Broccoli, sprouting	Start picking shoots when about 4 inches long and when showing first signs of flower buds. Gather tender shoots every few days. Cut the loose central head last.
Cabbage	When heads are solid and before they split. Splitting can be prevented by cutting off roots with a spade after rain.
Cauliflower	Before heads are ricey, discoloured, or blemished. Tie outer leaves above the head when curds are 2 to 3 inches in diameter; heads will be ready in 4 to 12 days after tying.
Cucumbers	When they are slender and dark green

and before colour becomes lighter. Harvest daily at season's peak. If large cucumbers are allowed to develop, production will be reduced. For pickles, harvest ridge sorts when of the desired size. Cut from plants with a short piece of stem attached to the cuke.

Kale — Cut and use the central, loose head. Later pick side-shoots when still young.

Kohlrabi — When balls are 2 to 3 inches in diameter.

Lettuce — When tightly-hearted and before bolting or deterioration occurs.

Onions — For salad use—when young and before bulbs are larger than $\frac{1}{4}$ inch in diameter; for cooking—select when bulbs are about $1\frac{1}{2}$ inches in diameter; for storage, when tops fall over, shrivel at the neck of the bulb, and turn brown. Allow to mature fully and dry off well before storing.

Parsnips — Delay digging parsnips until after a sharp frost. Roots may be safely left in ground over winter and used early the following spring before growth starts.

Peas — When pods are firm and well filled, but before the seeds reach their fullest size.

Potatoes — First Earlies—when tubers are large enough for use. Second Earlies— usually when haulm is dying. Maincrop for storage—only when haulm is dead.

Pumpkin — Well-matured on the vine. Skin should be hard and not easily punctured by the thumbnail. Cut fruit off vine with a portion of stem attached. Harvest before heavy frost.

Swedes	Lift and store in boxes of moist sand or peat in November. House containers in a shed or outhouse.
Sweet corn	When kernels are fully filled and in the milk stage as determined by the thumbnail test. Use before the kernels get doughy. Silks should be dry and brown.
Tomatoes	When fruits are a uniform red, but before they become soft.
Turnips (summer)	When 2 to 3 inches in diameter. Larger roots are coarse textured and bitter.
Turnips (winter)	Dig in early November and store in boxes of sand or peat in a shed or outhouse.
Vegetable marrow	Cut when still young and when the thumbnail pierces the skin easily. Small marrows (courgettes) are harvested regularly when no longer than 3 inches in length.

HOW HARVESTING CAN AFFECT VITAMIN QUALITY

When the housewife goes shopping to buy greens for her family she assumes that spinach is spinach regardless of variety, age, conditions of growth, and time of harvesting. She takes for granted that a pound of cabbage or spinach obtainable on one day is equal in quality to a pound on any other day, regardless of time and weather conditions. In the feeding of animals, the farmer even assumes that 2 hours pasturing of his stock in the early morning is the equivalent to 2 hours in the late afternoon.

Actually these assumptions do not agree with the facts. Definite differences in the amount of starches, sugars, proteins, fats, minerals, and of vitamins as well, may be found in plants subjected to different weather conditions especially at and near the time of harvesting, or even in plants picked at different times of day. Differences, which are particularly noticeable in the leaves, may be found also in plants of different ages.

To increase our knowledge of one of the vitamins, namely vitamin C, studies were made by the United States Public Health Service to determine the effect of age, conditions for growth, and time of harvesting upon the quantity of this substance in edible plants. It was assumed that the amount of food in a pound of spinach or peas might depend upon how old the plants were when the vegetables were picked, on the age of the vegetables themselves, on the time of day when they were picked, and on whether the weather had been prevailingly cloudy or sunny during their growth, particularly around the time of harvesting. It was found that light has a remarkable effect upon the accumulation of vitamin C. Seedlings sprouted in light contained, after 7 days, more than four times as much vitamin C as seedlings of the same age grown in darkness. Plants grown in the greenhouse during May and June in the neighbourhood of Washington, DC, contained twice as much vitamin C as plants grown during December and January. In more northerly latitudes, it might be expected that the differences at the two seasons would be even greater. However, recent tests with tomatoes conducted at USDA's Regional Laboratory at Ithaca, New York, yielded differences in vitamin C values in the summer and winter months similar to those which had been found with other types of plants at Washington, DC.

Fruit from the shaded side of a tree has been shown by other workers to have a lower vitamin C content than that from the sunny side, and even in individual fruits, the sunny side has been found to have more than the shaded side. The changes in the amount of vitamin C in a plant under varying conditions of sunlight as compared to shade are noticed first in the leaves, though later differences may be observed in other parts, even in the roots.

Losses of vitamin C at night amounting to as much as 20 per cent of the total quantity, and possibly even more, may occur in some types of plants. Appreciable losses at night occur only when the temperature is high enough to allow growth to take place. Similar losses of the vitamin may occur also during the day, but the quantity thus lost is not readily measurable because the vitamin is manufactured more rapidly than it is used. So the net result is an increase in vitamin C. Manufacture at a slow rate occurs at night, but its magnitude is difficult to determine because the vitamin is lost much more quickly than it is made. These facts suggest that the vitamin C is used by the plant in the process of growth. Just what it does with the vitamin is, so far, a secret with the plant. The evidence suggests, however, that it is used for some purpose in the growing regions such as in the tips of the roots and stems and in the development of the young leaves.

As a consequence of its own life processes, therefore, a plant starts the day with a lowered amount of vitamin C. If there then follows a succession of very cloudy days, and if the plant is growing rapidly, there tends to be a slow but progressive lowering of the amount of vitamin C. Comparable losses in the sugars and starches of plants under similar conditions have been recognized for a long time. Then comes a bright sunshiny day. Marked gains in the vitamin are to be observed during the course of the day. Some types of plants may, under these conditions, have more than 25 per cent more vitamin C by late afternoon than at break of day.

An interesting example of this variation in nutritional value of plants as related to time-of-day turned up in an experience in silkworm feeding. In sections of Italy where silkworm production has been an important industry from ancient times, it has been the practice to gather the mulberry leaves, used in feeding the silkworms, at dusk. These sericulturists have found by experience that leaves gathered at the end of the day tend to yield better results than leaves collected in the morning. Chemical studies of mulberry leaves have revealed why this is true. During the day, under the influence of sunlight, the leaves become enriched in nutritive substances, not only with carbohydrates such as starches and sugars but also with proteins, fats, minerals, and, presumably, vitamins, too, since Vitamin C, for example, is known to be present in relatively high concentrations in mulberry leaves. Moreover, the protein of young mulberry leaves nearing full size has been found to be superior in quality, quantity, and digestibility to that in well-matured leaves.

It seems strange indeed that one should have to turn to this lowly caterpillar for information on the subject of nutrition, but actually little is known of the influence of 'time-of-day' for collection of food plants, or even of shading, upon their nutritive value to humans and to animals other than silkworms. It is true that variations in protein and non-protein nitrogen have been observed in a number of types of plants harvested in late afternoon and evening in contrast to others collected in the morning. Just as in mulberry leaves, a greater amount of starches and sugars is found in plants kept in sunlight than in those kept in shade, and more also in plants collected in the evening than in those collected in the morning; but nothing was known until recently of the effect on variations in these different conditions on the amounts of any of the vitamins. It remains to be seen whether the amounts of the other vitamins in fruits and vegetables vary as does vitamin C with differences in light intensity, length-of-day, and time-of-day for harvesting. It seems probable that if differences occur, they won't be so great as those of vitamin C, unless the vitamin in question, like vitamin C, is also used up in the life processes of the plant.

When the time comes to harvest fruits and vegetables, particularly vegetables of the leafy type, due consideration should be given to variations in the amount of light. Present results suggest that for good vitamin C values, the harvesting of vegetables should not be done before mid-morning, say ten o'clock, after generally clear weather. It is preferable to harvest, if possible, after a spell of clear weather, or, if it must be done following cloudy days, collection should be made late in the day. Because of the tendency of vegetables, especially those of the leafy type, to lose vitamin C on standing, it would follow that when weather conditions permit, vegetables from the home garden should be freshly picked each day.

MARY E. REID
U.S. Public Health Service

FINAL CHECKLIST AT GARDEN CLOSING TIME

In late autumn, most gardeners, having harvested their crops, have entirely forgotten about their gardens, which will be something for them to think about again when the seed catalogues roll in next January. Actually the good gardener should be devoting a lot of time to his garden in autumn.

If you don't believe it, turn to nature. What is she doing in *her* garden? She is putting it to bed for the winter, blanketing it against the cold and the icy winds. If she has a garden in an open field, she lays down the grasses until they form a deep, matted mass, and she piles the dead stems of the higher plants on top to keep the grasses down. In the forest, she gently covers the floor with another layer of leaves and probably drops twigs and limbs on top; for forest trees are self-pruning. Look where you will, you will find that nature is scrupulous in blanketing the earth against the rigours of the wintertime.

The best time to start making a protective winter covering for your garden is long before the garden year ends. Accumulate all the organic matter that you can find, from residue crop materials, manures, cut weeds, or outside products. Then lay down a thick mulch over the area to be planted with crops next year. All plant residues should be strewn over your garden for winter cover unless they are seriously diseased. Otherwise, gather up the infected plant residues, compost them, scatter the compost on the soil, and rake it in.

If you would like to grow a soil-conserving cover

crop, cultivate the ground in the rows or rake it over and
sow rye grass or some other quick growing, sturdy crop.

Be sure to cut all weeds before they go to seed. The
old adage says that 'one year's seeding makes 7 years'
weeding'. Use the cut weeds as mulch. Add any organic
matter that will rot—the trimmings of your celery, the
outer leaves of your cabbage, the mowings from your
lawn, plant stems from your flower beds, the leaves from
your trees, and so on—provided, of course, that the
materials used are not diseased. A little earth may be
scattered over leaves to hold them down.

Don't ever burn tree leaves. There is nothing you can
use for mulch that may be as useful as tree leaves are.
Suppose you use carrot tops or bean plants or beet
leaves for mulch. How deeply do those plants forage?
A few inches only. Whatever plant foods they secure
must necessarily come from the top few inches of soil.
And in those top few inches, much of the original supply of plant food may be exhausted, leached out,
washed, or blown away. But the tree leaves contain
minerals that the roots brought up from deep down in
the earth. Even though some of the minerals may be
practically gone from the top 10 inches of soil, there
may be abundant supplies of these minerals 6 feet
below the surface of the ground. The tree roots will
bring up some of them. The leaves will contain a part
of what is brought up. Spread on your garden and eventually incorporated in your soil, these leaves will help
replenish the dwindling supplies of minerals. So you see
why tree leaves are especially valuable in your winter
mulch or in compost.

Perhaps you cannot collect enough organic material
to cover *all* of your garden thoroughly. In that case,
you can mulch the areas which you want to be especially
rich for your next summer's crops. This naturally sug-

gests that you should plan your next year's garden *this autumn*. Then you will know where you will plant this or that vegetable next spring. Summer cabbages demand less rich soil than say vegetable marrows, and radishes will do quite well in soil not rich enough for runner beans.

The gardener cannot put back into his garden all that came out of it, because he has to eat the potatoes, tomatoes, beans, and cabbage, etc. But he can return the *equivalent*—and more. His lawn mowings may make up for what is lost in the bean crop; his weeds may offset loss through carrot culture, and so on. If the gardener will put back into his soil, by composting, mulching, etc., all that it is possible for him to return to the ground, he may largely or wholly offset the annual loss of plant food. He can also add manure, tree leaves, and a host of other enriching products.

From time to time, he may need to sprinkle a little lime on his garden. Yet he should be careful where he puts it. Some plants do not thrive in soil that has been limed.

Although your soil is the primary interest in caring for your garden in the autumn, there are many adjuncts to your gardening that also need to be considered now. Tools should be carefully cleaned, oiled, and put away. All broken or damaged implements, etc., should be mended or replaced. Wire trellises should be rolled up and stored in a dry place. Your complement of bean poles, tomato stakes, and other similar pieces of equipment should be made ready for spring. For when the spring rush comes, you will find it difficult to do repair jobs. Digging, planting, and cultivating will keep you more than busy. If there is anyone who needs to take time by the forelock, it is the gardener. And the best time to do it is in the autumn.   LEWIS E. THEISS

Clean tools before storing

Gather all the rakes, hoes, spades, and other small tools which you won't be using until spring. Clean them well and paint with oil. Then hang them on the wall. If you have no regular hanging place for small tools, you can make one easily, using peg-board available at most hardware stores.

The care of power tools necessitates a little more work, but it will be rewarded with longer life and better operation.

PART VI

*THE ORGANIC WAY—ANTIDOTE
TO POLLUTION*

YOUR GARDEN IS ON THE FRONT LINE

There are still people around in favour of conservation who talk about banning DDT, but who spray DDT and worse in their own gardens. Perhaps they don't read the label (if there is one) on the aerosol or package and therefore don't know what it is they are using. More likely, they are still prisoners of the insect-hysteria reflex that grips a large percentage of people. Compulsively, they go after any bug that strays into their range. Also compulsively, the people who broadcast persistent poisons around their homes haven't yet learned that it is possible to share both living space and some of our food with the insects, and still be happy, content, and affluent.

Your garden is now on the front line of the pesticide battle, for several reasons. First, your garden is where you live, and if you are spraying persistent poisons, you are creating an impure environment at the place where such pollution can hurt you most. Second, we have the chemical people on the run because for the first time the facts about the harm of chemicals are making an impact at the high levels of government. Politically, your garden is the grass roots of a chain of influence that leads right up to Westminster. Just as each vote counts in an election, what you do in your garden has an impact on our national pesticide policy. As long as DDT sells in the stores to individuals who are willing to spray it where they live, the chemical industry can make the very strong point that people obviously want persistent poisons and want them right at home. A drying-up of the small-package sale of persistent pesticides would be the strongest possible vote in favour of a cleaner all-Britain environment.

Conservationists now recognize that a big battle in the pesticide war is being fought on the home front and they are encouraging us all to take a closer look at any pesticides purchased for use in the home and garden. Home and garden pesticides sales are Big Business … and Business is not noted for its high state of morality. The Ministry of Agriculture can hardly be regarded as the friend of the British environment but for those who bother to read Forewords in a booklet, the Ministry has this to say in its Foreword to *Chemicals for the Gardener*—'Misuse of chemicals may, however, cause harm to people, domestic animals, and wildlife, and they must be used with care and discrimination.' In the same booklet we are rightly told to 'Handle all chemicals with care. Only use them when really necessary. Do not use persistent chemicals if short-lived ones will do the job.' Among the many Ministry-approved control chemicals are two brands of sodium chlorate. Rather oddly, the British Broadcasting Corporation has film illustrating the explosion which could occur—and the terrific fire—even when sodium chlorate is handled correctly. The Ministry's booklet also fails to mention that sodium chlorate runs in the soil killing all before it. Thus, if you use it for killing weeds on paths (as the Ministry suggests) it may run into adjoining soil and kill your prize cabbages and parsnips. Worse still, it may run into your neighbour's soil and that could lead to a very unhappy neighbour with the possibility of court action for damages.

Loudest voice in Britain to yell against chemicalization of our soil, our environment, and of the food we eat comes from the Soil Association. Unfortunately, the Soil Association lacks the official status and the funds of a government Ministry so that its sane counsel is not heard by the greater part of the nation.

Do not be misled or lulled by halfway measures that the government is likely to take. It helps when our government bans the use of some highly poisonous, persistent chemicals to gardeners but the ban must also be binding on commercial agriculturists. Is it right that persistent and poisonous chemicals should continue to be used by farmers and commercial growers on large tracts of British soil to produce what are contaminated foods? Foolish, too, if the government prohibits the use of poisons in British agriculture (as it should do) but permits produce grown with the same poisons to be imported from abroad. Sometimes the authorities do take action to prevent us from being well-nigh poisoned. A case in point is when a shipload of apples polluted with arsenical pesticides arrived in the Port of London. Dump the lot—was the order of health officials.

The battle against poisons is just that—a battle. We are all in it, whether we want to be or not. The choice of being a victim or a fighter is up to you.

Can Britain's soil stand up much longer to poisoning? Can our bodies stand up much longer to a continued intake—possibly bigger intakes of poisonous residues on and in our food? What is your answer? Will the North Sea eventually become as polluted as America's Great Lakes and Europe's Baltic? Will chemicalized, dehedged British fields soon resemble America's Dust Bowls? Only the voice and the activity of you and me can stop the rot.

It could have been your child who was poisoned and killed after drinking a chemical solution in a lemonade bottle in your garden shed. If not your child—perhaps your neighbour's small boy or girl come round to play with your kiddies. It could have been your kiddy, too, so badly burned by exploding sodium chlorate used to kill your garden weeds.

What can you do? First stop using garden chemicals. Buy or lend a copy of this book to the neighbours on either side of you. Help them to see the menace of chemicalization of their environment, too. If you're an organizer, start an organic gardening club in your village, suburb, or town. Get a reporter down from the local paper. Tell him what you are up to. Cleaning up the environment is newsy stuff nowadays. Your local radio station is bound to be interested if you can contact the right chap there to deal with this sort of subject. Watch local parks department workmen. Ask them what they are spreading or spraying around. If the stuff is nasty and a possible health hazard like DDT is—complain to your local councillor. Make sure your M.P. knows what is going on. If the Council persists in using the stuff, collect signatures and send a petition to the Town Clerk—with copies, of course, to your local paper, local radio station, and to your M.P. You may even find a local doctor interested if the subject is related to public health ... although doctors seem more interested in trying to cure illness than prevent it.

Bang the drum hard. Make lots of noise. Somebody is bound to listen. Right round our homes is where action is needed and from whence it must come ... and the sooner people realize that the faster we are likely to get a total environment that isn't contaminated with persistent pesticides and other chemical hazards. When a lot of folk start thinking and acting alike, things begin to happen.

Millions of people who never used to worry about the

natural world very much are now forming the opinion that the land and water and the air have a deep and significant value when they are pure. It's time for all of us to use our gardens as a means to tell everyone that a pure environment is something that we can all have, especially around our homes. *Your* garden is on the front line.

Britain is ready for organic gardening—and organic gardening is ready for Britain.

DIG FOR YOUR HEALTH'S SAKE

If, and so far it seems the continued policy, monoculture and the increased use of inorganic fertilizers and chemical pesticides on a wide scale persist, then the earth will sicken. A failure of the North American wheat crop or of the south-east Asian rice crop due to over-chemicalization of soils will result in starvation. The political convulsion which will then occur will undoubtedly be as catastrophic as a hydrogen bomb explosion. What have and what are world politicians doing or planning? Let us consider our own country. Two world wars have clearly demonstrated that Britain cannot feed herself. Her population relies for 50 per cent (at least) of its food on imports from as far away as New Zealand and Australia. Yet, within a few years of the ending of World War Two the British government invited immigrants by the thousand to settle in these already over-populated, unable-to-feed-itself islands.

If, in the event of a failure of world crops rationing has to be reintroduced, no British government has, as yet, indicated that a plan to prevent starvation here is in

the pipeline. The danger round the corner is not publi-
cized and our children are not taught about this menace
to their generation. That the masses are not eager to
grow food in their gardens is due to their ignorance of
the hungry world beyond Europe. The Malthusian the-
ories and prophecies of 1798 are far removed from the
make-believe world of pop, football, and Bingo. Television and magazine pictures in colour of instances of
world hunger do not worry the masses who are not involved where supermarkets display unrationed foods
from all parts of the globe.

But are these home-produced and imported foodstuffs
health-giving? Are the British people already suffering
from malnutrition because of the eating of a preponder-
ate quantity of chemicalized, processed foodstuffs? Is
the National Health Service serving the health of the
nation or its diseases?

It is not difficult to foresee that with the greater pub-
licity to the organic way of thought and practice now
happening—due to the foresight of several enlightened
publishers—there is bound to be a demand in Britain
for land in which workers and redundants may grow at
least some unchemicalized food for themselves and their
children. So far most of the land available to the tower
flat dweller for food production is (where there is one)
a local government allotment site. The Labour Government appointed a Committee of Inquiry into Allotments
on August 2, 1965. Its Report* is 450 pages of facts
and figures—interesting but not light reading. If and
what the Conservative government intends to do about
putting into action some of the recommendations made
by Professor H. Thorpe and his colleagues in their Report is not known at the time this book is being pre-

* Departmental Committee of Inquiry into Allotments Report,
1969, London, H.M.S.O., Price £2.10.

pared for publication. Will the present government give
a lead in a 'Dig for Your Health's Sake' campaign or
will it be remembered as the government which gave 'A
Charter for Land-Grabbers' the front page headlines of
Garden News, August 13, 1971, with an editorial very
much worth quoting here.

> A big question mark today hangs over the great expecta-
> tions for a promised land of leisure gardens and weekend
> chalets in the development of Britain's allotments of the
> Seventies.
>
> And even the very existence of allotments in many
> areas is in jeopardy.
>
> Garden News this week pressed Government officials
> for a statement to clarify the vague and wholly unsatisfac-
> tory statement in the Commons two weeks ago by Local
> Government and Development Minister Graham Page on
> the future of allotments.
>
> Whitehall continues to be vague. But this is the picture
> that now begins to emerge: The 460-page report by Pro-
> fessor Harry Thorpe—heralded as the New Testament for
> plotholders—is unlikely to be enforced by Government
> legislation.
>
> In fact the only legislation that is on the horizon will lift
> all controls on allotments—and sites will thus become
> easy-meat for land-grabbing councils with plans for alter-
> native development.

BATTLE OF A STUBBORN GARDENER

Ever had an allotment? I've had one for 25 years. But
that's not quite truthful. In fact I've had three. Not that
I wanted three. One would have suited me fine but twice
I've had to suffer what most British allotmenteers get
now and then—an eviction notice for 'development'.
This can make you hopping mad!

The soil of my allotment had been rejuvenated with heavy dressings of garden compost for 14 years. In a soil like that plants burst with energy and good health; pests and diseases just don't have a chance. Then along came the quit notice so that the site could be 'developed'. What sort of development? Just 8 inches of concrete all over my fertile soil with garages around its perimeter. Of course I was offered an alternative plot. This time it was to be on the local authority's permanent allotment site. I got quite a shock when I paid my new plot a visit. Apart from being a sort of kiddies' playground it was also the spot where local folk dumped all junk the refuse collection people wouldn't take. My first job was to stack the junk. Yes, there was even a kitchen sink! The borough authorities kindly carted it all away. Next job was to clear the weed growth. It took me 44½ hours to skim off and stack the top couple of inches of couch grass and other weeds; 40 hours were then spent in forking the soil to a depth of about 4 inches and to remove every weed root I came across.

There was no shelter on the site and I got soaked to the skin twice before I built myself a temporary shed. This was a Sod Hut—made with weedy turves, a wooden door, and a corrugated tin roof. The plot was then fenced with 'Weldmesh' to keep out wandering dogs and I got down to potato planting. Now the potato plant is a hungry, thirsty sort. There was precious little food in the ground I had inherited and water just ran through the sandy stuff. There was a large compost heap standing on the plot I was to vacate so barrowload upon barrowload of rich garden compost was wheeled to the new plot and tipped over the potato bed—or over most of it. Local children turned out to be no problem at all. They had learnt a bit about compost making at school and also, to my surprise, about the earthworm as a soil improver. I put their knowledge and interest to good use. They collected—and still collect—weeds, discarded clothing, lawn mowings, newspapers, and hedge trimmings for my compost heaps. The bigger the heaps and the hotter they got, the more thrilled the youngsters became. Must say that some of the older-established plot-holders did not look all that happy at seeing so many kiddies on the allotment site. But the good folk in nearby houses noticed that the kids were being amused and occupied during the school holidays and out came soft drinks and coffee. On one occasion I was bending about so much that my gardening pants split. One good lady passed a pair of her husband's over the fence for me. Unfortunately the only spot for the pants was the compost heap. Organic gardeners don't carry a spare tyre of fat around the waist. Two of me could have been placed inside that waist-line! But the thought behind the gift was so kind—I thought.

Now each local household has a strong plastic bag into which all compostable wastes can be placed for adding to my compost heaps. The arrangement suits us all. Local gardens are small and mainly all lawn and privet. I get the lawn mowings and hedge trimmings for larger and larger compost heaps. They no longer need light up smelly, unneighbourly bonfires. A taste of organically grown cabbage, grapes, strawberries, and tomatoes is also appreciated by those who supply soil-feeding wastes.

The first compost heap made on the new allotment in April rotted down quickly and was ready for spreading over the soil in late May—just in time for setting out plants of tomatoes, sweet corn, cucumbers, marrows, and melons.

Trains pass the allotment site. One day when I was working hard to prepare the ground for planting a train stopped alongside. The motorman waved his hand and shouted out that I was wasting my time. He knew—he'd tried and failed. This was not very encouraging but when you have gardened organically for as long as I have you know in yourself that you are doing what is best for the soil and best for your plants and that apart from a monsoon or an earthquake—both rare in Britain —all will go well. The trouble is that gardening the organic way is so damned simple that people who see the results must so often complicate things by thinking up reasons for the good growth of my crops. After inspecting fruit and vegetables on my previous plot a journalist from Hong Kong told me that my success with Chinese and Japanese cucumbers was due to a current of warm air. He even pointed out the hill from whence the warm air came. It seemed odd to me that the warm air didn't help crops in gardens near by! An American plant breeder had a different idea. According to him the pylon wires above the allotment supplied some sort of electric force. He called it electro-culture. A farmer just down the road told me what he thought of that theory. The farmer has the same wires crossing a 10-acre field. There was just no difference in crop results below the wires. One of my neighbours knows for sure why my crops look and taste so good. It's all due to a secret potion I use in making garden compost. Fact is, it's so secret that even I don't know what it is! Perhaps hobgoblins bring it along and add it to my heaps at night!

But let's go back to that first summer on the new allotment. During July things looked reasonably good. Rainwater had been collected from the sod hut roof and stored in old steel tanks found on a local refuse tip. All sorts of mulches—peat, straw, autumn leaves, and wood shavings—helped retain moisture in the sandy soil and not much watering was necessary. Other plot holders had never seen an allotment tucked in straw like a barn yard and were interested in the idea of mulching to save water and save work in weeding.

But there hadn't been sufficient garden compost to fertilize the whole plot. A glance showed where compost had not been applied. None had been available for the last row of potatoes. Although the plants managed to show above the ground they promptly yellowed and died. A row of sprouting broccoli made a good show of tall, bushy plants where compost had been spread lavishly but three plants at the end of the row growing without the benefit of a compost dressing reached a height of 9 inches and stayed put.

A lot of time was spent during the following winter in tree planting for a regular supply of fruit and in digging and moving grape vines from the vacated allotment to the new one. I had no experience of moving established grape vines and found that the only way of digging out vines is to make a trench about 18 inches deep all around the vine. The soil between the trench and the trunk then has to be scooped out, roots in the trench chopped back with a spade and the vine then tugged until with a cracking noise other roots break and the vine comes out of the ground. After the vines had been replanted they were pruned drastically and within 2 years most were cropping normally again.

I had no intention of leaving all that plant-rich food in the ground which was due for covering with concrete so during the last season of the tenancy of the allotment I had sown mustard and lupins thickly all over it. During early autumn the thick stand of sappy plants was gathered and added to a compost heap being built on the new plot. This was a useful way of locking up lots of nitrogen, potassium, and phosphorus plus valuable trace elements and putting them to good use in the soil of the new plot.

The second summer on the new allotment was a very dry one and I had to use water liberally to keep my potato plants growing steadily and not to suffer the sad fate of unmulched and unwatered plants on other plots. These dry-at-the-roots plants just yellowed and died. The water did the trick and I got ready to lift a bumper crop in September. The crop was there all right but the damp conditions among the potato plants had attracted every thirsty slug on the allotment site and many of my choice potatoes had fat slugs in them. The goldfish in the pool alongside the sod hut enjoyed meals of crushed slug and I was left to work out a plan to defeat this menace to future crops. The answer was simple. In the following March the boys went out with pails and returned with lots of frog spawn. This hatched out well in my rainwater tanks and around 5,000 tiny frogs were released on the allotment in July. It's useless building up a frog colony unless there is a pool at hand where the frogs can breed. I now have three pools on the allotment ... and frogs everywhere. Slugs just haven't a chance of building up to pest proportions. Current work includes the establishment of a toad colony to complement the excellent work of the frogs in clearing slugs from the whole allotment site.

A bird I had not had dealings with before was the wood pigeon. Unless you have come up against the appetite of a dozen wood pigeons as large as hens you simply can't imagine the damage they can cause to summer and winter greens. They are such dirty birds, too. They perch on top of tall Brussels sprouts stems in winter and peck and mess over the plants. Scarecrows, black cotton, red tape, tinfoil, and mirrors are among the anti-pigeon tactics I have tried. I even tried to defeat them with a stuffed owl set among my plants. All tactics of this sort proved useless. There is only one way of keeping wood pigeons at bay and that is to sow and grow all brassicas beneath garden netting.

The thrush and the blackbird, because of their insect-eating habit, are two birds the gardener likes to have around the garden or the allotment. True, they will scoff every strawberry in June and, unless you have such bumper crops that you can afford to share them, will devour your raspberries in July and your blackberries in August. The answer to these fruit eaters is small-mesh garden netting. But garden netting is quite useless on 6-foot-high grape vines. The birds perch on the netting and peck at the grapes through it. My way to protect my ripening grape crop was to tie each cluster in a clear, perforated polythene bag. This gives complete protection but tying more than 1,000 bunches in bags is a long, boring job. Seeing bunches of grapes ripening just over their garden fences is something the kind people living near my allotment find fascinating. I was moaning a bit the other autumn to one of the local housewives as I was tying on bag number 200 and explaining that although I hated the job it's better than shooting or trapping song-birds. as is done in foreign vineyards. I'm always ready to learn but I was not all that convinced I was going to learn something really useful when the good lady said if I'd wait a minute she would show me how to protect my grapes by a far easier method. Within minutes she was handing me old nylon curtains and clothes pegs. A shout or two—and out came other housewives with more curtains and pegs. The allotment began to look like a Monday wash day but what a simple, effective, and quick way this is to protect grapes from birds. The method works equally well on loganberries and on bush fruits. Nylon curtaining is so different from cotton. Within minutes after the heaviest of rain showers the nylon is quite dry and there is no chance of damp conditions being built up to lead to grey mould on the protected fruit.

BRIAN FURNER

ORGANIZATIONS CONCERNED WITH ORGANIC METHODS AND ECOLOGICAL RESEARCH OR WITH ENVIRONMENTAL PROBLEMS

The Henry Doubleday Research Association, 20 Convent Lane, Bocking, Braintree, Essex.

This association of organic gardeners is named after Henry Doubleday (1813–1902), the Quaker smallholder who introduced Russian Comfrey to Britain. He sought no profit from his 30 years research on the crop he thought could feed a hungry world. His principles of 'Search always for the truth that harms no man' and 'Observe the works of God in humbleness' are followed by the Association founded in 1954 by Lawrence D. Hills. The objects of the Association are to find better methods of gardening and farming without chemicals and to study the nutritional, medicinal, agricultural, and horticultural uses of Comfrey, the only land plant so far known to extract Vitamin B.12 from the soil. Russian Comfrey is also the fastest builder of vegetable protein. Recent work of the Association includes investigations into such problems as slugs, carrot fly, club root, and potato eelworm. The Association keeps closely in touch with its members and has overseas groups in Australia and India. It publishes helpful booklets. One, *In Place of Poisons*, has a Braille edition. Annual subscription £2.00.

The Organic Gardening Society of Great Britain, 38
   Northend Road, Erith, Kent.
Pledged to practise organic methods and to publicize
them. No subscribing members.

The Soil Association, Walnut Tree Manor, Haughley,
   Stowmarket, Suffolk.

The Bio-Dynamical Agricultural Association, Rudolf
   Steiner House, 35 Park Road, London, NW1.

The Canadian Soil Association of Organic Husbandry,
   166, Joicey Boulevard, Toronto 12, Ontario, Canada.

The Soil and Health Foundation, 46 South West Street,
   Allentown, Pennsylvania, USA.

The Victorian Compost Society, PO Box 2605W, Mel-
   bourne, C1, Australia.

The New Zealand Organic Compost Society, PO Box
   318, Christchurch, New Zealand.

The Organic Soil Association of Southern Africa, PO
   Box 7736, Johannesburg, South Africa.

Organic Gardening and Farming, Organic Park, Em-
   maus, Penna. 18049, USA.

Organic Gardening and Farming, The Rodale Press,
   Berkhamsted, Herts.

GLOSSARY OF TERMS

ACIDITY-ALKALINITY. The soil condition is determined
by the kind of rock from which it comes, and the partial or complete decomposition of vegetation. In the
old times, a farmer tasted his soil. If it tasted sweet, he
knew he could expect high yields. But if it tasted sour
or bitter, he knew it wasn't good for crops. Today's
gardener depends on pH reading based on soil testing.

A pH of 7 is neutral; most plants do best around pH 6 or slightly acid.

ACTIVATORS. Compost activators are substances that some believe stimulate bacterial activity in a compost pile. This can work in two ways: (1) introduction of bacterial strains that break down organic matter; (2) increasing the nitrogen content of the pile to provide extra food for microorganisms. Good organic procedure calls for adding nitrogen-rich manures which also contain the bacteria necessary for complete decomposition.

AERATION. The exchange of air in the soil with air in the atmosphere. Air is needed in the soil for the proper working of bacteria and fungi and aids in the breakdown of organic matter, especially roots of previous crops. The average soil contains about 25 per cent air, and its fertility and optimum root functioning depend directly on the extent of air ventilation.

AEROBIC COMPOSTING. Decomposition of organic materials by airborne bacteria. The most common form of composting done by gardeners.

ALGAE. Microscopic green plants that live as single cells or as large colonies of one-celled plants. They are present both in the land and in the sea, and also in freshwater ponds.

ANAEROBIC COMPOSTING. Composting without air. The heap is completely enclosed in an airtight container, and is worked upon by bacteria that exist in the absence of air. Escaping odours can become a problem in anaerobic decomposition.

BLIGHT. Any of a number of plant diseases. Most blights are manifested by browning foliage caused by pathogenic organisms.

CARBON–NITROGEN RATIO. This means the proportion of the former to the latter in any organic matter. The C–N ratio of young sweet clover is 12 to 1; rotted manure is 10 to 1; sugar-cane trash is 50 to 1; straw is 80 to 1; and sawdust is 400 parts carbon to 1 part of nitrogen.

CATCH CROPS. Crops which mature quickly may be grown in ground reserved for the growing of a longer-growing crop later on. Radish and lettuce, for example, may be grown in spring/early summer in a plot where broccoli or kale plants are to be set out in June or July.

CHEMICALIZATION. Refers to soil-chemicalization. The principle that soil is inert and may be dosed with chemical fertilizers and pesticides in the production of food crops. A fallacy which, if its practice is not halted, may end mankind's tenure of planet Earth.

CLAY SOIL. The particles in a clay soil are so fine that it tends to compact, making cultivation difficult, and interfering with the oxygen supply of plant roots. A typical soil may be composed of about 60 per cent clay, 20 per cent silt, and 20 per cent sand.

COLD FRAME. Usually a glass-covered (plastic can also be used) frame, higher in the back, and slanting down towards the front to admit more of the sun's low winter-time rays. No heat is used inside the cold frame. The cover is usually hinged in the back for ventilation.

COMPACTION OF SOIL. The hardening of soil into a dense mass caused by the continuous passage of heavy weights or vehicles. Plants growing in soil compacted by heavy tractors or combines cannot develop healthy roots.

COMPANION CROPS. Good plant neighbours that occupy different levels in the soil or find in each other's company the light requirements best suited them. Runner beans and Jerusalem artichokes interfere with each other above and below the ground. But celery and leeks do fine together, also cabbages and dwarf French beans, beets and onions, ridge cucumbers, and sweet corn and carrots and peas. Do not grow your tomatoes next to kohlrabi.

COMPOST. Nature herself first made compost long before men began to garden. Leaves that fall to the forest floor and slowly decompose form compost. Last year's foliage, weeds, and grasses, combined with countless bodies of insects, birds, and animals are all part of the natural composting cycle. The compost pile in your garden is an intensified and somewhat speeded-up version of this seasonal transformation of protein into humus. Finished compost is the best-possible complete fertilizer for plants because it contains all the nutrients they require in readily assimilable form. Do not confuse home-made, plant-food-rich garden compost with special shop-bought seed and potting composts or with composted horse manure, composted fruit pulp, municipal composts, spent mushroom compost, etc.

CONTOUR GARDENING. Ploughing, planting, cultivating, and harvesting according to the terrain or prevailing slope of the ground. By fitting the furrows to the curves and swell of the land, water and soil are conserved. The curved furrows hold the rainfall, and reduce the amount of soil that is washed away. On the other hand, straight-up-and-down furrows mean washing away of soil, loss of water, and gullying.

COVER CROPS. Planting a crop before the main one in order to protect the soil and to add humus and nutrients to it by ploughing it under before the second is sown. A good cover crop makes a great amount of growth in the shortest possible time. It should be adapted to the prevailing soil and climate, and easily incorporated into the soil. Summer cover crops include buckwheat, millet, oats, soybeans, and Sudan grass. Winter crops comprise rye, ryegrass, and wheat.

CROP RESIDUES. Most of the nutrients plants obtain from the soil remain in the unharvested portion—the foliage or root systems. Research has shown that these crop residues increase subsequent yields with the right management. Burning these materials results in an almost complete loss of their nitrogen and carbon. They can, instead, be used in the compost pile when combined with nitrogenous manures, tilled into the soil, or used as bedding for livestock.

CULTIVATION. Refers to the entire job of caring for the soil surface, and in some cases the subsoil. Cultivation also includes the operations that are completed prior to planting the crop. Soil cultivation, after the crop is planted, is done to keep the weeds down, and to save moisture in the soil. Cultivation should never be done when the soil is wet; it tends to break up texture.

DAMPING OFF. The wilting and early death of young seedlings soon after they emerge from the soil. The fungus attacks the seedlings at the soil line and causes them to break off at that point. Remedial measures include proper ventilation and drying off of the soil. It can be prevented by sowing the seeds in a mixture of equal parts of compost and sand, and keeping the young seedlings in a well-ventilated and lighted cool place.

DRAINAGE. Inadequate or defective, it can take either of two extreme forms: (1) the soil drains too rapidly and does not hold moisture for its plant life; (2) it drains slowly or practically not at all and has degenerated into a swamp or bog. (*See* Aeration.)

EARTHWORM. Learn to rejoice when you see rainworms in your garden soil and red manure worms in the compost pile—it means you're doing things right. Our topsoils have been made by earthworms. Aristotle called them the 'intestines of the soil' because their castings are far richer minerally than the soil which they originally ingest. They also aerate the soil, going as far down as 6 feet, and making holes for the rain. They also break up hardpan, and their dead bodies add as much as 1,000 pounds of valuable nitrogenous fertilizer to an acre of highly organic soil.

ENZYME. Any of a group of complex organic substances that accelerate or catalyse specific chemical transformations such as the digestion of foods in plants and animals. Without enzymes, plants would not grow, seeds would not germinate, microbes would not function, and there would be no soil.

EROSION. Severe washing or wearing away of soil, generally by rainfall but also by wind. Sheet erosion occurs when rains puddle the soil and seal it so run-off occurs. Gully erosion is a further (and catastrophic) development in which the results of the steady loss in soil are made dramatically evident. Wind erosion such as occurred in the United States of America during the mid-1930s lifted topsoils from entire counties and deposited them hundreds of miles away. Most of the US soils are judged ruined when they lose 6 inches of topsoil and are generally abandoned before they lose the top 10 inches (*See* Cover crops *and* Mulch.)

FERTILIZER, ORGANIC. Plant fertilizers have three vital functions in addition to making the necessary nutrients available to plants: (1) improving soil tilth and structure; (2) improving the soil's water-holding capacity; (3) aiding nitrogen-fixation. Organic fertilizers such as animal manures and garden compost serve all these functions and serve to maintain a balanced soil economy by releasing their nutrients gradually over a period of time, making them available as needed. High nutrient chemical fertilizers do not add humus to the soil, tend to harm rather than help its texture and structure, and generally cause an imbalance by releasing too much of a single kind of nutrient immediately.

FERTILIZERS, ARTIFICIAL. The organic school does not accept the use of artificial chemical fertilizers for the following reasons: (1) they are quick-acting, short-term plant 'boosters' that are known to pollute waterways; (2) they contribute to the deterioration of soil texture, and actually create hardpans; (3) they destroy much beneficial soil life, including earthworms; (4) they alter the vitamin and protein content of some crops; (5) they make some crops more vulnerable to disease; (6) they prevent some plants from absorbing needed minerals, thus reducing flavour. The soil must be regarded as a living entity, and an acid fertilizer can dissolve some of its constituents which hold it together and thus injure its structure. The recent widespread dismay over pollution of the land, air, and water must serve to establish the validity of the organic fertilizer position.

FUNGUS. Any of a group of plants—moulds, mildews, rusts, smuts, mushrooms—that, destitute of chlorophyll, reproduce mainly by asexual spores. Most fungi are basically valuable, and essential to the processes of life. They help convert rock material into soil, and contribute to the manufacture of humus. They are also active in the decomposition of dead vegetation and animal bodies, restoring minerals to the soil. (*See* Microorganism *and* Mycorrhizal association.)

GARBAGE FOR COMPOST. Should be practised whenever and wherever possible. Kitchen refuse, vegetable and animal, is particularly rich in nitrogen and other nutrients so essential to plant growth. Use of garbage in garden compost-making helps to solve the overall pollution problem caused by uncontrolled tipping of household wastes by local authorities. Many local authorities burn this soil-valuable commodity.

GARDEN CALENDAR. It is difficult, if not impossible, to make a planting timetable which will agree exactly with the vagaries of the weather prevailing in your area. But the wise and observant gardener will read the seasonal signs and follow the monitions of the local weatherman and old-timer alike. Sometimes he will guess wrong, and his plantings will suffer accordingly. But holding to some sort of schedule is necessary and, with an elastic and accommodating mulching programme, the organic gardener should come through a 'normal' growing year with a minimum of damage and frustration.

GERMINATION. Viability in seeds (the power to grow) varies greatly with the species and varieties. Some seeds will take root and grow after many years, some will not germinate after a single year. You know a seed has germinated when the young stem and leaves appear at the surface.

GRASS CLIPPINGS. Can play an important role in improving soil. A good lawn doesn't need as much enrichment, added organic matter, or mulching as do the more heavily cropped plots. A rich source of nitrogen, these clippings can most often be better used elsewhere as a valuable fertilizer in the vegetable garden, a helpful addition in all mulches, and a major aid in converting leaves and other low-nitrogen wastes into best-quality compost.

GREEN MANURING. Special crops like rye grass, mustard, and lupins are sown in vacant soil. They fulfil three functions. As they grow they make use of plant foods in the topsoil and prevent their being leached into the subsoil; they provide a soil cover—and nature abhors bare soil in tropical, subtropical, and temperate climates; when dug into the soil the plant foods are released for the use of the crops to follow and the decaying vegetation slightly improves the soil quality. Green manures do not replace garden compost which is a unique manure. Allow about 6 weeks to elapse from digging in green manure to re-sowing or planting the ground with another crop—fruit or vegetable.

HARDENING OFF. Refers to the preparing of young plants to meet outside weather conditions. Young plants, especially non-hardy ones, are very vulnerable to sudden temperature changes. To put them outside, after their propagation in the protection of a greenhouse or other warm place, may easily be fatal. Therefore, young plants have to be introduced to the elements by degrees—the hardening-off process.

HARDINESS. That quality in plants that enables them to survive the climatic conditions of the particular area where they are to be placed. When gardeners speak of a 'hardy' plant, they usually mean one that will survive the winter. But the term can also be applied to plants of a northern climate which will survive the heat of a more temperate climate. *All* plants are hardy in their natural climates, but when transported by man to foreign environments, many cannot survive.

HARDPAN. Hardpans are impervious horizontal layers in the soil that may exist anywhere from 6 inches to about 2 feet below the surface. A true hardpan is formed by the cementing together of the soil grains into a hard, stone-like mass which is impervious to water. A more common condition is an impervious layer in the subsoil caused by the pore spaces becoming filled with fine clay particles. Such tight clay subsoils, called *claypans*, are generally associated with an extremely acid condition, so that from both the physical and chemical standpoint they are objectionable.

HEAVING. A type of winter injury in which plants are loosened and frequently lifted from the soil as a result of successive freezing and thawing. It occurs in soils containing a considerable amount of clay or silt which alternately freeze and thaw in the spring. Protecting the plants and soil with mulch should eliminate the condition. A long-range remedy is to compost heavily, adding large amounts of humus to the soil and reducing its clay content.

HEAVY SOIL. Contains a high percentage of clay and/or silt. Heavy soils generally hold too much moisture and have poor drainage.

HUMUS. Is organic matter in a more advanced stage of decomposition than compost in its early stages. In a compost heap, some of the organic matter has turned into humus, but the remainder will complete the decomposition process after it has been placed in the soil. Organic matter in the soil, in the early stages of decomposition, cannot be called humus. It must still be called organic matter. The process where organic matter turns to humus is called *humification*.

IRRIGATION. The objective of irrigation is to keep a readily available supply of moisture in contact with plant roots at all times. But all too often farmers and some gardeners depend on irrigation to the exclusion of soil building and management practices. Their soil is not in condition to receive and properly utilize the water falling upon it as rain or applied by irrigation. A soil rich in organic matter will catch and hold nearly all the rain falling on it. Thus much less irrigation water will be needed, and what is applied will be held better. Mulching, green manuring, strip cropping, contour ploughing, and terracing are vital to cut irrigation costs and save the underground sources from going dry.

KITCHEN WASTES. Represent a tremendous potential of organic matter which can be returned to the soil. Reports show that the average person creates about 300 pounds of garbage a year. At present, most cities destroy garbage, burning it, burying it, or dumping it into the sea. In recent years, however, some cities have been adopting various methods of municipal composting, whereby all the city's garbage is composted and reduced to a fine material suitable for garden and agricultural use.

LAYERING. This refers to a method of plant propagation in which the rooting of branches of woody plants takes place while they are still attached to the parent plant. Layering is used on certain woody plants, usually those which have become too 'leggy', that is, too tall and gangling, with a few leaves growing at the end of a long stem. Its purpose is to produce shorter, stockier, more robust-looking, and better foliage plants. The bark and cambium layer are cut or 'wounded', and the injured area covered with sphagnum moss or selected soil. New, young roots generally form within 30 to 60 days.

LEACHING. Rainwater and irrigation are known to dissolve a certain amount of plant food elements from the soil, carrying them down to greater depths where they will be lost by the roots. This leaching is inevitable and should be remembered when fertilizing. Leaching also occurs in house plants, but this kind of leaching can be prevented by not over-watering plants. Remember that every time water runs out of the drainage hole and is thrown away in excess, it carries with it some soil nutrients.

LICHENS. Actually flowerless plants, active in the initial stages of soil fermentation. Long before men appeared on earth, lichens grew endlessly on flinty rock and sterile sand, in steaming tropics and icy tundra, perhaps the best example of the teamwork that is the very cornerstone of nature. Other organisms that work together to build soil from the inert substances of the earth's crust include aerobic and anaerobic bacteria,

and earthworms that take over where fungi and moulds
leave off. All these tiny creatures form links in a chain,
the end product of which is life-sustaining, fertile soil.
But the lichen is the indispensable 'starter' link in the
chain.

LOAM. Soil which is composed of a friable mixture of
clay, silt, sand, and organic matter. The mixture of mineral and organic material in a good loam should provide 50 per cent solid matter, and 50 per cent space
between the solids. Of the space, about half should be
filled with water and half with air for optimum plant
growth. Clay, silt, and sand are particles of rock, usually
of the rock which underlies the field on which they are
found. Silt is composed of rock particles of less than
$\frac{1}{16}$ mm in diameter which is or has been deposited on
the bed of a body of water. Sand is coarser material,
clay is finer rock material. If the mineral content of a
loam is composed of more than half sand, it is said
to be a sand loam. If clay predominates, it is a clay
loam, or if it is mostly silt, it is a silt loam.

MANURE. The excreta of agricultural animals, along
with stable litter, constitutes one of the oldest and most
effective fertilizers known to man. The rise of chemical
fertilizers in the twentieth century has led to a decrease
in the amount of manure utilized by world agriculturists. This wasteful misuse of natural fertilizer is often
rationalized by farmers and agriculturists, who allege
that the supply is not adequate for the need for fertilizers. No British figures are available to contradict this
assumption. For the United States the assumption shows
faulty reasoning. In 1889 there were 13,663,000 horses
in the United States and 50,331,000 head of cattle.
Today there are far fewer horses—but almost

100,000,000 cattle. There has also been a subsequent rise in the number of other livestock. The problem in the United States is not insufficient manure, but its misuse. In Britain there are vast quantities of manure available from battery hen houses, animal sweat boxes, and from the turkey industry. The organic gardener who may be offered manures from these sources may not be keen on accepting them. They may be riddled with chemical residues—hormones, vaccines, pesticides. You name it—they've got it!

MICROORGANISM. There are many kinds and weights of microorganisms in the surface foot of soil in large numbers. Each kind of organism plays some significant role in the decomposition of plant and animal residues, liberation of plant nutrients, or in the development of soil structure. Many groups are dependent on each other; consequently one kind may tend to follow another.

MULCH. A layer of material, preferably organic material, that is placed on the soil surface to conserve moisture, hold down weeds, and ultimately improve soil structure and fertility. As with composting, mulching is a basic practice in the organic method. It is a practice which nature employs constantly, that of always covering a bare soil. In addition, mulching also protects plants in the winter by reducing the dangers of freezing and heaving. Practically any organic waste material can be used as mulch.

MYCORRHIZAL ASSOCIATION. Usually symbiotic (two plants necessary to each other which benefit from their proximity) of the mycelium (filamentary threadlike growths) of various fungi and the roots of seed plants.

The fungi make various nutrients more available to plant assimilation.

NEUTRAL. Referring to soils that are balanced between acidity and alkalinity, having a pH of about 7.

NO-DIGGING METHOD. A school of gardening which adheres to the belief that no digging or soil spading is necessary to attain best garden results. Here are the basic principles: (1) to imitate nature closely by not inverting the soil; (2) to economize on compost and other organic materials by using them as a surface mulch, where nature keeps its fertility promoting materials; (3) to reduce weed growth by not bringing more and more seeds to the surface; (4) and, by all these methods, to maintain a balance of air, moisture, biological life, and plant foods.

NUTRITION. Proper nutrition is an integral part of the organic method of gardening and farming. Aside from the many other advantages of the organic method of gardening, the sound nutrition that is achieved from eating naturally grown foods is reason enough to follow the organic method. The relation between soil and health is as basic as the very process of nature; the axiom 'you are what you eat' assumes greater and greater impact as experiments show the wonderful results of eating carefully selected, organically grown foods.

ORGANIC GARDENING AND FARMING. Calls for the maintenance of soil fertility and texture by replenishing soil with its own materials and readily decomposable matter which can be easily reassimilated. Natural animal manures, crop residues of every kind, plus compost are used as plant fertilizers and applied as mulch to conserve moisture and regulate soil temperature. The organic method also bans the use of artificial chemical fertilizers and toxic pesticides while permitting the use of naturally occurring minerals such as calcium in ground chalk or in ground limestone. What the gardener knows as 'lime'.

ORGANIC MATERIAL. Or organic matter, is any part of any substance which once had life—animal, vegetable, or a byproduct thereof. Almost all organic matter can be composted to return its nutritive substances to the soil, thus continuing the cycle of nature. The wise gardener will avail himself of these various forms of organic matter and use them in the compost heap.

PESTICIDES. Powders or liquids which kill pests. Many pesticides used on the farm and in the garden are poisonous and dangerous to man, his pets and stock, to wildlife, and to the soil. The use of this sort of pesticide is not condoned in the organic method because of the harm it does and because of the potential threat to human health.

PHOTOSYNTHESIS. The process of forming starches and sugars that takes place in leaves in the presence of water and plant nutrients brought up from the roots, carbon dioxide from the air, chlorophyll in the leaf tissues, and light. Chloroplasts, microscopic bodies in the leaves, manufacture carbohydrates using radiant energy from the sun for their power source. Thus, leaves are the only known agents capable of transforming the sun's energy to food energy.

PROPAGATION. The great majority of plants can be propagated by seeds, cutting, division, and layering. For vegetables—annuals, biennials, and perennials—the most common reproducing method is by seeds.

PRUNING. Trimming out unwanted or unhealthy portions of a plant in order to help the portions which remain. The time of pruning varies with the type of plant that you want to prune, and with the results you wish to achieve through pruning. Some pruning is done at any time suitable to the gardener's convenience; some pruning must be done at a specific season. Pruning is not a mysterious process but a garden technique that requires an understanding of growth habits of plants plus an intelligent programme of plant care and an appreciation of the beauty of plant forms.

RABBIT MANURE. A fine source of nitrogen and other fertilizer values. The analyses differ according to the feeding practices, but an average sample is rich enough in nitrogen to produce good heating in a compost heap. The manure should not be applied to the soil as it is taken from the hutches but should either be used as a compost heap activator or layered between wetted straw, grass, sawdust, or wood shavings for the making of composted rabbit manure. The resultant product should be applied with discretion to vacant land or as a fertilizer around growing plants.

ROOT CROP. A vegetable grown for its edible root. Popular root crops are beetroot, carrot, turnip, swede, and parsnip. Potatoes are tubers and are not true roots. The onion is a bulb.

ROTATION. All vegetables do not utilize the same amounts of plant foods in the soil. Where one vegetable has a liking for potash, another prefers more nitrogen.

So, if we grow the same vegetable on the same plot of ground year after year we are liable to exhaust the soil of one or more plant foods. It stands to reason, too, that if the same vegetable is grown in the same place for several years, there is every likelihood of a build-up of the pests and diseases to which the vegetable is subject. Thus a patch of soil may become cabbage-sick and infected with the dangerous club-root disease. To prevent these troubles from occurring, the gardener rotates his crops. For the medium-sized garden, the following 3-year plan is suggested. In a really large kitchen garden the rotation could be based on a 4-year plan.

First year	Second year	Third year
Potatoes	Brassicas (all kinds of cabbage)	Other vegetables
Soil manured or composted during winter digging	*Soil limed, if necessary, in the autumn. Manured or composted later*	*No manure or garden compost for root crops. Compost may be applied for other crops (if available) or, if considered helpful, other organic fertilizers may be used*

It is not always practicable to stick to such a programme but any plan based on the practice of not growing the same vegetable in the same patch for 2 years running is a help.

SANDY SOIL. A typical 'light sandy' soil may be composed of approximately 70 per cent sand, 20 per cent silt, and 10 per cent clay. The particles in a sandy soil are comparatively large, permitting water to enter the soil and to pass through it so quickly that it dries out very rapidly, and often carries nutrients with it. Organic matter is especially important in improving the structure of sandy soils.

SANITATION. In gardening, this means the destruction of diseased, injured, or insect-infested plants or parts of plants, and certain other clean-up techniques that further aid in promoting the health and productivity of plants. Prompt removal of diseased or insect-damaged plants is the first rule of sanitation. It's a good idea to cultivate the habit of watching carefully for anything abnormal in the growth of your plants. Sometimes removing just a few sickly leaves or a single plant may prevent a bad infestation of bugs or the spread of a disease.

SEAWEED. Seaweed used as fertilizer belongs to two main groups according to habitat. Brown weeds grow between high and low water on rocky sites and also on rock below low water, down to a depth of 60 feet. Rockweeds are relatively small plants, but their growth is usually dense, and they are easily collected by pulling or cutting from the rocks; 200 pounds per hour can be gathered easily from a good site. One of the basic tenets of seaside gardening is to never leave the ground bare to the drying action of the wind. Chopped seaweed makes a good mulch when used alone or it can be mixed with compost, autumn leaves, or lawn mowings. You can also dig finely chopped seaweed into the upper few inches of your soil at the rate of 50 to 200 pounds per 100 square feet during winter digging. Seaweed is low in phosphorus, so it's a good practice to mix in some bone meal.

SILT. Particles are microscopic pieces of rock—much smaller than sand—that help make up soil. Silt of the non-quartz minerals is rich in plant food.

SOIL FAUNA. This is one of most important gardening assets. They include mites, worms, grubs, centipedes, etc. All feed either on each other, or the crop residues and leaves deposited on the soil. Through continual activity—biting, chewing, tunnelling, crawling—they loosen and aerate the soil and thoroughly mix its various components. Where there is an abundance of organic matter, there is also a proportionate number of functioning soil fauna.

SOIL TEMPERATURE. Soil temperatures vary just as much as air temperatures. One part of a garden is probably hotter (or colder) than another, depending upon its location, chemical and physical make-up. Here are some examples of how soil temperatures influence your gardening results:

1. Germination of seeds depends upon warmth of soil below as well as upon air above.

2. Sowing your first crop as soon as soil has warmed up enough in spring can mean that you'll have time for a sowing or a planting of another crop in the same spot later in the season. Cloches are excellent soil warmers and the gardener who has a set of cloches can make a much earlier start with spring sowings.

3. A mulch or cover crop regulates the soil's temperature to your advantage.

4. You'll learn how to save plants from frost damage.

5. You can aid the work of helpful soil bacteria if you know at what soil temperature they work best.

BACTERIA. Organic gardeners are well aware that their soil is alive, and that it provides a home for many beneficial bacteria. These bacteria require special conditions of warmth, moisture, and free aeration of soil to do their best job. These conditions are found only in the upper cultivated layers of the soil, and are more easily obtained in sandy loams than in clays, where the moisture content is too high and the supply of oxygen is lacking.

THINNING. Consists of pulling up certain seedlings in a row to give room to those that are left. Sometimes the pulled seedlings are kept and replanted, in which case the procedure is called pricking out. Disbudding, the removal of some flower buds to make the remaining ones grow larger blooms, is also a form of thinning, which in fruit growing consists of pruning out some of the fruitlets as soon as they are set to prevent too much small fruit production.

TILTH. As ordinarily understood, tilth refers to the physical condition of the soil. Good soil tilth means a loosening to the depth necessary for root penetration and plant growth. A friable soil is one that has good tilth. In addition, soil tilth is also used to mean cultivation.

TOP-DRESSING. The application of compost, lime, manure, and fertilizers to the surface of the soil. Usually the material is lightly raked into the ground around growing plants and along rows.

TRACE ELEMENTS. Trace elements are minor mineral nutrients needed by all plants, animals, and humans in extremely small or 'trace' amounts. In order to be present, these micronutrients must be available in the soil in which the plants and foods are grown. Too little of one or more elements produces deficiencies which result in plant or animal disease. On the other hand, an excessive quantity of any trace element similarly brings about a host of toxic conditions in plants and sicknesses in animals and people. Just how important these elements are can be seen by the fact that although trace elements may constitute less than 1 per cent of the total dry matter of a plant, they are often the factor that determines the vigour of the plant. Even where good crops have been thought to be produced, trace elements additions to the soil have raised yields and improved crop quality often amazingly. Most soils originally contain a sufficient supply of these elements to sustain good plant growth. But intensive cropping, erosion, chemical fertilization, and the replacement of manure-producing animals with machines have caused widespread deficiencies to occur.

TRANSPLANTING. When seedlings are about a $\frac{1}{2}$ inch high or have their true leaves (those resembling the species, instead of the ones known as 'seed leaves' which appear first), they have reached the proper stage for transplanting into other containers. These containers for transplanting purposes are practically the same as those used for sowing. Use a somewhat richer potting mixture, so that the seedlings will have plenty of available plant food. Dampen the soil and fill the containers loosely, smooth it off, and press it down with a flat board. With a small round stick, make holes in which to set the young seedlings. Be sure that these holes are wide and deep enough to accommodate the roots in their natural position without crowding.

SOURCES OF SUPPLY

Vegetable Seedsmen

Samuel Dobie & Son Ltd., Grosvenor Street, Chester, CHI IXD.

Thompson & Morgan (Ipswich) Ltd., London Road, Ipswich.

Alexander & Brown, Perth.

Suttons Seeds, Reading, Berks.

G. Winfield & Son Ltd., 26 Westgate Street, Gloucester, GL1 2NH.

W. J. Unwin Ltd., Histon, Cambridge.

Webbs Garden Seeds, Sealand, Chester CHI 6BA.

S. E. Marshall & Co. Ltd., Oldfield Lane, Wisbech, Cambs.

J. W. Boyce, Soham, Ely, Cambs.

Chase Compost Seeds Ltd., Benhall, Saxmundham, Suffolk.

Nurserymen Supplying Fruit Trees, Bushes and Plants

Blackmoor Nurseries, Blackmoor, Liss, Hampshire.

Laxton & Bunyard Nurseries Ltd., Sealand, Chester.

Rivers, The Nurseries, Sawbridgeworth, Herts.

Toynbee's Nurseries, Barnham, Bognor Regis, Sussex.

George Jackman & Son (Woking Nurseries) Ltd., Woking, Surrey.

Garden Herbs

Laxton & Bunyard Nurseries Ltd., Sealand, Chester.

INDEX

Most Magazine Advertisements Offer You Big Savings — We Promise You A Better Way Of Life

ORGANIC GARDENING & FARMING is catching the imagination of everyone concerned with preventing further environmental pollution not only by revealing the hazards *but by showing how you can put a stop to using chemical sprays and fertilizers,* when growing tastier vegetables and better blooms.

How to improve the quality of the foods you eat.

It shows you where to start, what to do, whether you live in the heart of the city or out in the country.

It is one of the few British magazines that shows how, as an individual—you can create a more natural life for yourself and your family. And we've got the best organic journalists explaining these methods.

It's packed with practical tips and guidance on how to save money.

15 pence monthly.

Don't Delay

Write today for a free specimen copy of ORGANIC GARDENING & FARMING to:—

Specimen Copy Offer XYZ, ORGANIC GARDENING & FARMING, Berkhamsted, Herts, England.